The Theory of Timed I/O Automata

Second Edition

Synthesis Lectures on Distributed Computing Theory

Editor
Nancy Lynch, *Massachusetts Institute of Technology*

Synthesis Lectures on Distributed Computing Theory is edited by Nancy Lynch of the Massachusetts Institute of Technology. The series will publish 50- to 150 page publications on topics pertaining to distributed computing theory. The scope will largely follow the purview of premier information and computer science conferences, such as ACM PODC, DISC, SPAA, OPODIS, CONCUR, DialM-POMC, ICDCS, SODA, Sirocco, SSS, and related conferences. Potential topics include, but not are limited to: distributed algorithms and lower bounds, algorithm design methods, formal modeling and verification of distributed algorithms, and concurrent data structures.

The Theory of Timed I/O Automata - Second Edition
Dilsun K. Kaynar, Nancy Lynch, Roberto Segala, and Frits Vaandrager
2010

Principles of Transactional Memory
Rachid Guerraoui and Michal Kapalka
2010

Fault-tolerant Agreement in Synchronous Message-passing Systems
Michel Raynal
2010

Communication and Agreement Abstractions for Fault-Tolerant Asynchronous Distributed Systems
Michel Raynal
2010

The Mobile Agent Rendezvous Problem in the Ring
Evangelos Kranakis, Danny Krizanc, and Euripides Markou
2010

The Theory of Timed I/O Automata - Second Edition
Dilsun K. Kaynar, Nancy Lynch, Roberto Segala, and Frits Vaandrager

ISBN:978-3-031-00875-7 paperback
ISBN:978-3-031-02003-2 ebook

DOI 10.1007/978-3-031-02003-2

A Publication in the Springer series
SYNTHESIS LECTURES ON DISTRIBUTED COMPUTING THEORY

Lecture #5
Series Editor: Nancy Lynch, *Massachusetts Institute of Technology*
Series ISSN
Synthesis Lectures on Distributed Computing Theory
Print 2155-1626 Electronic 2155-1634

The Theory of Timed I/O Automata

Second Edition

Dilsun K. Kaynar
CyLab, Carnegie Mellon University

Nancy Lynch
MIT Computer Science and Artificial Intelligence Laboratory

Roberto Segala
Dipartimento di Informatica, Università di Verona

Frits Vaandrager
Institute for Computing and Information Sciences, Radboud University Nijmegen

SYNTHESIS LECTURES ON DISTRIBUTED COMPUTING THEORY #5

ABSTRACT

This monograph presents the *Timed Input/Output Automaton (TIOA)* modeling framework, a basic mathematical framework to support description and analysis of timed (computing) systems. Timed systems are systems in which desirable correctness or performance properties of the system depend on the timing of events, not just on the order of their occurrence. Timed systems are employed in a wide range of domains including communications, embedded systems, real-time operating systems, and automated control. Many applications involving timed systems have strong safety, reliability, and predictability requirements, which make it important to have methods for systematic design of systems and rigorous analysis of timing-dependent behavior.

The TIOA framework also supports description and analysis of timed distributed algorithms—distributed algorithms whose correctness and performance depend on the relative speeds of processors, accuracy of local clocks, or communication delay bounds. Such algorithms arise, for example, in traditional and wireless communications, networks of mobile devices, and shared-memory multiprocessors. The need to prove rigorous theoretical results about timed distributed algorithms makes it important to have a suitable mathematical foundation.

An important feature of the TIOA framework is its support for decomposing timed system descriptions. In particular, the framework includes a notion of *external behavior* for a timed I/O automaton, which captures its discrete interactions with its environment. The framework also defines what it means for one TIOA to *implement* another, based on an inclusion relationship between their external behavior sets, and defines notions of *simulations*, which provide sufficient conditions for demonstrating implementation relationships. The framework includes a *composition* operation for TIOAs, which respects external behavior, and a notion of *receptiveness*, which implies that a TIOA does not block the passage of time.

The TIOA framework also defines the notion of a property and what it means for a property to be a safety or a liveness property. It includes results that capture common proof methods for showing that automata satisfy properties.

KEYWORDS

timed computing systems, distributed algorithms, formal modeling and verification,
I/O automata

Contents

Acknowledgments

The authors thank Sayan Mitra for his extensive collaborations with us on developing language support for TIOA, carrying out numerous case studies, developing proof methods, and extending TIOA to include probabilistic behavior. We also thank Shinya Umeno for his work on case studies and proof methods for TIOA.

We thank the many members of the Tempo tool development project, including Alex Shvartsman, Laurent Michel, Steve Garland, Scott Smolka, Radu Grosu, Myla Archer, Nancy Griffeth, Paul Attie, and their students, for their extensive TIOA-related work. This tool development work certainly helped to exercise and evaluate the TIOA model. Among the Tempo participants, Nancy Griffeth was especially helpful in applying TIOA and Tempo extensively to practical communication protocols. She provided great feedback on the tools and the model.

We thank Rui Fan, Seth Gilbert, Tina Nolte, and Matt Brown for using TIOA as the mathematical foundation for their theses and related papers. All four carried out extremely thorough algorithms studies, using the TIOA definitions and results in a deep way. We are glad to see that TIOA provided them with an adequate foundation for their work. In particular, Seth and Tina developed new results for TIOAs, some of which have found their way into this edition of the book.

We thank Sayan Mitra and Nancy Griffeth for reviewing the manuscript.

Dilsun Kaynar and Nancy Lynch were supported by DARPA/AFOSR MURI Contract F49620-02-1-0325, DARPA SEC contract F33615-01-C-1850, NSF ITR grant CCR-0121277, and Air Force Aerospace Research-OSR Contract F49620-00-1-0097.

Dilsun Kaynar was also supported by the US Army Research Office contract on Perpetually Available and Secure Information Systems (DAAD19-02-0389) to CMU's CyLab.

Nancy Lynch was also supported by AFOSR contract FA9550-08-1-0159 and NSF grants CCF-0702670, CNS-0614414, and CNS-0715397.

Frits Vaandrager was supported by EU IST project IST-2001-35304 (Advanced Methods for Timed Systems, AMETIST), PROGRESS project TES4999 (Verification of Hard and Softly Timed Systems, HaaST), NWO/EW project 612.000.103 (Fault-tolerant Real-time Algorithms Analyzed Incrementally, FRAAI), and EU FP7 project 214755 (Quantitative System Properties in Model-Driven-Design of Embedded Systems, QUASIMODO).

Dilsun K. Kaynar, Nancy Lynch, Roberto Segala, and Frits Vaandrager
November 2010

Notations

a, b	action
f, g, h	function
i, j	index
l	locally controlled action
t	time point
v, x	variable
A	set of actions
C	task
E	set of external actions
F	set of functions
H	set of internal (hidden) actions
I	set of input actions, invariants
J	interval
K	set of time points
L	set of locally controlled actions
O	set of output actions
P	set of elements in cpo, properties
Q	set of automaton states
R	(simulation) relation
S	set
T	set of trajectories
V	set of variables
X	set of internal variables
$\mathbf{x}$	state
$\mathbf{v}$	valuation
$\mathcal{A}, \mathcal{B}, \mathcal{C}$	timed (I/O) automaton
$\mathcal{D}$	set of discrete transitions
$\mathcal{T}$	set of trajectories
N	the natural numbers
R	the real numbers
T	the time axis
Z	the integers
V	the universe of variables

α, β, δ	(A, V)-sequence
γ	sequence
λ	the empty sequence
π	projection function
σ, ρ	sequence
τ, υ	trajectory
Θ	set of start states

CHAPTER 1

Introduction

1.1 OVERVIEW

This book presents the *Timed Input/Output Automaton (TIOA)* modeling framework, a basic mathematical framework to support description and analysis of timed computing systems and timed distributed algorithms.

Timed systems and timed algorithms: Timed computing systems are systems in which desirable correctness or performance properties of the system depend on the timing of events, not just on the order of their occurrence. A typical timed system consists of computer components, which operate in discrete steps, and timing-related components such as physical or logical clocks, whose behavior involve continuous transformation over time. Timed systems are employed in a wide range of domains including communications, embedded systems, real-time operating systems, and automated control. Many applications involving timed systems have strong safety, reliability and predictability requirements, which makes it important to have methods for systematic design of systems and rigorous analysis of timing-dependent behavior. Timed distributed algorithms are distributed algorithms whose correctness and performance depend on factors related to timing, such as the relative speeds of processors, the accuracy of local clocks, or communication delay bounds. Such algorithms arise, for example, in traditional and wireless communications, networks of mobile devices, and shared-memory multiprocessors. The need to prove rigorous theoretical results about timed distributed algorithms makes it important to have a suitable mathematical foundation.

Modeling plays a key role in all stages in the design and analysis of systems. Models represent system designs at a level of abstraction that is suitable for isolating and focusing on their most crucial aspects. They can be modified and experimented with more easily than real implementations. Moreover, if the modeling is performed using the concepts provided by a formal framework, the modeling can be done more precisely, and analysis and verification methods supported by that framework can be applied. Timed systems, which combine discrete steps with continuous evolution of state over time, exhibit complex behaviors that are typically hard to describe and analyze in the absence of a carefully developed modeling framework [34, 108, 109].

Modeling is equally important for distributed algorithms. To be meaningful, rigorous theoretical results about algorithm behavior must rest on some type of mathematical model. Many, perhaps most, papers about distributed algorithms define special-purpose models from scratch; a general modeling framework can be used as a foundation for defining special-purpose models, making it unnecessary to redefine general concepts and reprove general results. For timed distributed algorithms, defining models is especially challenging; a general framework can make the job much easier.

A good modeling framework can support algorithm description at different levels of abstraction. It can serve as the basis for algorithm simulation, and can support formal analysis.

A modeling framework must support designing systems and algorithms in structured ways, viewing them at multiple levels of abstraction and as compositions of interacting components. If a framework is to provide flexibility and generality, it must also support nondeterminism. A system or algorithm designer might wish to allow several potential behaviors at certain points in the computation of a system, for example, to avoid making assumptions about how the environment will behave, or to allow several correct implementations for the same design. Such liberty in specification would not be possible to accommodate without nondeterminism. In addition to supporting all of these features, modeling frameworks for timed systems and algorithms must provide mechanisms for representing continuously evolving components such as clocks and timers.

An interesting complication that arises in modeling timed systems and algorithms is that time can progress in ways that conflict with our intuition about physical time. For example, we may force time to stop entirely to "urge" some discrete action to happen, or schedule infinitely many discrete actions to happen in a finite amount of time. A framework needs to provide concepts that identify the conditions under which a timed system behaves according to our intuitions, that is, the conditions under which time diverges as the system continues to run.

Timed I/O Automata: In this work, we introduce a basic mathematical framework – the *Timed Input/Output Automaton* modeling framework – to support description and analysis of timed systems. In this framework, a system is represented as a *Timed I/O Automaton (TIOA)*, which is a kind of nondeterministic, possibly infinite-state, state machine. The state of a TIOA is described by a valuation of state variables that are internal to the automaton. The state of a TIOA can change in two ways: instantaneously by the occurrence of a *discrete transition*, which is labeled by a discrete action, or according to a *trajectory*, which is a function that describes the evolution of the state variables over intervals of time. Trajectories may be continuous or discontinuous functions.

The TIOA framework supports decomposition of system description and analysis. A key to this decomposition is the rigorously-defined notion of *external behavior* for timed I/O automata. The external behavior of each TIOA is defined by a simple mathematical object called a *trace*–essentially, a sequence of actions interspersed with time-passage steps. *Abstraction* and *parallel composition* are other important notions for decomposition of system description and analysis.

For abstraction, the framework includes notions of *implementation* and *simulation*, which can be used to view timed systems and algorithms at multiple levels of abstraction, starting from a high-level version that describes required properties, and ending with a low-level version that describes a detailed design or implementation. In particular, the TIOA framework defines what it means for one TIOA, $\mathcal{A}$, to *implement* another TIOA, $\mathcal{B}$, namely, any trace that can be exhibited by $\mathcal{A}$ is also allowed by $\mathcal{B}$. In this case, $\mathcal{A}$ might be more deterministic than $\mathcal{B}$, in terms of either discrete transitions or trajectories. For instance, $\mathcal{B}$ might be allowed to perform an output action at an arbitrary time before noon, whereas $\mathcal{A}$ produces the same output sometime between 10 and 11 AM. The notion of a *simulation relation* from $\mathcal{A}$ to $\mathcal{B}$ provides a sufficient condition for demonstrating that $\mathcal{A}$ implements $\mathcal{B}$. A simulation relation is defined to satisfy three conditions, one relating start states, one relating discrete transitions, and one relating trajectories of $\mathcal{A}$ and $\mathcal{B}$.

For parallel composition, the framework provides a *composition operation*, by which TIOAs modeling individual timed system components can be combined to produce a model for a larger timed system. The model for the composed system can describe interactions among the components, which involves joint participation in discrete transitions. Composition requires certain "compatibility" conditions, namely, that each output action be controlled by at most one automaton, and that internal actions of one automaton cannot be shared with any other automaton. The composition operation respects traces, for example, if $\mathcal{A}_1$ implements $\mathcal{A}_2$ then the composition of $\mathcal{A}_1$ and $\mathcal{B}$ implements the composition of $\mathcal{A}_2$ and $\mathcal{B}$. Composition also satisfies *projection* and *pasting* results, which are fundamental for compositional design and verification of systems: a trace of a composition of TIOAs "projects" to give traces of the individual TIOAs, and traces of components are "pastable" to give behaviors of the composition.

If a TIOA approaches a finite point in time without quite reaching it, or by scheduling infinitely many discrete actions to happen in a finite amount of time, it is said to exhibit *Zeno behavior*, in reference to Zeno's paradox [76]. The TIOA framework includes a notion of *receptiveness*, which is used to classify automata that do not contribute to producing Zeno behavior, and which is preserved by composition. Receptiveness of a TIOA, $\mathcal{A}$, in the TIOA framework is defined in terms of the existence of a strategy, which is defined as a subautomaton of $\mathcal{A}$ that chooses some of the evolutions from each state of $\mathcal{A}$.

The TIOA framework also supports a notion of a property, which is defined for sequences of alternating actions and trajectories, and includes a definition of what it means for an automaton to satisfy a property. The framework also includes basic results about the classification of properties as safety and liveness properties and common proof methods for showing automata satisfy the stated properties.

The TIOA framework presented in this work is purely mathematical. However, it constitutes a natural basis for computer support tools [57]. A preliminary version of a toolset is available at http://www.veromodo.com.

1.2 EVOLUTION OF THE TIOA FRAMEWORK

The TIOA modeling framework presented in this book evolved from the *Hybrid Input/Output Automaton (HIOA)* modeling framework for hybrid systems [79] by Lynch, Segala and Vaandrager. The HIOA framework, in turn, evolved from the I/O automata of [83, 84, 76, 53, 54], a fundamental modeling framework for (untimed) asynchronous systems. Our approach is based on the assumption that a timed system can be viewed as a special kind of a hybrid system where the continuous transformation is limited to internal system components that determine the timing of events. Therefore, we define a TIOA as a restricted HIOA where the only essential difference between an HIOA and a TIOA is that an HIOA may have *external variables* to model the continuous information flowing into and out of the system, in addition to state variables. A major consequence of this definition is that the communication between TIOAs is restricted to shared-action communication only. The TIOA model does not impose any further restrictions on the expressive power of the HIOA model.

We developed this new modeling framework even though there are several timed automaton models that extend the basic I/O automaton model [91, 107, 87, 86], because we have observed that the new HIOA modeling framework offered a way of improving and simplifying previous work on timed I/O automaton models [107, 87, 86]. For example, the use of trajectories as first-class objects to represent the external behavior of a timed automaton, the definition of a strategy as an automaton rather than a two-player game, and the variable structure on states are all new features that were motivated by what we learned in developing the HIOA framework and that gave rise to more elegant definitions and simpler proofs for timed automata.

We intend the TIOA model to serve as a general semantic framework in which previous results for timed I/O automata [87, 91, 107, 86] and other related models [7, 88, 100, 23] can be re-cast in a style that is upwardly compatible with the new HIOA model. Limiting the communication to discrete interactions is an apt choice since the previous timed I/O automaton models also adopt this type of communication. On the other hand, by avoiding any further restrictions on the general hybrid model, we obtain an expressive model suitable for specifying complex timing behavior. For example, our model does not require variables to be either discrete or to evolve at the same rate as real time as in some other models [7, 100]. Consequently, algorithms such as clock synchronization algorithms that use local clocks evolving at different and varying rates can be formalized naturally in our framework. The TIOA model can also naturally describe systems undergoing dynamic changes and reconfigurations through component failures, joins, recoveries, etc.

The fact that HIOAs subsume TIOAs as a special case does not eliminate the need for a separate modeling framework for timed systems. Having no external variables in the TIOA model gives rise to considerable simplifications in the theory. For example, proving that the composition of two timed automata is a well-defined automaton becomes simpler in the absence of external variables; no extra compatibility conditions as in the general HIOA framework are needed to obtain the desirable composition theorems for TIOAs.

In the past few years, we and others have developed the Tempo formal language for describing TIOAs, along with a collection of basic tools for analyzing Tempo programs. The syntax of the language corresponds closely to the pseudocode style used in this book. The tools consist of: (a) a front-end processor for Tempo, incorporating syntax and static semantic checking; (b) a simulation tool allowing simulation of Tempo specifications; (c) a model-checking link through an interface to the model-checker UPPAAL [100, 66]; and (d) a theorem-proving link through an interface to the theorem-prover PVS [98]. We refer to [57, 56, 32, 33] for more information on the TIOA toolset, and to the Tempo project web site [51]. The web site includes a user manual for Tempo, which contains comprehensive information about the language and several detailed examples. The Tempo project builds upon our prior work on the IOA language [35].

TIOAs have been used to specify and analyze many timed systems, from a variety of domains including vehicle and air-traffic control systems [44, 120, 119, 68, 117, 27, 74, 72, 70, 43, 77], communications [111, 112, 71, 73, 69, 29, 62, 116], and mobile robotics [78, 39, 40]. The TIOA framework has also been used as the foundation for describing and analyzing many timed distributed algorithms, including algorithms for implementing atomic memory [82, 38, 41, 20], for synchronizing clocks [28, 30, 63, 61], and for implementing applications in mobile wireless networks [26, 25, 96, 97, 16, 19]. Some of this work has involved development of new application-dependent structure in terms of TIOA; for instance, Nolte [96] defined concepts related to self-stabilization of wireless network algorithms.

1.3 RELATED WORK

There are several formalisms and tools for timed systems that are based on automata and state transition models. In this section, we briefly introduce those lines of work that we think are most closely related to ours. Note that we do not focus on the toolsets and their capabilities, but rather on the underlying formal models and languages.

One of the widely used formal frameworks for timed systems is that of Alur-Dill timed automata [7, 5]. An Alur-Dill automaton is a finite directed multigraph augmented with a finite set of clock variables. The semantics of such a timed automaton are defined as a state transition system in which each state consists of a location and a clock valuation. Clocks are assumed to change with the same rate as real-time, that is, with rate 1. Timed automata accept timed languages consisting of sequences of events tagged with their occurrence times. The main technical result for timed automata is that emptiness and reachability are decidable. Decision problems such as universality and language inclusion are undecidable for timed automata. A slight generalization of Alur-Dill timed automata are the linear hybrid automata of [6]. In this model, apart from clocks that progress with rate 1, one can also use continuous variables whose derivatives are contained in some arbitrary interval. The reachability problem for linear hybrid automata is undecidable [6].

The aim of facilitating automated verification has motivated the restrictions on the expressive power in the Alur-Dill and linear hybrid automata models. Over the two last decades, numerous papers have refined the decidability boundary of [7, 5]; for instance, see [50, 64, 18, 13, 8, 118]. The timed automaton model presented in this book is much more expressive than the Alur-Dill and linear hybrid automata models. In our model, there are no finiteness assumptions and no restrictions imposed on the dynamic types of variables. Our focus has been to develop a general formal framework with a well-defined notion of external behavior, parallel composition and abstraction that supports reasoning with simulation relations.

Uppaal [100, 66] is a widely used modeling and verification tool for timed systems. It supports the description of systems as a network of Alur-Dill timed automata and enhances that model with CCS-style communication [92] along with other notions such as committed and urgent locations. Uppaal also supports (synchronous) broadcast communication and communication via shared variables. Uppaal has a sophisticated model-checker that explores the whole state space of the modeled system to verify timing properties. Therefore, finiteness assumptions are built into the model to make such verification possible and the operations on clocks are restricted. Uppaal can be used as a model-checker for restricted TIOAs. We have done some preliminary work in this direction [104].

A compositional simulation-based verification method for Uppaal was presented in [11] and is applied to the Zeroconf protocol in [10]. It would be interesting to work on an alternative compositional semantics for (a subset of) Uppaal based on some variation of our restricted hybrid I/O automaton model. There are several small mismatches due to the style of communication and notions such as committed locations. It remains to be seen to what extent we can use the communication mechanisms of our automata to model these formally. We could, for example, allow a nonempty set of external variables with restricted dynamic types and seek restrictions on the use of shared variables in Uppaal, which would allow us to view these variables as external variables in the HIOA sense. Recently, an extension of Uppaal with input and output actions, also called *timed I/O automata*, was proposed in [21] aiming at compositional design using the concepts of timed games [17].

Kronos [121, 22] is another verification tool for timed systems that uses Alur-Dill automata. This tool requires systems to be represented as timed automata and the correctness conditions to be expressed in the real-time temporal logic TCTL [4]. Kronos, as Uppaal, can perform model-checking using a symbolic representation of the infinite state space by sets of linear constraints. Kronos can model-check full TCTL and implements the symbolic algorithm developed by [46]. It would be possible to use Kronos as a model-checker for restricted TIOAs.

The IF notation, which is the intermediate representation used in the IF toolset [15], is based on Alur-Dill automata extended with discrete data variables, communication primitives, dynamic process creation and destruction. This notation has been designed such that it can serve as a target for the translation of higher-level modeling languages, such as real-time extensions of SDL and UML. The support for dynamic process creation and destruction appears to be a distinguishing feature of the IF notation.

A well-known model checking tool for linear hybrid automata (based on a semi-decision procedure) is HyTech [47]. The input language of HyTech can be translated into our TIOA model, to apply TIOA verification methods. Likewise, TIOAs whose continuous variables conform to the linearity conditions of HyTech could be verified using model-checking capabilities of HyTech. For an overview of verification tools for hybrid systems we refer to [99].

The timed I/O automaton modeling framework presented in this monograph can be used to express models that use lower and upper time bounds on tasks or actions [91, 88]. Our framework includes an operation for adding time bounds on a subset of the actions of a timed automaton. As a result of this operation, lower bounds are transformed to appropriate preconditions for transitions and upper bounds are transformed to stopping conditions for trajectories.

An interesting timed automaton model called "Clock GTA " was introduced in [23]. The model was used for describing algorithms that behave in accordance with their timing constraints in certain intervals but may exhibit timing failures for some other intervals. The possibility of expressing such an ability turns out to be crucial for performance and fault-tolerance analysis for practical algorithms [23, 75]. We are interested in finding a systematic way of describing such behavior with our timed I/O automaton model.

1.4 ORGANIZATION OF THE BOOK

The rest of this book is organized as follows. Chapter 2 contains mathematical preliminaries. Chapter 3 defines notions that are useful for describing the behavior of timed systems, most importantly, trajectories and timed sequences. Chapter 4 defines *timed automata (TAs)*, which contain all of the structure of TIOAs except for the classification of external actions as inputs or outputs. It also defines external behavior for TAs and implementation and simulation relationships between TAs. Chapter 5 presents composition and hiding operations for TAs, along with operations for adding bounds that relate TAs to other timed automaton models. Chapter 6 presents definitions and results on the classification of properties of TAs as safety and liveness properties. Chapter 7 defines *timed I/O automata (TIOAs)* by adding an input/output classification to TAs, and extends the theory of TAs to TIOAs. It also defines special kinds of TIOAs such as progressive and receptive TIOAs. Chapter 8 presents compositionality results for TIOAs in general, and for the special classes of progressive and receptive TIOAs. Finally, Chapter 9 presents some conclusions and discusses future work. Examples are included throughout.

An earlier edition of this book was published in 2006 [59]. In this second edition, some minor errors in the first edition have been corrected and some clarifications and references have been added. We have also included new material in Chapter 6 on properties, and several other results about composition. A still earlier version of the work appeared in [58].

CHAPTER 2

Mathematical Preliminaries

In this chapter, we give basic mathematical definitions and notation that will be used as a foundation for our definitions of timed automata and timed I/O automata. These definitions involve functions, sequences, partial orders, and untimed automata. Many readers might prefer to skip directly to Chapter 4, referring back to Chapters 2 and 3 as needed.

2.1 FUNCTIONS AND RELATIONS

If f is a function, then we denote the domain and range of f by $dom(f)$ and $range(f)$, respectively. If S is a set, then we write $f \lceil S$ for the restriction of f to S, that is, the function g with $dom(g) = dom(f) \cap S$ such that $g(c) = f(c)$ for each $c \in dom(g)$.

We say that two functions, f and g, are *compatible* if $f \lceil dom(g) = g \lceil dom(f)$. If f and g are compatible functions then we write $f \cup g$ for the unique function h with $dom(h) = dom(f) \cup dom(g)$ satisfying the condition: for each $c \in dom(h)$, if $c \in dom(f)$ then $h(c) = f(c)$ and if $c \in dom(g)$ then $h(c) = g(c)$. More generally, if F is a set of pairwise compatible functions then we write $\bigcup F$ for the unique function h with $dom(h) = \bigcup\{dom(f) \mid f \in F\}$ satisfying the condition: for each $f \in F$ and $c \in dom(f)$, $h(c) = f(c)$.

If f is a function whose range is a set of functions and S is a set, then we write $f \downarrow S$ for the function g with $dom(g) = dom(f)$ such that $g(c) = f(c) \lceil S$ for each $c \in dom(g)$.

The restriction operation $\downarrow$ is extended to sets of functions by pointwise extension. Also, if f is a function whose range is a set of functions, all of which have a particular element d in their domain, then we write $f \downarrow d$ for the function g with $dom(g) = dom(f)$ such that $g(c) = f(c)(d)$ for each $c \in dom(g)$.

We say that two functions, f and g, whose ranges are sets of functions are *pointwise compatible* if for each $c \in dom(f) \cap dom(g)$, $f(c)$ and $g(c)$ are compatible. If f and g have the same domain and are pointwise compatible, then we denote by $f \dot\cup g$ the function h with $dom(h) = dom(f)$ such that $h(c) = f(c) \cup g(c)$ for each c.

A relation over sets X and Y is defined to be any subset of $X \times Y$. If R is a relation, then we denote the domain and range of R by $dom(R)$ and $range(R)$, respectively. A relation over X and Y is *total* over X if $dom(R) = X$. If R is a relation over X and Y, and $x \in X$, we define $R(x) = \{y \in Y \mid (x, y) \in R\}$. We say that a relation R over X and Y is *image-finite* if for each $x \in X$, $R(x)$ is finite.

2.2 SEQUENCES

Let S be any set. A *sequence* σ over S is a function from a downward-closed subset of $\mathsf{Z}^{>0}$ to S. Thus, the domain of a sequence is either the set of all positive integers, or is of the form $\{1, \ldots, k\}$ for some k. In the first case, we say that the sequence is infinite, and in the second case finite. We use $|\sigma|$ to denote the cardinality of $dom(\sigma)$. The sets of finite and infinite sequences over S are denoted by S^* and S^ω, respectively. *Concatenation* of a finite sequence ρ with a finite or infinite sequence σ is denoted by $\rho \frown \sigma$. The *empty sequence*, that is the sequence with the empty domain, is denoted by λ. The sequence containing one element $c \in S$ is abbreviated as c. We say that a sequence σ is a *prefix* of a sequence ρ, denoted by $\sigma \leq \rho$, if $\sigma = \rho \lceil dom(\sigma)$. Thus, $\sigma \leq \rho$ if either $\sigma = \rho$, or σ is finite and $\rho = \sigma \frown \sigma'$ for some sequence σ'. If σ is a nonempty sequence then $head(\sigma)$ denotes the first element of σ and $tail(\sigma)$ denotes σ with its first element removed. Moreover, if σ is finite, then $last(\sigma)$ denotes the last element of σ and $init(\sigma)$ denotes σ with its last element removed. Let σ and σ' be sequences over S. Then σ' is a *subsequence* of σ provided that there exists a monotone increasing function $f : dom(\sigma') \to dom(\sigma)$ such that $\sigma'(i) = \sigma(f(i))$ and $f(i+1) = f(i) + 1$ for all $i \in dom(\sigma')$. If $1 \leq j_1 \leq j_2 \leq |\sigma|$, then we define $\sigma(j_1 \ldots j_2)$ to be the subsequence of σ obtained by extracting the elements in positions $j_1, \ldots, j_2$; that is, σ' is the subsequence obtained from function f of length $j_2 - j_1 + 1$, where $f(i) = i + j_1 - 1$ for all $i \in dom(\sigma')$.

2.3 PARTIAL ORDERS

We recall some basic definitions and results regarding partial orders, and in particular, complete partial orders (cpos) from [42, 45]. A *partial order* is a set S together with a binary relation $\sqsubseteq$ that is reflexive, antisymmetric, and transitive. In the sequel, we usually denote posets by the set S without explicit mention to the binary relation $\sqsubseteq$.

A subset $P \subseteq S$ is *bounded (above)* if there is a $c \in S$ such that $d \sqsubseteq c$ for each $d \in P$; in this case, c is an *upper bound* for P. A *least upper bound (lub)* for a subset $P \subseteq S$ is an upper bound c for P such that $c \leq d$ for every upper bound d for P. If P has a lub, then it is necessarily unique, and we denote it by $\bigsqcup P$. A subset $P \subseteq S$ is *directed* if every finite subset Q of P has an upper bound in P. A poset S is *complete*, and hence is a *complete partial order (cpo)* if every directed subset P of S has a lub in S.

A finite or infinite sequence of elements, $c_0\, c_1\, c_2 \ldots$, of a partially ordered set $(S, \sqsubseteq)$ is called a *chain* if $c_i \sqsubseteq c_{i+1}$ for each nonfinal index i. We define the *limit* of the chain, $\lim_{i\to\infty} c_i$, to be the lub of the set $\{c_0, c_1, c_2, \ldots\}$ if S contains such a bound; otherwise, the limit is undefined. Since a chain is a special case of a directed set, each chain of a cpo has a limit.

A function $f : S \to S'$ between posets S and S' is *monotone* if $f(c) \sqsubseteq f(d)$ whenever $c \sqsubseteq d$. If f is monotone and P is a directed set, then the set $f(P) = \{f(c) \mid c \in P\}$ is directed as well. If f is monotone and $f(\bigsqcup P) = \bigsqcup f(P)$ for every directed P, then f is said to be *continuous*.

An element c of a cpo S is *compact* if, for every directed set P such that $c \sqsubseteq \bigsqcup P$, there is some $d \in P$ such that $c \sqsubseteq d$. We define $K(S)$ to be the set of compact elements of S. A cpo S is *algebraic* if every $c \in S$ is the lub of the set $\{d \in K(S) \mid d \sqsubseteq c\}$. A simple example of an algebraic cpo is the set of finite or infinite sequences over some given domain, equipped with the prefix ordering. Here the compact elements are the finite sequences.

2.4 A BASIC GRAPH LEMMA

We require the following lemma, a slight generalization of König's Lemma [60]. If G is a directed graph, then a *root* of G is defined to be a node with no incoming edges.

Lemma 2.1 *Let G be an infinite directed graph that satisfies the following properties.*

1. *G has finitely many roots.*
2. *Each node of G has finite outdegree.*
3. *Each node of G is reachable from some root of G.*

Then, there is an infinite path in G starting from some root.

Proof. An extension of the usual proof of König's Lemma [60]. □

CHAPTER 3

Describing Timed System Behavior

In this chapter, we give basic definitions that are useful for describing discrete and continuous changes to the system's state. The key notions are *static* and *dynamic types* for variables, *trajectories*, and *hybrid sequences*. Most of the material in this chapter comes from the paper on the HIOA modeling framework [79]. The reader is referred to [79] for the proofs that are not included here. Again, the reader might prefer to skip directly to Chapter 4 and refer back to this chapter as needed.

3.1 TIME

Throughout this monograph, we fix a *time axis* T, which is a subgroup of $(\mathsf{R}, +)$, the real numbers with addition. We assume that every infinite, monotone, bounded sequence of elements of T has a limit in T. The reader may find it convenient to think of T as the set R of real numbers, but the set Z of integers and the singleton set $\{0\}$ are also examples of allowed time axes. We define $\mathsf{T}^{\geq 0} \triangleq \{t \in \mathsf{T} \mid t \geq 0\}$.

An *interval* J is a nonempty, convex subset of T. We denote intervals as usual: $[t_1, t_2] = \{t \in \mathsf{T} \mid t_1 \leq t \leq t_2\}$, $[t_1, t_2) = \{t \in \mathsf{T} \mid t_1 \leq t < t_2\}$, etc. An interval J is *left-closed* (*right-closed*) if it has a minimum (resp., maximum) element, and *left-open* (*right-open*) otherwise. It is *closed* if it is both left-closed and right-closed. We write $\min(J)$ and $\max(J)$ for the minimum and maximum elements, respectively, of an interval J (if they exist), and $\inf(J)$ and $\sup(J)$ for the infimum and supremum, respectively, of J in $\mathsf{R} \cup \{-\infty, \infty\}$. For $K \subseteq \mathsf{T}$ and $t \in \mathsf{T}$, we define $K + t \triangleq \{t' + t \mid t' \in K\}$. Similarly, for a function f with domain K, we define $f + t$ to be the function with domain $K + t$ satisfying, for each $t' \in K + t$, $(f + t)(t') = f(t' - t)$.

In some definitions and theorems in the monograph where we use R as the time domain, we assume that the relation $\leq$ on R extends to a relation on $\mathsf{R} \cup \{\infty\}$ such that $\infty \leq \infty$ and for all $t \in \mathsf{R}$, $t < \infty$.

3.2 STATIC AND DYNAMIC TYPES

We assume a universal set V of *variables*. A variable represents a location within the state of a system. For each variable v, we assume both a *(static) type*, which gives the set of values it may take on, and a *dynamic type*, which gives the set of trajectories it may follow. Formally, for each variable v we assume the following:

- $type(v)$, the *(static) type* of v. This is a nonempty set of values.
- $dtype(v)$, the *dynamic type* of v. This is a set of functions from left-closed intervals of T to $type(v)$ that satisfies the following properties:
  1. *(Closure under time shift)*
     For each $f \in dtype(v)$ and $t \in \mathsf{T}$, $f + t \in dtype(v)$.
  2. *(Closure under subinterval)*
     For each $f \in dtype(v)$ and each left-closed interval $J \subseteq dom(f)$, $f \lceil J \in dtype(v)$.
  3. *(Closure under pasting)*
     Let $f_0\, f_1\, f_2, \ldots$ be a sequence of functions in $dtype(v)$ such that, for each nonfinal index i, $dom(f_i)$ is right-closed and $\max(dom(f_i)) = \min(dom(f_{i+1}))$. Then the function f defined by $f(t) \triangleq f_i(t)$, where i is the smallest index such that $t \in dom(f_i)$, is in $dtype(v)$.

Example 3.1 (Discrete variables). Let v be any variable and let *Constant* be the set of constant functions from a left-closed interval of T to $type(v)$. Then *Constant* is closed under time shift and subinterval. If the dynamic type of v is obtained by closing *Constant* under the pasting operation, then v is called a *discrete* variable. This is essentially the same as the definition of a discrete variable in [88].

Example 3.2 (Analog variables). Assume that $\mathsf{T} = \mathsf{R}$. Let v be any variable whose static type is an interval of R and *Continuous* be the set of continuous functions from a left-closed interval of T to $type(v)$. Then *Continuous* is closed under time shift and subinterval. If the dynamic type of v is obtained by closing *Continuous* under the pasting operation, then v is called an *analog* variable. Figure 3.1 shows an example of a function f in the dynamic type of an analog variable. Function f is defined on the interval $[0, 4)$ and is obtained by pasting together four pieces. At the boundary points between these pieces, f takes the value specified by the leftmost piece, which makes f continuous from the left. Note that f is undefined at time 4. Also note that, in a setting with $\mathsf{T} = \mathsf{R}$, a real-valued discrete variable is a special kind of analog variable as constant functions are also continuous.

Example 3.3 (Standard real-valued function classes). If we take $\mathsf{T} = \mathsf{R}$ and $type(v) = \mathsf{R}$, then other examples of dynamic types can be obtained by taking the pasting closure of standard function classes from real analysis, the set of differentiable functions, the set of functions that are differentiable k times (for any k), the set of smooth functions, the set of integrable functions, the set of L^p functions (for any p), the set of measurable locally essentially bounded functions [113], or the set of all functions.

Standard function classes are closed under time shift and subinterval, but not under pasting. A natural way of defining a dynamic type is as the pasting closure of a class of functions that is closed under time shift and subinterval. In such a case, it follows that the new class is closed under all three operations.

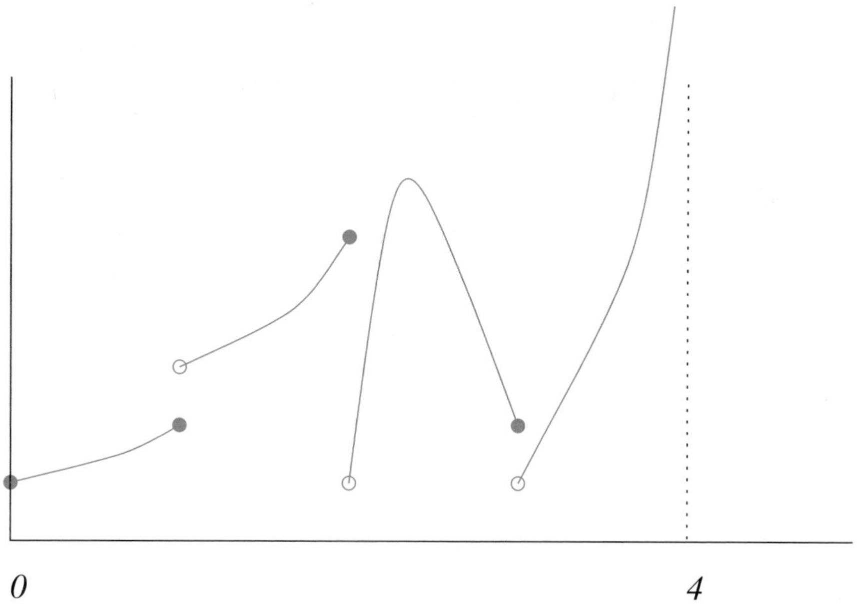

Figure 3.1: Example of a function in the dynamic type of an analog variable.

3.3 TRAJECTORIES

In this section, we define the notion of a *trajectory*, define operations on trajectories, and prove simple properties of trajectories and their operations. A trajectory is used to model the evolution of a collection of variables over an interval of time.

3.3.1 BASIC DEFINITIONS

Let V be a set of variables, that is, a subset of V. A *valuation* $\mathbf{v}$ for V is a function that associates with each variable $v \in V$ a value in $type(v)$. We write $val(V)$ for the set of valuations for V. Let J be a left-closed interval of T with left endpoint equal to 0. Then a J*-trajectory* for V is a function $\tau : J \to val(V)$, such that for each $v \in V$, $\tau \downarrow v \in dtype(v)$. A *trajectory* for V is a J-trajectory for V, for any J. We write $trajs(V)$ for the set of all trajectories for V. If Q is a set of valuations for some set V of variables, we write $trajs(Q)$ for the set of all trajectories whose range is a subset of Q.

A trajectory for V where $V = \emptyset$ is simply a function from a time interval to the special function with the empty domain. Thus, the only interesting information represented by such a trajectory is the length of the time interval that constitutes the domain of the trajectory. We use trajectories over the empty set of variables when we wish to capture the amount of time-passage but abstract away the evolution of variables.

A trajectory for V with domain $[0, 0]$ is called a *point* trajectory for V. If $\mathbf{v}$ is a valuation for V then $\wp(\mathbf{v})$ denotes the point trajectory for V that maps 0 to $\mathbf{v}$. We say that a J-trajectory is *finite* if J is a finite interval, *closed* if J is a (finite) closed interval, *open* if J is a right-open interval, and *full* if $J = \mathsf{T}^{\geq 0}$. If T is a set of trajectories, then *finite*(T), *closed*(T), *open*(T), and *full*(T) denote the subsets of T consisting of all the finite, closed, open, and full trajectories in T, respectively.

If τ is a trajectory then $\tau.ltime$, the *limit time* of τ, is the supremum of $dom(\tau)$. We define $\tau.fval$, the *first valuation* of τ, to be $\tau(0)$, and if τ is closed, we define $\tau.lval$, the *last valuation* of τ, to be $\tau(\tau.ltime)$. For τ a trajectory and $t \in \mathsf{T}^{\geq 0}$, we define

$$
\begin{aligned}
\tau \trianglelefteq t &\triangleq \tau \lceil [0, t], \\
\tau \triangleleft t &\triangleq \tau \lceil [0, t), \\
\tau \trianglerighteq t &\triangleq (\tau \lceil [t, \infty)) - t.
\end{aligned}
$$

Note that, since dynamic types are closed under time shift and subintervals, the result of applying the above operations is always a trajectory, except when the result is a function with an empty domain. By convention, we also write $\tau \trianglelefteq \infty \triangleq \tau$ and $\tau \triangleleft \infty \triangleq \tau$.

3.3.2 PREFIX ORDERING

Trajectory τ is a *prefix* of trajectory υ, denoted by $\tau \leq \upsilon$, if τ can be obtained by restricting υ to a subset of its domain. Formally, if τ and υ are trajectories for V, then $\tau \leq \upsilon$ iff $\tau = \upsilon \lceil dom(\tau)$. Alternatively, $\tau \leq \upsilon$ iff there exists a $t \in \mathsf{T}^{\geq 0} \cup \{\infty\}$ such that $\tau = \upsilon \trianglelefteq t$ or $\tau = \upsilon \triangleleft t$. If $\tau \leq \upsilon$ then clearly $dom(\tau) \subseteq dom(\upsilon)$. If T is a set of trajectories for V, then *pref*(T) denotes the *prefix closure* of T, defined by:

$$
pref(T) \triangleq \{\tau \in trajs(V) \mid \exists \upsilon \in T : \tau \leq \upsilon\}.
$$

We say that T is *prefix closed* if $T = pref(T)$.

The following lemma gives a simple domain-theoretic characterization of the set of trajectories over a given set V of variables.

Lemma 3.4 *Let V be a set of variables. The set $trajs(V)$ of trajectories for V, together with the prefix ordering $\leq$, is an algebraic cpo. Its compact elements are the closed trajectories. In fact, each element of the cpo is the limit of a chain of compact elements.*

We say that a set P of trajectories is *closed under limits* if the limit of each chain of elements of P is contained in P.

3.3.3 CONCATENATION

The concatenation of two trajectories is obtained by taking the union of the first trajectory and the function obtained by shifting the domain of the second trajectory until the start time agrees with the limit time of the first trajectory; the last valuation of the first trajectory, which may not be the same as the first valuation of the second trajectory, is the one that appears in the concatenation. Formally, suppose τ and τ' are trajectories for V, with τ closed. Then the *concatenation* $\tau \frown \tau'$ is the function given by

$$\tau \frown \tau' \quad \triangleq \quad \tau \cup (\tau' \lceil (0, \infty) + \tau.ltime).$$

Because dynamic types are closed under time shift and pasting, it follows that $\tau \frown \tau'$ is a trajectory for V. Observe that $\tau \frown \tau'$ is finite (resp., closed, full) if and only if τ' is finite (resp., closed, full). Observe also that concatenation is associative.

The following lemma, which is easy to prove, shows the close connection between concatenation and the prefix ordering.

Lemma 3.5 *Let τ and υ be trajectories for V with τ closed. Then*

$$\tau \leq \upsilon \quad \Leftrightarrow \quad \exists \tau' : \upsilon = \tau \frown \tau'.$$

Note that if $\tau \leq \upsilon$, then the trajectory τ' such that $\upsilon = \tau \frown \tau'$ has an arbitrary value for $\tau'.fval$ and the remainder of the trajectory is unique. Note also that the "$\Leftarrow$" implication in Lemma 3.5 would not hold if the first valuation of the second argument, rather than the last valuation of the first argument, were used in the concatenation.

We extend the definition of concatenation to any (finite or countably infinite) number of arguments. Let $\tau_0\, \tau_1\, \tau_2 \ldots$ be a (finite or infinite) sequence of trajectories such that τ_i is closed for each nonfinal index i. Define trajectories $\tau'_0, \tau'_1, \tau'_2, \ldots$ inductively by

$$\begin{aligned} \tau'_0 &\triangleq \tau_0, \\ \tau'_{i+1} &\triangleq \tau'_i \frown \tau_{i+1} \text{ for nonfinal } i. \end{aligned}$$

Lemma 3.5 implies that for each nonfinal i, $\tau'_i \leq \tau'_{i+1}$. We define the *concatenation* $\tau_0 \frown \tau_1 \frown \tau_2 \cdots$ to be the limit of the chain $\tau'_0, \tau'_1, \tau'_2, \ldots$; existence of this limit follows from Lemma 3.4.

3.4 HYBRID SEQUENCES

In this section, we introduce the notion of a *hybrid sequence*, which is used to model a combination of changes that occur instantaneously and changes that occur over intervals of time. Our definition is parameterized by a set A of *actions*, which are used to model instantaneous changes and instantaneous synchronizations with the environment, and a set V of *variables*, which are used to model changes over intervals of time. We also define some special kinds of hybrid sequences and some operations on hybrid sequences, and give basic properties.

3.4.1 BASIC DEFINITIONS

Fix a set A of actions and a set V of variables. An (A, V)-*sequence* is a finite or infinite alternating sequence $\alpha = \tau_0\, a_1\, \tau_1\, a_2\, \tau_2 \ldots$, where:

1. each τ_i is a trajectory in $trajs(V)$;
2. each a_i is an action in A;
3. if α is a finite sequence then it ends with a trajectory; and
4. if τ_i is not the last trajectory in α then τ_i is closed.

We write $\mathsf{S}(A, V)$ to denote the set of (A, V)-sequences. A *hybrid sequence* is an (A, V)-sequence for some A and V.

Since the trajectories, in a hybrid sequence can be point trajectories, our notion of hybrid sequence allows a sequence of discrete actions to occur at the same real time, with corresponding changes of variable values. An alternative approach is described in [102], where state changes at a single real time are modeled using a notion of "superdense time". Specifically, hybrid behavior is modeled in [102] using functions from an extended time domain, which includes countably many elements for each real time, to states.

If α is a hybrid sequence, with notation as above, then we define the *limit time* of α, $\alpha.ltime$, to be $\sum_i \tau_i.ltime$. A hybrid sequence α is defined to be:

- *time-bounded* if $\alpha.ltime$ is finite.
- *admissible* if $\alpha.ltime = \infty$.
- *closed* if α is a finite sequence and its final trajectory is closed.
- *open* if α is a finite sequence and its final trajectory is open.
- *Zeno* if α is neither closed nor admissible, that is, if α is time-bounded and is either open or an infinite sequence.
- *nonZeno* if α is not Zeno.

We write $\mathsf{A}(A, V)$ and $\mathsf{C}(A, V)$ to denote the sets of admissible and closed (A, V)-sequences, respectively. Figure 3.2 illustrates the classification of hybrid sequences. Observe that finite admissible hybrid sequences are always open, and infinite time-bounded sequences are always Zeno. Finite time-bounded sequences can be either closed or Zeno and open. For any hybrid sequence α, we define the *first valuation* of α, $\alpha.fval$, to be $head(\alpha).fval$. Also, if α is closed, we define the *last valuation* of α, $\alpha.lval$, to be $last(\alpha).lval$, that is, the last valuation in the final trajectory of α.

If α is a closed (A, V)-sequence, where $V = \emptyset$ and $\beta \in trajs(\emptyset)$, we call $\alpha \frown \beta$ a *time-extension* of α.

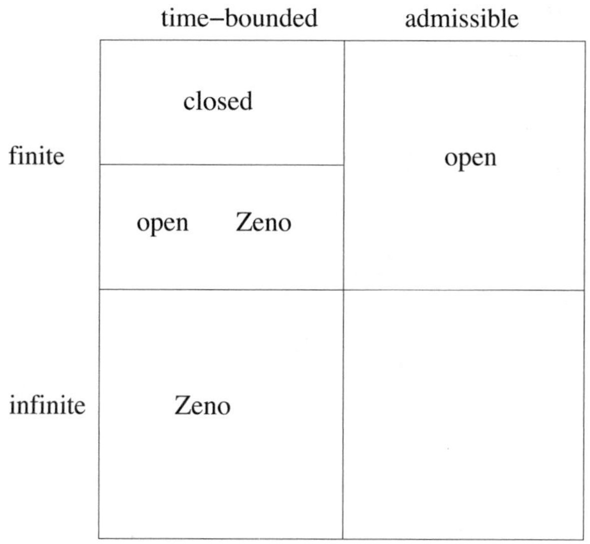

Figure 3.2: Classification of hybrid sequences.

3.4.2 PREFIX ORDERING

We say that (A, V)-sequence $\alpha = \tau_0\, a_1\, \tau_1 \ldots$ is a *prefix* of (A, V)-sequence $\beta = \upsilon_0\, b_1\, \upsilon_1 \ldots$, denoted by $\alpha \leq \beta$, provided that (at least) one of the following holds:

1. $\alpha = \beta$.

2. α is a finite sequence ending in some τ_k; $\tau_i = \upsilon_i$ and $a_{i+1} = b_{i+1}$ for every i, $0 \leq i < k$; and $\tau_k \leq \upsilon_k$.

Like the set of trajectories over V, the set of (A, V)-sequences is an algebraic cpo:

Lemma 3.6 *Let V be a set of variables and A a set of actions. The set of (A, V)-sequences, together with the prefix ordering $\leq$, is an algebraic cpo. Its compact elements are the closed (A, V)-sequences. In fact, each element of the cpo is the limit of a chain of compact elements.*

We say that a set P of (A, V)-sequences is *closed under limits* if the limit of each chain of elements of P is contained in P. Set P is *closed under time-bounded limits* if, for each chain of elements of P with a limit α that is time-bounded, α is contained in P. In a similar way, we define closure under admissible limits, finite limits, Zeno limits, etc.

3.4.3 CONCATENATION

Suppose α and α' are (A, V)-sequences with α closed. Then the *concatenation* $\alpha \frown \alpha'$ is the (A, V)-sequence given by

$$\alpha \frown \alpha' \triangleq init(\alpha)\ (last(\alpha) \frown head(\alpha'))\ tail(\alpha').$$

(Here, *init*, *last*, *head*, and *tail* are ordinary sequence operations.)

Lemma 3.7 *Let α and β be (A, V)-sequences with α closed. Then*

$$\alpha \leq \beta \quad \Leftrightarrow \quad \exists \alpha' : \beta = \alpha \frown \alpha'.$$

Note that if $\alpha \leq \beta$, then the (A, V)-sequence α' such that $\beta = \alpha \frown \alpha'$ is unique except that it has an arbitrary value in $val(V)$ for $\alpha'.fval$.

As we did for trajectories, we extend the concatenation definition for (A, V)-sequences to any finite or infinite number of arguments. Let $\alpha_0\, \alpha_1 \ldots$ be a finite or infinite sequence of (A, V)-sequences such that α_i is closed for each nonfinal index i. Define (A, V)-sequences $\alpha'_0, \alpha'_1, \ldots$ inductively by

$$\begin{aligned} \alpha'_0 &\triangleq \alpha_0, \\ \alpha'_{i+1} &\triangleq \alpha'_i \frown \alpha_{i+1} \text{ for nonfinal } i. \end{aligned}$$

Lemma 3.7 implies that for each nonfinal i, $\alpha'_i \leq \alpha'_{i+1}$. We define the *concatenation* $\alpha_0 \frown \alpha_1 \cdots$ to be the limit of the chain $\alpha'_0, \alpha'_1, \ldots$; existence of this limit is ensured by Lemma 3.6.

3.4.4 RESTRICTION

Let A and A' be sets of actions and let V and V' be sets of variables. The (A', V')*-restriction* of an (A, V)-sequence α, denoted by $\alpha \lceil (A', V')$, is obtained by first projecting all trajectories of α on the variables in V', then removing the actions not in A', and finally concatenating all adjacent trajectories. Formally, we define the (A', V')-restriction first for closed (A, V)-sequences and then extend the definition to arbitrary (A, V)-sequences using a limit construction. The definition for closed (A, V)-sequences is by induction on the length of those sequences:

$$\begin{aligned} \tau \lceil (A', V') &= \tau \downarrow V' \text{ if } \tau \text{ is a single trajectory}, \\ \alpha\, a\, \tau \lceil (A', V') &= \begin{cases} (\alpha \lceil (A', V'))\, a\, (\tau \downarrow V') & \text{if } a \in A', \\ (\alpha \lceil (A', V')) \frown (\tau \downarrow V') & \text{otherwise.} \end{cases} \end{aligned}$$

It is easy to see that the restriction operator is monotone on the set of closed (A, V)-sequences. Hence, if we apply this operation to a directed set, the result is again a directed set. Together with Lemma 3.6, this allows us to extend the definition of restriction to arbitrary (A, V)-sequences by:

$$\alpha \lceil (A', V') = \sqcup \{\beta \lceil (A', V') \mid \beta \text{ is a closed prefix of } \alpha\}.$$

The next four lemmas state some basic properties of the restriction operation.

Lemma 3.8 *(A', V')-restriction is a continuous operation.*

Lemma 3.9 $(\alpha_0 \frown \alpha_1 \frown \cdots) \lceil (A, V) = \alpha_0 \lceil (A, V) \frown \alpha_1 \lceil (A, V) \frown \ldots$.

Lemma 3.10 $(\alpha \lceil (A, V)) \lceil (A', V') = \alpha \lceil (A \cap A', V \cap V')$.

Lemma 3.11 *Let α be a hybrid sequence, A a set of actions and V a set of variables.*

1. *α is time-bounded if and only if $\alpha \lceil (A, V)$ is time-bounded.*
2. *α is admissible if and only if $\alpha \lceil (A, V)$ is admissible.*
3. *If α is closed then $\alpha \lceil (A, V)$ is closed.*
4. *If α is nonZeno then $\alpha \lceil (A, V)$ is nonZeno.*

Example 3.12 (A Zeno execution with a closed (A, V)-restriction). In order to understand why in Lemma 3.11 we have an implication in only one direction in items 3 and 4, consider the Zeno sequence α of the form $\wp(\mathbf{v})\ a\ \wp(\mathbf{v})\ a\ \wp(\mathbf{v}) \ldots$. Let A be a set such that $a \notin A$ and let V consist of the variables in $dom(\mathbf{v})$. Obviously, $\alpha \lceil (A, V)$, which is $\wp(\mathbf{v})$, is closed, and hence also nonZeno. This shows that the fact that $\alpha \lceil (A, V)$ is closed (resp., nonZeno) does not imply that α is closed (resp., nonZeno).

CHAPTER 4

Timed Automata

In this chapter, as a preliminary step toward defining timed I/O automata, we define a slightly more general *timed automaton* model. In timed automata, actions are classified as external or internal, but external actions are not further classified as input or output; the input/output distinction is added in Chapter 7. We define how timed automata execute and define implementation and simulation relations between timed automata.

4.1 DEFINITION OF TIMED AUTOMATA

A timed automaton is a state machine whose states are divided into *variables*, and that has a set of discrete *actions*, some of which may be internal and some external. The state of a timed automaton may change in two ways: by *discrete transitions*, which change the state atomically, and by *trajectories*, which describe the evolution of the state over intervals of time. The discrete transitions are labeled with actions; this will allow us to synchronize the transitions of different timed automata when we compose them in parallel. The evolution described by a trajectory may be described by continuous or discontinuous functions.

Formally, a *timed automaton (TA)* $\mathcal{A} = (X, Q, \Theta, E, H, \mathcal{D}, \mathcal{T})$ consists of:

- A set X of *internal variables*.
- A set $Q \subseteq val(X)$ of *states*.
- A nonempty set $\Theta \subseteq Q$ of *start states*.
- A set E of *external actions* and a set H of *internal actions*, disjoint from each other. We write $A \triangleq E \cup H$.
- A set $\mathcal{D} \subseteq Q \times A \times Q$ of *discrete transitions*. We use $\mathbf{x} \xrightarrow{a}_{\mathcal{A}} \mathbf{x}'$ as shorthand for $(\mathbf{x}, a, \mathbf{x}') \in \mathcal{D}$. Here and elsewhere, we sometimes drop the subscript and write $\mathbf{x} \xrightarrow{a} \mathbf{x}'$, when we think $\mathcal{A}$ should be clear from the context. We say that a is *enabled* in $\mathbf{x}$ if $\mathbf{x} \xrightarrow{a} \mathbf{x}'$ for some $\mathbf{x}'$. We say that a set C of actions is enabled in a state $\mathbf{x}$ if some action in C is enabled in $\mathbf{x}$.
- A set $\mathcal{T} \subseteq trajs(Q)$ of trajectories. Given a trajectory $\tau \in \mathcal{T}$ we denote $\tau.fval$ by $\tau.fstate$ and, if τ is closed, we denote $\tau.lval$ by $\tau.lstate$. When $\tau.fstate = \mathbf{x}$ and $\tau.lstate = \mathbf{x}'$, we write $\mathbf{x} \xrightarrow{\tau}_{\mathcal{A}} \mathbf{x}'$. We require that the following axioms hold:

T0 *(Existence of point trajectories)*
If $\mathbf{x} \in Q$ then $\wp(\mathbf{x}) \in \mathcal{T}$.

T1 *(Prefix closure)*
For every $\tau \in \mathcal{T}$ and every $\tau' \leq \tau$, $\tau' \in \mathcal{T}$.

T2 *(Suffix closure)*
For every $\tau \in \mathcal{T}$ and every $t \in dom(\tau)$, $\tau \trianglerighteq t \in \mathcal{T}$.

T3 *(Concatenation closure)*
Let $\tau_0 \, \tau_1 \, \tau_2 \ldots$ be a sequence of trajectories in $\mathcal{T}$ such that, for each nonfinal index i, τ_i is closed and $\tau_i.lstate = \tau_{i+1}.fstate$. Then $\tau_0 \frown \tau_1 \frown \tau_2 \cdots \in \mathcal{T}$.

A timed automaton is essentially a hybrid automaton in the sense of [79] in which W, the set of external variables, is empty. Apart from that, the only difference is the addition of Axiom **T0**, a small restriction that does not affect any of the results of [79] but that we need to prove Theorem 8.8. Axioms **T1-3** express some natural further conditions on the set of trajectories that we need to construct our theory. A key part of this theory is a parallel composition operation for timed automata. In a composed system, any trajectory of any component automaton may be interrupted at any time by a discrete transition of another (possibly independent) component automaton. Axiom **T1** ensures that the part of the trajectory up to the discrete transition is a trajectory, and Axiom **T2** ensures that the remainder is a trajectory. Axiom **T3** is required because the environment of a timed automaton, as a result of its own internal discrete transitions, may change its dynamics repeatedly, and the automaton must be able to follow this behavior. Axiom **T3** implies that the set $\mathcal{T}$ of trajectories is closed under limits.

Our definition of a timed automaton differs from previous definitions of timed automata [86, 107] in two major respects. First, the states are structured using variables, which have dynamic types with specific closure properties. The variable structure is convenient for writing specifications and the dynamic types are useful in analyzing continuous evolution of the state. Second, the set of trajectories is defined as an explicit component of an automaton. In the previous definitions, time-passage was represented by special time-passage actions and trajectories were defined implicitly, as auxiliary functions describing the effects of time-passage actions on states.

Notation: We often denote the components of a TA $\mathcal{A}$ by $X_{\mathcal{A}}$, $Q_{\mathcal{A}}$, $\Theta_{\mathcal{A}}$, $E_{\mathcal{A}}$, etc., and the components of a TA $\mathcal{A}_i$ by X_i, Q_i, Θ_i, E_i, etc. We sometimes omit these subscripts, where no confusion seems likely. For example, we typically specify sets of trajectories using differential and algebraic equations and inclusions. Below, we explain a few notational conventions that help us in doing this. Suppose the time domain T is R, τ is a (fixed) trajectory over some set of variables V, and $v \in V$. With some abuse of notation, we use the variable name v to denote the function $\tau \downarrow v$ in $dom(\tau) \rightarrow type(v)$, which gives the value of v at all times during trajectory τ. That is, for all $t \in dom(\tau)$, we have $v(t) = (\tau \downarrow v)(t) = \tau(t)(v)$. Similarly, we view any expression e containing variables from V as a function with domain $dom(\tau)$. Suppose that v is a variable and e is a real-valued expression containing variables from V. Using these conventions we can say, for example, that τ satisfies the algebraic equation

$$v \;=\; e$$

which means that, for every $t \in dom(\tau)$, $v(t) = e(t)$, that is, the constraint on the variables expressed by the equation $v = e$ holds for each state on trajectory τ. Now suppose also that e, when viewed as a function, is integrable. Then we say that τ satisfies

$$d(v) \;=\; e$$

if, for every $t \in dom(\tau)$, $v(t) = v(0) + \int_0^t e(t')dt'$. Equivalently, for every $t_1, t_2 \in dom(\tau)$ such that $t_1 \leq t_2$, $v(t_2) = v(t_1) + \int_{t_1}^{t_2} e(t')dt'$. Note that this interpretation of the differential equation makes sense even at points where v is not differentiable. A similar interpretation of differential equations is used by Polderman and Willems [103], who call functions defined in this way "weak solutions".

We generalize this notation to handle inequalities as well as equalities. Suppose that v is a variable and e is a real-valued expression containing variables from V. The inequality

$$e \;\leq\; v$$

means that, for every $t \in dom(\tau)$, $e(t) \leq v(t)$. That is, the constraint expressed by the inequality $e \leq v$ holds for each state of trajectory τ. Similarly, the inequality

$$v \;\leq\; e$$

means that, for every $t \in dom(\tau)$, $v(t) \leq e(t)$. Now suppose that e is integrable when viewed as a function. Then we say that τ satisfies

$$e \;\leq\; d(v)$$

if, for every $t_1, t_2 \in dom(\tau)$ such that $t_1 \leq t_2$, $v(t_1) + \int_{t_1}^{t_2} e(t')dt' \leq v(t_2)$, and τ satisfies

$$d(v) \;\leq\; e$$

if, for every $t_1, t_2 \in dom(\tau)$ such that $t_1 \leq t_2$, $v(t_2) \leq v(t_1) + \int_{t_1}^{t_2} e(t')dt'$.

Conventions for automata specifications: In all the examples of this monograph we assume the time axis T to be R and specify timed automata by using a variant of the *TIOA* language presented in [93, 56, 32, 33].

An automaton specification consists of four main parts: a signature, which lists the actions along with their kinds (**external** or **internal**), and parameter types, a state variables list, which declares the names and types of state variables, a collection of transition definitions and a trajectories definition.

Unless specified otherwise, the set of states of an automaton equals the set of all valuations of its state variables. Static types of variables are always declared explicitly in the state variables list. For example, we write `v:t` for a variable `v` of static type `t`. Moreover, a variable can be initialized to a specific value allowed by its type. For example, in order to initialize the variable `v` above to the value `val`, we write `v:t := val`. If no initial value is specified it is assumed to be arbitrary. The state variables list in an automaton specification can be followed by an **initially** clause, which consists of a predicate that constrains the automaton parameters and initial values of state variables. All of the static types used in the examples have standard interpretations, except possibly for the type **AugmentedReal**, which denotes $\mathsf{R} \cup \{\infty\}$.

The dynamic types of variables are specified implicitly. By default, variables of type `Real` are assumed to be analog and variables of types other than `Real` are assumed to be discrete. The definition of what it means for a variable to be discrete or analog is given in Examples 3.1 and 3.2. The keyword **discrete** is used to qualify a discrete variable of type `Real`. Although timed automata may contain variables that are neither discrete nor analog, none of our examples use such variables.

The transitions are specified in precondition-effect style. A **pre** clause specifies the enabling condition for an action. An **eff** clause contains a list of statements that specify the effect of performing that action on the state. All the statements in an effect clause are assumed to be executed sequentially in a single indivisible step. The absence of a specified precondition for an action means that the action is always enabled and the absence of a specified effect means that performing the action does not change the state.

The trajectories are specified using a combination of algebraic and differential equations and inequalities, and stopping conditions. A trajectory belongs to the set of legal trajectories of an automaton if it satisfies the stopping condition expressed by the **stop when** clause, and the equations or inequalities in the **evolve** clause. The stopping condition is satisfied by a trajectory if the only state in which the condition holds (if any) is the last state of that trajectory. That is, time cannot advance beyond the point where the stopping condition is true. The **evolve** clause specifies the algebraic and differential equations that must be satisfied by the trajectories. We write $\mathbf{d}(v) = e$ for $d(v) = e$, $\mathbf{d}(v) \leq e$ for $d(v) \leq e$ and $e \leq \mathbf{d}(v)$ for $e \leq d(v)$. We assume that the evolution of each variable follows a continuous function throughout a trajectory. This implies that the value of a discrete variable is constant throughout a trajectory: time-passage does not change the value of discrete variables.

Example 4.1 (Time-bounded channel). The automaton `TimedChannel` in Fig. 4.1 is the specification of a reliable FIFO channel that delivers its messages within a certain time bound, represented by the automaton parameter `b` of type `Real` which is nonnegative. The other automaton parameter `M` is an arbitrary type parameter that represents the type of messages communicated by the channel.

The variable `queue` is used to hold a sequence of pairs consisting of a message that has been sent and its delivery deadline. The variable `now` is used to describe real time. Every `send(m)` transition adds to the queue a new pair whose first component is `m` and whose second component is the deadline `now + b`. A `receive(m)` transition can occur only when `m` is the first message in the queue and it results in the removal of the first message from the queue.

The trajectory specification shows that the variable `now` increases with rate `1`, that is, at the same rate as real time. The stopping condition implies that, within a trajectory, time cannot pass beyond the point where `now` becomes equal to the delivery deadline of some message in the queue.

```
automaton TimedChannel(b: Real, M: Type) where b ≥ 0
type Packet = tuple of message: M, deadline: Real
  signature
     external send(m: M), receive(m: M)
  states
     queue: Queue[Packet] := {},
     now: Real := 0
  transitions
     external send(m)
       eff
         queue := append([m,now+b],queue)
     external receive(m)
       pre
         head(queue).message = m
       eff
         queue := tail(queue)
  trajectories
     stop when
       ∃p: Packet p ∈ queue ∧ (now = p.deadline)
     evolve
       d(now) = 1
```

Figure 4.1: Time-bounded channel.

Example 4.2 (Periodic sending process). The automaton `PeriodicSend` in Fig. 4.2 is the specification of a process that sends messages periodically, every u time units, where u is an automaton parameter of type `Real` which is nonnegative. The type parameter `M` represents the type of the messages sent by the process.

The analog variable `clock` is a timer whose value records the amount of time that has elapsed since it was last reset to 0. A `send(m)` transition can occur only when `clock = u`, and it causes `clock` to be reset. The trajectory specification says that `clock` increases at the same rate as real time and time cannot pass beyond the point where `clock = u`.

Example 4.3 (Periodic sending process with failures). The specification of the `PeriodicSend` process from Example 4.2 does not model failures. We now consider a variant of `PeriodicSend` where the process may fail and stop doing any discrete actions. The specification of this new automaton is given in Fig. 4.3.

The discrete variable `failed` in automaton `PeriodicSend2` is a boolean flag that records whether the process is failed. It is initialized to `false` and is set to `true` when a `fail` action occurs. The trajectory specification of `PeriodicSend2` shows that time can advance without any bound when the process is failed.

```
automaton PeriodicSend(u: Real, M: Type) where u ≥ 0
  signature
    external send(m: M)
  states
    clock: Real := 0
  transitions
    external send(m)
      pre
        clock = u
      eff
        clock := 0
  trajectories
    stop when
      clock = u
    evolve
      d(clock) = 1
```

Figure 4.2: Periodic sending process.

Example 4.4 (Timeout process). The automaton `Timeout` in Fig. 4.4 is the specification of a process that awaits the receipt of a message from another process. If `u` time units elapse without such a message arriving, `Timeout` performs a `timeout` action, thereby "suspecting" the other process. When a message arrives it "unsuspects" the other process. `Timeout` may suspect and unsuspect repeatedly.

The discrete variable `suspected` is a flag that shows whether `Timeout` suspects that the other process is failed. The variable `clock` is a timer that records the amount of time that has elapsed since the receipt of the last message. A `receive(m)` transition can occur at any time; this causes the variable `clock` to be reset and the flag `suspected` to be set to `false`. If `clock` reaches `u` before the arrival of a message then the `timeout` action becomes enabled. The process sets `suspected` to `true` as a result of a `timeout`.

The trajectory specification shows that `clock` increases at the same rate as real time and, if `suspected = false`, then time cannot go beyond the point where `clock = u`. Note that if `suspected = true`, there is no restriction on the amount of time that can elapse.

Example 4.5 (Fischer's algorithm). The timed automaton `FischerME` presented in Figs. 4.5 and 4.6 is the specification of a shared memory mutual exclusion algorithm which uses a single shared variable that can be read and written by all the participants. We fix here the number of participants to be four, by defining `Index` to be an enumeration consisting of four elements. Note, however, that this specification can be generalized to any finite number of participants.

The automaton parameters `u_set` and `l_check` represent upper and lower time bounds for the `set(i)` and `check(i)` actions respectively. We assume that `u_set < l_check`.

```
automaton PeriodicSend2(u: Real, M: Type) where u ≥ 0
  signature
    external send(m: M), fail
  states
    failed: Bool := false,
    clock: Real := 0
  transitions
    external send(m)
      pre
        ¬failed ∧ clock = u
      eff
        clock := 0
    external fail
      eff
        failed := true
  trajectories
    stop when
      ¬failed ∧ clock = u
    evolve
      d(clock) = 1
```

Figure 4.3: Periodic sending process with failures.

The shared variable `x` can be assigned any value of type `Index` plus one additional special value `nil`. If a process is in the critical region, then the variable `x` contains the index of that process. If all users are in the remainder region, then the variable `x` contains the value `nil`. The array variable `pc` records the program counters of all processes. The array variable `lastset` keeps track of the deadlines by which the processes' `set` actions must occur. Similarly, the array variable `firstcheck` keeps track of the earliest time the processes' `check` actions may occur. The analog variable `now` models real time.

The transition definitions for external actions `try(i)`, `crit(i)`, `exit(i)`, and `rem(i)` are straightforward. When a process performs one of these actions, its program counter is updated to record the region entered by the process. The most interesting transition definitions are `test(i)`, `set(i)`, and `check(i)` since they are the ones that involve timing constraints of the algorithm. When a process `i` performs a `test` action and observes `x` to be `nil`, it sets `lastset[i]` to `now` + `u_set`. This sets the deadline for the performance of the `set(i)` action. Note that this deadline is enforced through the stopping condition in the trajectory specification. The transition `set(i)` sets `firstcheck[i]` to `now` + `l_check`. The value of `firstcheck[i]` determines the earliest time `check(i)` may occur. The `check(i)` action is enabled only when the current time has at least this value.

```
automaton Timeout(u: Real, M: Type) where u > 0
  signature
    external receive(m: M), timeout
  states
    suspected: Bool := false,
    clock: Real := 0
  transitions
    external receive(m)
      eff
        clock := 0;
        suspected := false
    external timeout
      pre
        ¬suspected ∧ clock = u
      eff
        suspected := true
  trajectories
    stop when
      clock = u and ¬suspected
    evolve
      d(clock) = 1
```

Figure 4.4: Timeout.

The stopping condition implies that if the value of `now` reaches the value of `lastset[i]` for some process `i` at some point in time, then that point must be the limit time of the trajectory.

Example 4.6 (Clock synchronization). The automaton `ClockSync(u,r:Real, i:Index)` in Fig. 4.7 is the specification of a single process in a clock synchronization algorithm. Each process has a physical clock and generates a logical clock. The goal of the algorithm is to achieve "agreement" and "validity" among the logical clock values. Agreement means that the logical clocks are close to one another. Validity means that the logical clocks are within the range of the physical clocks.

The algorithm is based on the exchange of physical clock values between different processes in the system. The parameter `u` determines the frequency of sending messages. Processes in the system are indexed by the elements of the type `Index` which we assume to be pre-defined. `ClockSync(u,r:Real, i:Index)` has a physical clock `physclock`, which may drift from the real time with a drift rate bounded by `r`. It uses the variable `maxother` to keep track of the largest physical clock value of the other processes in the system. The variable `nextsend` records when it is supposed to send its physical clock to the other processes. The logical clock, `logclock`, is defined to be the maximum of `maxother` and `physclock`. Formally `logclock` is a *derived variable*, which is a function whose value is defined in terms of the state variables.

```
type Index = enumeration of p1, p2, p3, p4

type PcValue =  enumeration of rem, test, set, check,
                               leavetry, crit, reset, leaveexit

automaton FischerME(u_set, l_check: Real)
 where u_set ≥ 0 ∧ l_check ≥ 0 ∧ u_set < l_check
 signature
  external try(i:Index), crit(i:Index), exit(i:Index), rem(i:Index)
  internal test(i:Index), set(i:Index),
           check(i:Index), reset(i:Index)

 states
   x: Null[Index] := nil,
   pc: Array[Index,PcValue] := constant(rem),
   lastset: Array[Index,discrete AugmentedReal] := constant(infty),
   firstcheck: Array[Index,discrete AugmentedReal] := constant(0),
   now: Real := 0
```

Figure 4.5: Fischer's mutual exclusion algorithm: signature and states.

A `send(m,i)` transition is enabled when `m = physclock` and `nextsend = physclock`. It causes the value of `nextsend` to be updated so that the next send can occur when `physclock` has advanced by `u` time units. The transition definition for `receive(m,j,i)` specifies the effect of receiving a message from another process `j` in the system. Upon the receipt of a message `m` from `j`, `i` sets `maxother` to the maximum of `m` and the current value of `maxother`, thereby updating its knowledge of the largest physical clock value of other processes in the system.

The trajectory specification is slightly different from that in the previous examples. In this example, the analog variable `physclock` does not change at the same rate as real time but it drifts with a rate that is bounded by `r`. The periodic sending of physical clocks to other processes is enforced through the stopping condition in the trajectory specification. Time is not allowed to pass beyond the point where `physclock = nextsend`.

4.2 EXECUTIONS AND TRACES

We now define execution fragments, executions, trace fragments, and traces, which are used to describe automaton behavior. An *execution fragment* of a timed automaton $\mathcal{A}$ is an (A, V)-sequence $\alpha = \tau_0\, a_1\, \tau_1\, a_2\, \tau_2 \ldots$, where (1) each τ_i is a trajectory in $\mathcal{T}$, and (2) if τ_i is not the last trajectory in α then $\tau_i.lstate \overset{a_{i+1}}{\rightarrow} \tau_{i+1}.fstate$. An execution fragment records what happens during a particular run

```
transitions
  external try(i)
    pre
      pc[i] = rem
    eff
      pc[i] := test
  internal test(i)
    pre
      pc[i] = test
    eff
      if x = nil then
         pc[i] := set;
         lastset[i] := now + u_set
  internal set(i)
    pre
      pc[i] = set
    eff
      x := embed(i);
      pc[i] := check;
      lastset[i] := infty;
      firstcheck[i] := now + l_check
  internal check(i)
    pre
      pc[i] = check ∧
            now ≥ firstcheck[i]
    eff
      if x = embed(i) then pc[i] := leavetry
      else pc[i] := test

  external crit(i)
    pre
      pc[i] = leavetry
    eff
      pc[i] := crit
  external exit(i)
    pre
      pc[i] = crit
    eff
      pc[i] := reset

  internal reset(i)
    pre
      pc[i] = reset
    eff
      x := nil;
      pc[i] := leaveexit

  external rem(i)
    pre
      pc[i] = leaveexit
    eff
      pc[i] := rem
trajectories
  stop when
    ∃i: Index now = lastset[i]
  evolve
    d(now) = 1
```

Figure 4.6: Fischer's mutual exclusion algorithm: transitions and trajectory definitions.

of a system, including all the instantaneous, discrete state changes and all the changes to the state that occur while time advances. We write $frags_{\mathcal{A}}$ for the set of all execution fragments of $\mathcal{A}$.

If α is an execution fragment, with notation as above, then we define the *first state* of α, $\alpha.fstate$, to be $\alpha.fval$. An *execution fragment* of a timed automaton $\mathcal{A}$ *from* a state $\mathbf{x}$ of $\mathcal{A}$ is an execution fragment of $\mathcal{A}$ whose first state is $\mathbf{x}$. We write $frags_{\mathcal{A}}(\mathbf{x})$ for the set of execution fragments of $\mathcal{A}$ from $\mathbf{x}$. An execution fragment α is defined to be an *execution* if $\alpha.fstate$ is a start state, that

```
automaton ClockSync(u, r: Real, i: Index) where  u > 0 ∧ (0 ≤ r < 1)
  signature
    external send(m: Real, const i: Index),
             receive(m: Real, j: Index, const i: Index) where j ≠ i
  states
    nextsend: discrete Real := 0,
    maxother: discrete Real := 0,
    physclock: Real := 0

  derived variables
    logclock = max(maxother, physclock)

  transitions
    external send(m, i)
      pre
        m = physclock ∧ physclock = nextsend
      eff
        nextsend := nextsend + u
    external receive(m, j, i)
      eff
        maxother := max(maxother, m)
  trajectories
    stop when
      physclock = nextsend
    evolve
      (1 - r) ≤ d(physclock) ≤ (1 + r)
```

Figure 4.7: Clock synchronization.

is, $\alpha.\mathit{fstate} \in \Theta$. We write $\mathit{execs}_{\mathcal{A}}$ for the set of all executions of $\mathcal{A}$. If α is a closed (A, V)-sequence then we define the *last state* of α, $\alpha.\mathit{lstate}$, to be $\alpha.\mathit{lval}$.

Like trajectories also execution fragments are closed under countable concatenation.

Lemma 4.7 *Let $\alpha_0\,\alpha_1\,\ldots$ be a finite or infinite sequence of execution fragments of $\mathcal{A}$ such that, for each nonfinal index i, α_i is closed and $\alpha_i.\mathit{lstate} = \alpha_{i+1}.\mathit{fstate}$. Then $\alpha_0 \frown \alpha_1 \frown \cdots$ is an execution fragment of $\mathcal{A}$.*

Proof. Follows easily from the definitions, using Axiom **T3**. □

The characterization of the prefix ordering on (A, V)-sequences from Lemma 3.7 carries over to execution fragments.

Lemma 4.8 *Let α and β be execution fragments of $\mathcal{A}$ with α closed. Then*

$$\alpha \leq \beta \quad \Leftrightarrow \quad \exists \alpha' \in \mathit{frags}_{\mathcal{A}} : \beta = \alpha \frown \alpha'.$$

Proof. Implication "$\Leftarrow$" follows from the corresponding implication in Lemma 3.7. Implication "$\Rightarrow$" follows from the definitions and **T2**. □

The external behavior of a timed automaton is captured by the set of "traces" of its execution fragments, which record external actions and the trajectories that describe the intervening passage of time. A trace consists of alternating external actions and trajectories over the empty set of variables, $\emptyset$; the only interesting information contained in these trajectories is the amount of time that elapses.

Formally, if α is an execution fragment, then the *trace* of α, denoted by *trace*(α), is the $(E, \emptyset)$-restriction of α, $\alpha \lceil (E, \emptyset)$. A *trace fragment* of a timed automaton $\mathcal{A}$ *from* a state $\mathbf{x}$ of $\mathcal{A}$ is the trace of an execution fragment of $\mathcal{A}$ whose first state is $\mathbf{x}$. We write $\mathit{tracefrags}_{\mathcal{A}}(\mathbf{x})$ for the set of trace fragments of $\mathcal{A}$ from $\mathbf{x}$. Also, we define a *trace* of $\mathcal{A}$ to be a trace fragment from a start state, that is, the trace of an execution of $\mathcal{A}$, and write $\mathit{traces}_{\mathcal{A}}$ for the set of traces of $\mathcal{A}$.

In the earlier timed automaton models [86, 107], execution fragments were defined in a similar style to the one presented here, that is, as an alternating sequence of trajectories and actions. However, the traces were not derived from execution fragments by a simple restriction to external actions and the empty set of variables. Rather, a trace was defined as a sequence consisting of actions paired with their time of occurrence together with a limit time. The new definition increases uniformity; the definitions, results and proof techniques for hybrid sequences apply to both execution fragments and traces.

We now revisit some of the automata presented earlier in this chapter and give sample executions and traces for these automata.

Example 4.9 (Periodic sending process). Consider the automaton `PeriodicSend` from Example 4.2 where u is instantiated to the real number 3 and the message type parameter `M` is instantiated to the set {`m1`, `m2`, ...}. The following sequence is an execution of the automaton:

$$\alpha = \tau\ \texttt{send(m1)}\ \tau\ \texttt{send(m2)}\ \tau\ \texttt{send(m3)}\ \tau \ldots$$

where $\tau : [0, 3] \rightarrow \mathit{val}(\{\texttt{clock}\})$ is defined such that $\tau(t)(\texttt{clock}) = t$ for all $t \in [0, 3]$. The function τ is defined for closed intervals of length 3, starting at time 0. It describes the evolution of the variable `clock`, which is 0 at the start of τ and increases with rate 1 for 3 time units. The discrete `send` events occur periodically, every 3 time units and reset the `clock` variable to 0.

The trace of the above execution fragment, *trace*(α), is the sequence

$$\alpha' = \tau'\ \texttt{send(m1)}\ \tau'\ \texttt{send(m2)}\ \tau'\ \texttt{send(m3)}\ \tau' \ldots$$

where $\tau' : [0, 3] \rightarrow \mathit{val}(\emptyset)$. Since the range of function τ' contains only the function with the empty domain, *trace*(α) does not contain any information about what happens to the value of `clock` as time progresses. Since the domains of τ and τ' are identical, α and α' express the same information about the amount of time that elapses between discrete steps.

Example 4.10 (Timeout process). We now present an execution of the automaton `Timeout` from Example 4.4 where the the maximum waiting time u for a message is 5 and the message alphabet M is the set {m1, m2}. The following finite sequence is an execution of `Timeout`:

$$\alpha = \tau_0 \ \texttt{receive(m1)} \ \tau_1 \ \texttt{timeout} \ \tau_2 \ \texttt{receive(m2)} \ \tau_3 \ \texttt{timeout} \ \tau_4$$

where $Val = val(\{\texttt{suspected}, \texttt{clock}\})$ and the functions $\tau_0, \tau_1, \tau_2, \tau_3, \tau_4$ are defined as follows:

$\tau_0 : [0, 2] \to Val$ where $\tau_0(t)(\texttt{suspected}) = \texttt{false}$ and $\tau_0(t)(\texttt{clock}) = t$ for all $t \in [0, 2]$.
$\tau_1 : [0, 5] \to Val$ where $\tau_1(t)(\texttt{suspected}) = \texttt{false}$ and $\tau_1(t)(\texttt{clock}) = t$ for all $t \in [0, 5]$.
$\tau_2 : [0, 1] \to Val$ where $\tau_2(t)(\texttt{suspected}) = \texttt{true}$ and $\tau_2(t)(\texttt{clock}) = 5 + t$ for all $t \in [0, 1]$.
$\tau_3 : [0, 5] \to Val$ where $\tau_3(t)(\texttt{suspected}) = \texttt{false}$ and $\tau_3(t)(\texttt{clock}) = t$ for all $t \in [0, 5]$.
$\tau_4 : [0, \infty) \to Val$ where $\tau_4(t)(\texttt{suspected}) = \texttt{true}$ and $\tau_4(t)(\texttt{clock}) = 5 + t$ for all $t \in [0, \infty)$.

In this sample execution, the first awaited message arrives at time 2. Since no other message arrives within the next 5 time units, the process performs a timeout. A new message arrives 1 time unit after the timeout and the variable `clock` is reset to 0. Since no new message arrives in the next 5 time units the process performs another timeout. The time elapses forever after this timeout since no further message arrives.

This example illustrates that the automaton `Timeout` can perform multiple timeout transitions. Another point to note is that the sample execution consists of a finite (A, V)-sequence ending with a trajectory, as opposed to an infinite sequence as in Example 4.9 . The final trajectory here is a trajectory whose domain is right open and the execution is admissible and nonZeno. Replacing τ_4 with a function on a closed interval would yield a nonZeno execution that is not admissible.

The trace of the execution α can be obtained by letting the range of τ_i be the set consisting of the function with the empty domain, as we did in the previous example. That is, by hiding the values of the internal variables `clock` and `suspected` during trajectories.

The following lemma states that some properties of executions carry over to their traces and vice versa.

Lemma 4.11 *If α is an execution of $\mathcal{A}$ then:*

1. *α is time-bounded if and only if trace(α) is time-bounded;*
2. *α is admissible if and only if trace(α) is admissible;*
3. *If α is closed then trace(α) is closed;*
4. *If α is nonZeno then trace(α) is nonZeno.*

Proof. Follows directly from the corresponding properties for the restriction of (A,V)-sequences (Lemma 3.11). □

Lemma 4.12 *If β is a trace of $\mathcal{A}$ then:*

1. *If β is closed then there exists an execution α of $\mathcal{A}$ such that $trace(\alpha) = \beta$ and α is closed;*

2. *If β is nonZeno then there exists an execution α of $\mathcal{A}$ such that $trace(\alpha) = \beta$ and α is nonZeno.*

Proof. For the first part of the lemma, let $\beta = trace(\alpha)$ be a closed trace of $\mathcal{A}$. By definition of a trace, we know that $\beta.ltime = \alpha.ltime$. We also know that α is either closed or has a suffix which is an infinite sequence of alternating point trajectories and internal actions. Now, let α' be the least closed prefix of α such that $\alpha'.ltime = \beta.ltime$. Clearly, α' is a closed execution of $\mathcal{A}$ and $\beta = trace(\alpha')$.

For the second part of the lemma, observe that a nonZeno trace is either closed or admissible. Let $\beta = trace(\alpha)$. For the case where β is closed, we have already shown how we can find a closed execution. For the case where $\beta = trace(\alpha)$ is admissible, we know that $\alpha.ltime = \infty$. Hence, α is admissible, as needed. □

Example 4.13 (Constructing a closed execution from a closed trace). Consider the Zeno hybrid sequence $\alpha = \wp(\mathbf{v})\, a\, \wp(\mathbf{v})\, a\, \wp(\mathbf{v}) \ldots$ given in Example 3.12. Suppose that α is an execution of $\mathcal{A}$ and that a is an internal action of $\mathcal{A}$. Then, $trace(\alpha) = \wp(\mathbf{v}')$ where $\wp(\mathbf{v}')$ is a trajectory over the empty set of variables. However, the fact that $trace(\alpha)$ is closed does not imply that α is closed. Thus, we see why we have a one way implication in item 3 of Lemma 4.11. On the other hand, we can construct a closed execution of $\mathcal{A}$ with trace $\wp(\mathbf{v}')$ as explained in the proof of Lemma 4.12. The execution consisting of the point trajectory $\wp(\mathbf{v})$ is a closed execution of $\mathcal{A}$ with trace $\wp(\mathbf{v}')$.

4.3 INVARIANTS

A state of a timed automaton $\mathcal{A}$ is *reachable* if it is the last state of some closed execution of $\mathcal{A}$. If X is the set of state variables of $\mathcal{A}$ and I is a set of valuations of X, then we say that I is an *invariant* of $\mathcal{A}$ if I contains all reachable states of $\mathcal{A}$. We often describe invariants by *assertions*, formulas that are constructed by applying boolean connectives and quantifications to atomic formulas over the state variables. Define the *i-length* of a finite (A, V)-sequence β to be equal to the length of β if β ends with a point trajectory, and equal to the length of β plus 1 otherwise. Invariants can be proved by induction on the i-length of executions. Sometimes we may also use the following simple lemma. In order to state the lemma we use some terminology from [90]. A set of valuations I of $\mathcal{A}$ is *stable* if it is preserved by discrete transitions and by trajectories, that is, for all states $\mathbf{x}, \mathbf{x}' \in Q$ and trajectories $\tau \in \mathcal{T}$,

$$\begin{aligned} \mathbf{x} \in I \ \wedge\ \mathbf{x} \xrightarrow{a}_{\mathcal{A}} \mathbf{x}' \quad &\Rightarrow \quad \mathbf{x}' \in I \\ \tau.fstate \in I \ \wedge\ \tau \text{ closed} \quad &\Rightarrow \quad \tau.lstate \in I. \end{aligned}$$

Set I is *inductive* if it is stable and moreover contains all the start states, that is $\Theta \subseteq I$.

Lemma 4.14 *Let I be a set of states of $\mathcal{A}$ that is inductive. Then I is an invariant.*

Proof. We must establish that I contains all reachable states of $\mathcal{A}$. Let $\mathbf{x}$ be a reachable state. Then $\mathbf{x}$ is the final state of some closed execution α. We prove $\mathbf{x} \in I$ by induction on the i-length k of execution α. If $k = 1$ then α consists of a point trajectory and hence $\mathbf{x}$ is an initial state. Because I is inductive, $\Theta \subseteq I$ and hence $\mathbf{x} \in I$. If $k > 1$ then we distinguish between two cases: either α ends with a point trajectory or it does not.

1. In the first case, α has the form $\alpha' a \tau$ where τ is a point trajectory containing state $\mathbf{x}$ and the i-length of α' is either $k-2$ or $k-1$ (depending on whether α' ends with a point trajectory or not). Let $\mathbf{x}'$ be the last state of α'. Then by induction hypothesis $\mathbf{x}' \in I$. But since I is stable and $\mathbf{x}' \xrightarrow{a} \mathbf{x}$, also $\mathbf{x} \in I$.

2. In the second case, α can be written as $\alpha' \frown \tau$ where α' ends with a point trajectory, τ is a closed trajectory, $\alpha'.\mathit{lstate} = \tau.\mathit{fstate}$, and the i-length of α' equals $k-1$. Hence, by induction hypothesis, $\alpha'.\mathit{lstate} = \tau.\mathit{fstate} \in I$. Since I is stable, also $\tau.\mathit{lstate} \in I$. Hence, $\mathbf{x} \in I$.

□

Example 4.15 (Time-bounded channel). Consider the time-bounded channel automaton from Example 4.1. It is easy to observe that time cannot pass beyond any delivery deadline recorded in the message queue and that each deadline in the queue is less than or equal to the sum of the current time and the bound `b`. This property can be stated as an invariant assertion as follows.

Invariant 1 *In any reachable state* $\mathbf{x}$ *of automaton* `TimedChannel`, *for all* $\mathtt{p} \in \mathbf{x}(\mathtt{queue})$, $\mathbf{x}(\mathtt{now}) \leq \mathtt{p.deadline} \leq \mathbf{x}(\mathtt{now}) + \mathtt{b}$.

We can prove this invariant using Lemma 4.14. Let I be the set of states that satisfy the assertion, that is, the set of states $\mathbf{x}$ such that for all $\mathtt{p} \in \mathbf{x}(\mathtt{queue})$, $\mathbf{x}(\mathtt{now}) \leq \mathtt{p.deadline} \leq \mathbf{x}(\mathtt{now}) + \mathtt{b}$. In the (unique) initial state $\mathbf{x}$, $\mathbf{x}(\mathtt{queue})$ is empty and so $\mathbf{x} \in I$.

Discrete transitions do not modify variable `now` and either add or remove a single message from `queue`. A `send(m)` transition from state $\mathbf{x}$ adds a single message `p` with $\mathtt{p.deadline} = \mathbf{x}(\mathtt{now}) + \mathtt{b}$. A `receive(m)` transition removes a single message. Clearly, both types of actions preserve the invariant.

Let τ be a closed trajectory with $\tau.\mathit{fstate} = \mathbf{x}' \in I$ and $\tau.\mathit{lstate} = \mathbf{x}$. Suppose that $\mathbf{x} \notin I$. This means that there is some $\mathtt{p} \in \mathbf{x}(\mathtt{queue})$ for which it does not hold that $\mathbf{x}(\mathtt{now}) \leq \mathtt{p.deadline} \leq \mathbf{x}(\mathtt{now}) + \mathtt{b}$. But since $\mathbf{x}(\mathtt{queue}) = \mathbf{x}'(\mathtt{queue})$, we know that $\mathbf{x}'(\mathtt{now}) \leq \mathtt{p.deadline} \leq \mathbf{x}'(\mathtt{now}) + \mathtt{b}$. Since `now` increases along trajectories, $\mathbf{x}'(\mathtt{now}) < \mathbf{x}(\mathtt{now})$. It follows that $\mathtt{p.deadline} < \mathbf{x}(\mathtt{now})$. But since $\mathbf{x}'(\mathtt{now}) \leq \mathtt{p.deadline}$ and `now` increases continuously along τ, there exists a nonfinal state $\mathbf{x}''$ on τ with $\mathtt{p.deadline} = \mathbf{x}''(\mathtt{now})$. But this contradicts the stopping condition for the time-bounded channel. Hence, $\mathbf{x} \in I$.

We conclude that I is inductive and hence an invariant.

In practice, we often encounter invariants that are not inductive. In order to prove such invariants we typically first need to establish some auxiliary invariants. This style of reasoning can be formalized using a slight generalization of Lemma 4.14. Again, we use terminology from [90]. Let I_1 and I_2 be sets of states of $\mathcal{A}$. Then I_2 is *stable relative to* I_1 if, for all states $\mathbf{x}, \mathbf{x}' \in Q$ and trajectories $\tau \in \mathcal{T}$,

$$\begin{array}{rcl} \mathbf{x} \in I_1 \cap I_2 \ \wedge \ \mathbf{x} \xrightarrow{a}_{\mathcal{A}} \mathbf{x}' & \Rightarrow & \mathbf{x}' \in I_2 \\ \tau.\mathit{fstate} \in I_1 \cap I_2 \ \wedge \ \tau \text{ closed} & \Rightarrow & \tau.\mathit{lstate} \in I_2. \end{array}$$

Set I_2 is *inductive relative to* I_1 if I_2 is stable relative to I_1 and contains all the start states, that is $\Theta \subseteq I_2$.

Lemma 4.16 *Let I_1 and I_2 be sets of states of $\mathcal{A}$ such that I_1 is invariant and I_2 is inductive relative to I_1. Then I_2 is an invariant.*

Proof. Similar to the proof of Lemma 4.14. □

Example 4.17 (Fischer's mutual exclusion). The main safety property that needs to be satisfied by the automaton `FischerME` from Example 4.5 is mutual exclusion. This safety property can be expressed as an invariant assertion.

Invariant 2 *In any reachable state* $\mathbf{x}$ *of* `FischerME`, *there do not exist* `i:Index` *and* `j:Index` *such that* $\mathtt{i} \neq \mathtt{j}$, $\mathbf{x}(\mathtt{pc})[\mathtt{i}] = \mathtt{crit}$ *and* $\mathbf{x}(\mathtt{pc})[\mathtt{j}] = \mathtt{crit}$.

Even though the invariant does not refer to time, its proof depends on the timing constraints of the automaton. For example, the following auxiliary invariant can be used in proving Invariant 2.

Invariant 3 *In any reachable state* $\mathbf{x}$ *of* `FischerME`, *if* $\mathbf{x}(\mathtt{pc})[\mathtt{i}] = \mathtt{check}$, $\mathbf{x}(\mathtt{x}) = \mathtt{embed(i)}$, *and* $\mathbf{x}(\mathtt{pc})[\mathtt{j}] = \mathtt{set}$, *then* $\mathbf{x}(\mathtt{firstcheck})[\mathtt{i}]) > \mathbf{x}(\mathtt{lastset})[\mathtt{j}]$.

This invariant states that if the program counter of process `i` has the value `check`, the program counter of process `j` has the value `set`, and the variable `x` has the value `embed(i)`, then `i` will allow enough time for `j` to set `x` to `embed(j)`, before performing the check. If this timing constraint were not satisfied, it would be possible for `i` to check that `x = embed(i)` before `j` sets `x` to `embed(j)`. Both of the processes would then observe `x` to contain their own index and enter the critical region.

4.4 SPECIAL KINDS OF TIMED AUTOMATA

This section describes several restricted forms of timed automata and gives definitions that are needed for theorems that are presented later on in this monograph.

Timed Automata with Finite Internal Nondeterminism: We are sometimes interested in bounding the amount of internal nondeterminism in a timed automaton. Thus, we say that a timed automaton $\mathcal{A}$ *has finite internal nondeterminism (FIN)* provided that:

1. the set Θ of start states is finite, and
2. for every state $\mathbf{x}$ of $\mathcal{A}$ and every trace fragment β of $\mathcal{A}$ from $\mathbf{x}$, the set $\{\alpha.lstate \mid \alpha \in frags_{\mathcal{A}}(\mathbf{x}) \wedge trace(\alpha) = \beta\}$ is finite.

Example 4.18 (Automata with FIN). It is not hard to see that the automata `TimedChannel`, `PeriodicSend`, `PeriodicSend2`, and `Timeout` given in Section 4.1 all have FIN. The first property of the definition of FIN is satisfied since each of these automata has a unique start state. The second property follows from the fact that in each automaton, for every state $\mathbf{x}$ and every trace fragment β from $\mathbf{x}$, there is a unique execution fragment α such that $trace(\alpha) = \beta$.

Example 4.19 (Automata without FIN). We show that automata `FischerME` and `ClockSync(a,r:Real, i:Index)` from Section 4.1 do not have FIN. For each automaton, we specify a trace, describe the set of all executions that have the specified trace, and argue that the second property in the definition of FIN fails for the chosen trace.

Let $\mathbf{x}$ be the start state of `FischerME` and $\beta = \tau_0$ `try(i)` τ_1 be a trace of the same automaton where the domains of the functions τ_0 and τ_1 are, respectively, the single point interval $[0, 0]$ and the interval $[0, u]$, and the range of both functions is the set consisting of the function with the empty domain. For any execution α, $trace(\alpha) = \beta$, if and only if $\alpha.ltime =$ `u`, `try(i)` occurs at time 0, and all the actions in α that occur after `try(i)` are internal actions. There are infinitely many different times that the internal actions may occur, and infinitely many values `lastcheck` and `firstcheck` could have, by the time u. Therefore, the set $\{\alpha.lstate \mid \alpha \in frags_{\mathcal{A}}(\mathbf{x}) \wedge trace(\alpha) = \tau_0$ `try(i)` $\tau_1\}$ is not finite and `FischerME` does not have FIN.

Now, let $\mathbf{x}$ be the start state of `ClockSync(a,r:Real, i:Index)` where $\mathbf{x}($`physclock`$) = \mathbf{x}($`nextsend`$) = \mathbf{x}($`maxother`$) = 0$ and $\beta = \tau_0$ `send(0)` τ_1 be a trace of `ClockSync(a,r:Real, i:Index)` where the domains of functions τ_0 and τ_1 are, respectively, the interval $[0, 0]$ and the interval $[0, u]$, and the range of both functions is the set consisting of the function with the empty domain. For any α in which `send(0)` occurs at time 0 and is followed by a trajectory τ such that $\tau.ltime = u$, we have $trace(\alpha) = \beta$. For any such α, $\alpha.lstate($`physclock`$)$ can be any value in the interval `[u (1 - r), u (1 + r)]`. Therefore, the set $\{\alpha.lstate \mid \alpha \in frags_{\mathcal{A}}(\mathbf{x}) \wedge trace(\alpha) = \tau_0$ `send(0)` $\tau_1\}$ is not finite and `ClockSync(a,r:Real, i:Index)` does not have FIN.

The following lemma states that if a timed automaton has FIN, then its set of traces is limit-closed.

Lemma 4.20 *Suppose that timed automaton $\mathcal{A}$ has FIN and $\mathbf{x} \in Q$. Suppose that $\beta_1, \beta_2, \ldots$ is a chain of trace fragments of $\mathcal{A}$ from $\mathbf{x}$. Then the hybrid sequence $\lim_i \beta_i$ is a trace fragment of $\mathcal{A}$ from $\mathbf{x}$.*

Proof. This is analogous to the proof of Lemma 4.3 of [86]. Suppose that $\mathcal{A}$ is a timed automaton that has FIN, $\mathbf{x}$ is a state of $\mathcal{A}$, and $\beta_1, \beta_2, \ldots$ is a chain of trace fragments of $\mathcal{A}$ from $\mathbf{x}$. We define a relation *after* between trace fragments from $\mathbf{x}$ and states of $\mathcal{A}$: $\mathit{after} = \{(\beta, \mathbf{y}) \mid \exists \alpha \in \mathit{frags}_{\mathcal{A}}(\mathbf{x}).\ \mathit{trace}(\alpha) = \beta \wedge \alpha.\mathit{lstate} = \mathbf{y}\}$.

We construct a directed graph G whose nodes are pairs $(\beta_i, \mathbf{y}) \in \mathit{after}$ where β_i is an element of the given chain. In G, there is an edge from $(\beta_i, \mathbf{y})$ to $(\beta_{i+1}, \mathbf{y}')$ exactly if $\beta_{i+1} = \beta_i \frown \gamma$ such that $\gamma = \mathit{trace}(\alpha)$ for some $\alpha \in \mathit{frags}_{\mathcal{A}}(\mathbf{y})$, and $\alpha.\mathit{lstate} = \mathbf{y}'$. By the definition of property FIN, there are finitely many roots of G of the form $(\beta_1, \mathbf{y})$. By the definition of FIN and the construction of G, each node of G has finite outdegree.

We claim that each node $(\beta_i, \mathbf{y})$ of G is reachable from some root $(\beta_1, \mathbf{z})$ for some $\mathbf{z}$. By definition of the node set, there exists $\alpha \in \mathit{frags}_{\mathcal{A}}(\mathbf{x})$ such that $\mathit{trace}(\alpha) = \beta_i$ and $\alpha.\mathit{lstate} = \mathbf{y}$. Choose $\alpha' \in \mathit{frags}_{\mathcal{A}}(\mathbf{x})$ to be a prefix of α such that $\mathit{trace}(\alpha') = \beta_1$ and let $\mathbf{z} = \alpha'.\mathit{lstate}$. By definition of the edge set of G, $(\beta_i, \mathbf{y})$ is reachable from $(\beta_1, \mathbf{z})$.

Hence, G satisfies the hypotheses of Lemma 2.1, which implies that there is an infinite execution fragment starting from $\mathbf{x}$ whose trace is $\lim_i \beta_i$. Lemma 2.1 is an extension of Konig's lemma. □

There are two references to automata with FIN later in the monograph. The first one is in Theorem 4.21, which lists some sufficient conditions for establishing an implementation relationship between two automata. The second reference appears in the discussion about the kinds of automata that satisfy the assumptions of Theorem 8.8.

Feasible Timed Automata: A timed automaton $\mathcal{A}$ is *feasible* provided that, for every state $\mathbf{x}$ of $\mathcal{A}$, there exists an admissible execution fragment of $\mathcal{A}$ from $\mathbf{x}$.

Feasibility is a basic requirement that any "reasonable" timed automaton should satisfy. Theorems 4.21 and 7.2 establish some results about feasible automata.

Timing-Independent Timed Automata: A timed automaton $\mathcal{A}$ is said to be *timing-independent* provided that all its state variables are discrete variables, and its set of trajectories is exactly the set of constant-valued functions over left-closed time intervals with left endpoint 0.

We refer to timing-independent automata later in Examples 5.14 and 8.10, and in our discussion about Theorem 8.8.

4.5 IMPLEMENTATION RELATIONSHIPS

Timed automata $\mathcal{A}_1$ and $\mathcal{A}_2$ are *comparable* if they have the same external interface, that is, if $E_1 = E_2$. If $\mathcal{A}_1$ and $\mathcal{A}_2$ are comparable then we say that $\mathcal{A}_1$ *implements* $\mathcal{A}_2$, denoted by $\mathcal{A}_1 \leq \mathcal{A}_2$, if the traces of $\mathcal{A}_1$ are included among those of $\mathcal{A}_2$, that is, if $\mathit{traces}_{\mathcal{A}_1} \subseteq \mathit{traces}_{\mathcal{A}_2}$.[1]

[1] In [86, 36, 80, 81], definitions of the set of traces of an automaton and of one automaton implementing another are based on closed and admissible executions only. The results we obtain in this monograph using the newer, more inclusive definition imply corresponding results for the earlier definition. For example, we have the following property: If $\mathcal{A}_1 \leq \mathcal{A}_2$ then the set of traces

Other preorders between timed automata could also be used as implementation relationships, for example, if $\mathcal{A}_1$ and $\mathcal{A}_2$ are comparable timed automata, we could consider:

- Every closed trace of $\mathcal{A}_1$ is a trace of $\mathcal{A}_2$.
- Every admissible trace of $\mathcal{A}_1$ is a trace of $\mathcal{A}_2$.
- Every nonZeno trace of $\mathcal{A}_1$ is a trace of $\mathcal{A}_2$.

Theorem 4.21 *Let $\mathcal{A}_1$ and $\mathcal{A}_2$ be comparable TAs.*

1. *If every closed trace of $\mathcal{A}_1$ is a trace of $\mathcal{A}_2$ and $\mathcal{A}_2$ has FIN, then $\mathcal{A}_1 \leq \mathcal{A}_2$.*
2. *If every admissible trace of $\mathcal{A}_1$ is a trace of $\mathcal{A}_2$ and $\mathcal{A}_1$ is feasible, then every closed trace of $\mathcal{A}_1$ is a trace of $\mathcal{A}_2$.*
3. *If every admissible trace of $\mathcal{A}_1$ is a trace of $\mathcal{A}_2$, $\mathcal{A}_1$ is feasible, and $\mathcal{A}_2$ has FIN, then $\mathcal{A}_1 \leq \mathcal{A}_2$.*

Proof. Part 1 follows from Lemma 4.20.

For Part 2, consider a closed trace β of $\mathcal{A}_1$. By feasibility of $\mathcal{A}_1$, we may extend β to an admissible trace β' of $\mathcal{A}_1$. Then by assumption, β' is also a trace of $\mathcal{A}_2$. By prefix closure of the set of traces, β is a trace of $\mathcal{A}_2$.

Part 3 follows from Parts 1 and 2. □

4.6 SIMULATION RELATIONS

In this section, we define simulation relations between timed automata. Simulation relations may be used to show that one TA implements another, in the sense of inclusion of sets of traces. We define two main types of simulation relations (forward and backward simulations) and three derived notions (refinements, history relations and prophecy relations).

Forward simulations are more commonly used than backward simulations because they are easier to think about and are general enough to cover most interesting situations that arise in practice. Backward simulations are sometimes necessary, in particular, when nondeterministic choices are resolved earlier in the specification than in the implementation. In proving implementation relations, we prefer to use forward simulation relations whenever they exist, since backward simulations are harder to think about.

that arise from closed or admissible executions of $\mathcal{A}_1$ is a subset of the set of traces that arise from closed or admissible executions of $\mathcal{A}_2$. This follows from Lemmas 4.11 and 4.12.

4.6.1 FORWARD SIMULATIONS

Let $\mathcal{A}$ and $\mathcal{B}$ be comparable TAs. A *forward simulation* from $\mathcal{A}$ to $\mathcal{B}$ is a relation $R \subseteq Q_{\mathcal{A}} \times Q_{\mathcal{B}}$ satisfying the following conditions, for all states $\mathbf{x}_{\mathcal{A}}$ and $\mathbf{x}_{\mathcal{B}}$ of $\mathcal{A}$ and $\mathcal{B}$, respectively.

1. If $\mathbf{x}_{\mathcal{A}} \in \Theta_{\mathcal{A}}$ then there exists a state $\mathbf{x}_{\mathcal{B}} \in \Theta_{\mathcal{B}}$ such that $\mathbf{x}_{\mathcal{A}}\ R\ \mathbf{x}_{\mathcal{B}}$.

2. If $\mathbf{x}_{\mathcal{A}}\ R\ \mathbf{x}_{\mathcal{B}}$ and α is an execution fragment of $\mathcal{A}$ consisting of one action surrounded by two point trajectories, with $\alpha.\mathit{fstate} = \mathbf{x}_{\mathcal{A}}$, then $\mathcal{B}$ has a closed execution fragment β with $\beta.\mathit{fstate} = \mathbf{x}_{\mathcal{B}}$, $\mathit{trace}(\beta) = \mathit{trace}(\alpha)$, and $\alpha.\mathit{lstate}\ R\ \beta.\mathit{lstate}$.

3. If $\mathbf{x}_{\mathcal{A}}\ R\ \mathbf{x}_{\mathcal{B}}$ and α is an execution fragment of $\mathcal{A}$ consisting of a single closed trajectory, with $\alpha.\mathit{fstate} = \mathbf{x}_{\mathcal{A}}$, then $\mathcal{B}$ has a closed execution fragment β with $\beta.\mathit{fstate} = \mathbf{x}_{\mathcal{B}}$, $\mathit{trace}(\beta) = \mathit{trace}(\alpha)$, and $\alpha.\mathit{lstate}\ R\ \beta.\mathit{lstate}$.

The first condition states that for each start state of $\mathcal{A}$ there exists a related start state of $\mathcal{B}$. The second and third condition, which are referred to as *transfer properties*, assert that each discrete transition resp. trajectory of $\mathcal{A}$ can be simulated by a corresponding execution fragment of $\mathcal{B}$ with the same trace.

If both R and R^{-1} are forward simulations then we say that R is a *bisimulation* from $\mathcal{A}$ to $\mathcal{B}$. Bisimulation relations play an important role in the automated analysis of timed and hybrid systems, see e.g. [6, 67, 122]. However, the bisimulations used for automated analysis are usually *time abstracted bisimulations*, whereas in our definition a trajectory α of one automaton must be simulated by a trajectory β of the other automaton with exactly the same duration ($\mathit{trace}(\beta) = \mathit{trace}(\alpha)$), these durations may be different in a time abstracted bisimulation.

Forward simulation relations induce a preorder between timed automata.

Theorem 4.22 *Let $\mathcal{A}$, $\mathcal{B}$, and $\mathcal{C}$ be comparable TAs. If R_1 is a forward simulation from $\mathcal{A}$ to $\mathcal{B}$ and R_2 is a forward simulation from $\mathcal{B}$ to $\mathcal{C}$, then $R_2 \circ R_1$ is a forward simulation from $\mathcal{A}$ to $\mathcal{C}$.*

Even though the definition of a forward simulation only refers to closed trajectories it also yields a correspondence for open trajectories.

Lemma 4.23 *Let $\mathcal{A}$ and $\mathcal{B}$ be comparable TAs and let R be a forward simulation from $\mathcal{A}$ to $\mathcal{B}$. Let $\mathbf{x}_{\mathcal{A}}$ and $\mathbf{x}_{\mathcal{B}}$ be states of $\mathcal{A}$ and $\mathcal{B}$, respectively, such that $\mathbf{x}_{\mathcal{A}}\ R\ \mathbf{x}_{\mathcal{B}}$. Let α be an execution fragment of $\mathcal{A}$ from state $\mathbf{x}_{\mathcal{A}}$ consisting of a single open trajectory. Then $\mathcal{B}$ has an execution fragment β with $\beta.\mathit{fstate} = \mathbf{x}_{\mathcal{B}}$ and $\mathit{trace}(\beta) = \mathit{trace}(\alpha)$.*

Proof. Let τ be the single open trajectory in α. Using Axioms **T1** and **T2**, we construct an infinite sequence $\tau_0\, \tau_1 \ldots$ of closed trajectories of $\mathcal{A}$ such that $\tau = \tau_0 \frown \tau_1 \frown \cdots$. Then, working recursively, we construct a sequence $\beta_0\, \beta_1 \ldots$ of closed execution fragments of $\mathcal{B}$ such that $\beta_0.\mathit{fstate} = \mathbf{x}_{\mathcal{B}}$ and, for each i, $\tau_i.\mathit{lstate}\ R\ \beta_i.\mathit{lstate}$, $\beta_i.\mathit{lstate} = \beta_{i+1}.\mathit{fstate}$, and $\mathit{trace}(\tau_i) = \mathit{trace}(\beta_i)$. This construction

uses induction on i, using Property 3 of the definition of a forward simulation in the induction step. Now let $\beta = \beta_0 \frown \beta_1 \frown \cdots$. By Lemma 4.7, β is an execution fragment of $\mathcal{B}$. Clearly, $\beta.\mathit{fstate} = \mathbf{x}_{\mathcal{B}}$. By Lemma 3.9 applied to both α and β, $\mathit{trace}(\beta) = \mathit{trace}(\alpha)$. Thus, β has the required properties.
□

Theorem 4.24 *Let $\mathcal{A}$ and $\mathcal{B}$ be comparable TAs and let R be a forward simulation from $\mathcal{A}$ to $\mathcal{B}$. Let $\mathbf{x}_{\mathcal{A}}$ and $\mathbf{x}_{\mathcal{B}}$ be states of $\mathcal{A}$ and $\mathcal{B}$, respectively, such that $\mathbf{x}_{\mathcal{A}}\ R\ \mathbf{x}_{\mathcal{B}}$. Then $\mathit{tracefrags}_{\mathcal{A}}(\mathbf{x}_{\mathcal{A}}) \subseteq \mathit{tracefrags}_{\mathcal{B}}(\mathbf{x}_{\mathcal{B}})$.*

Proof. Suppose that δ is the trace of an execution fragment of $\mathcal{A}$ that starts from $\mathbf{x}_{\mathcal{A}}$; we prove that δ is also a trace of an execution fragment of $\mathcal{B}$ that starts from $\mathbf{x}_{\mathcal{B}}$. Let $\alpha = \tau_0\ a_1\ \tau_1\ a_2\ \tau_2 \ldots$ be an execution fragment of $\mathcal{A}$ such that $\alpha.\mathit{fstate} = \mathbf{x}_{\mathcal{A}}$ and $\delta = \mathit{trace}(\alpha)$. We consider the following cases.

1. α is an infinite sequence.

   Using Axioms **T1** and **T2**, we can write α as an infinite concatenation $\alpha_0 \frown \alpha_1 \frown \alpha_2 \cdots$, in which the execution fragments α_i with i even consist of a trajectory only, and the execution fragments α_i with i odd consist of a single discrete step surrounded by two point trajectories.

   We define inductively a sequence $\beta_0\, \beta_1\, \ldots$ of closed execution fragments of $\mathcal{B}$, such that $\beta_0.\mathit{fstate} = \mathbf{x}_{\mathcal{B}}$ and, for all i, $\beta_i.\mathit{lstate} = \beta_{i+1}.\mathit{fstate}$, $\alpha_i.\mathit{lstate}\ R\ \beta_i.\mathit{lstate}$, and $\mathit{trace}(\beta_i) = \mathit{trace}(\alpha_i)$. We use Property 3 of the definition of a simulation for the construction of the β_i's with i even, and Property 2 for the construction of the β_i's with i odd. Let $\beta = \beta_0 \frown \beta_1 \frown \beta_2 \cdots$. By Lemma 4.7, β is an execution fragment of $\mathcal{B}$. Clearly, $\beta.\mathit{fstate} = \mathbf{x}_{\mathcal{B}}$. By Lemma 3.9, $\mathit{trace}(\beta) = \mathit{trace}(\alpha)$. Thus, β has the required properties.

2. α is a finite sequence ending with a closed trajectory.

   Similar to the first case.

3. α is a finite sequence ending with an open trajectory.

   Similar to the first case, using Lemma 4.23.

□

The next corollary states that forward simulations constitute a sound technique for proving trace inclusion between timed automata.

Corollary 4.25 *Let $\mathcal{A}$ and $\mathcal{B}$ be comparable TAs and let R be a forward simulation from $\mathcal{A}$ to $\mathcal{B}$. Then $\mathcal{A} \leq \mathcal{B}$.*

Proof. Suppose $\beta \in \mathit{traces}_{\mathcal{A}}$. Then $\beta \in \mathit{tracefrags}_{\mathcal{A}}(\mathbf{x}_{\mathcal{A}})$ for some start state $\mathbf{x}_{\mathcal{A}}$ of $\mathcal{A}$. Property 1 of the definition of simulation implies the existence of a start state $\mathbf{x}_{\mathcal{B}}$ of $\mathcal{B}$ such that $\mathbf{x}_{\mathcal{A}}\ R\ \mathbf{x}_{\mathcal{B}}$. Then Theorem 4.24 implies that $\beta \in \mathit{tracefrags}_{\mathcal{B}}(\mathbf{x}_{\mathcal{B}})$. Since $\mathbf{x}_{\mathcal{B}}$ is a start state of $\mathcal{B}$, this implies that $\beta \in \mathit{traces}_{\mathcal{B}}$, as needed. □

Example 4.26 (Time-bounded channels). Consider two instances of the specification in Fig. 4.1, `TimedChannel(b1, M)` and `TimedChannel(b2, M)` where b1 $\leq$ b2. We define a forward simulation R from `TimedChannel(b1, M)` to `TimedChannel(b2, M)` below. If $\mathbf{x}$ is a state of `TimedChannel(b1, M)` and $\mathbf{y}$ is a state of `TimedChannel(b2, M)`, then $\mathbf{x}\ R\ \mathbf{y}$ provided that the following conditions are satisfied:

1. $\mathbf{x}$(now) = $\mathbf{y}$(now);
2. |$\mathbf{x}$(queue)| = |$\mathbf{y}$(queue)|. We use $|q|$ to denote the length of an object q of type queue;
3. $\forall i.\ 1 \leq i \leq$ |$\mathbf{x}$(queue)|, if $\mathbf{x}$(queue)(i) = `[m,u1]` then $\mathbf{y}$(queue)(i) = `[m,u2]`, for some u2 with u1 $\leq$ u2.

We can prove that R is a forward simulation from the automaton `TimedChannel(b1, M)` to the automaton `TimedChannel(b2, M)` by showing that R satisfies each of the three properties in the definition of a forward simulation relation. In each automaton there is a unique initial state that maps the variable `now` to 0 and `queue` to the empty sequence. It is obvious that the initial states, which are identical, are related by R and so the first property is satisfied.

For the rest of the proof, we let $\mathbf{x}$ and $\mathbf{y}$ be, respectively, states of `TimedChannel(b1, M)` and `TimedChannel(b2, M)` such that $\mathbf{x}\ R\ \mathbf{y}$. In order to show that the second property is satisfied, we need to consider two cases, one for each discrete action that may be performed by `TimedChannel(b1, M)`.

If `TimedChannel(b1, M)` performs a `send(m)` action, and the state changes from $\mathbf{x}$ to $\mathbf{x}'$ then we need to find an execution fragment β of `TimedChannel(b2,M)` from $\mathbf{y}$ ending in $\mathbf{y}'$, such that $\mathbf{x}'\ R\ \mathbf{y}'$ and $trace(\beta)$ is the same as the trace of $\wp(\mathbf{x})$ `send(m)` $\wp(\mathbf{x}')$. The execution fragment $\beta = \wp(\mathbf{y})$ `send(m)` $\wp(\mathbf{y}')$ satisfies the required conditions. This follows from the hypothesis that $\mathbf{x}\ R\ \mathbf{y}$ and the definition of R, using the fact that the effect of a `send(m)` action of `TimedChannel(b1, M)`, `TimedChannel(b2, M)` are, respectively, adding the entry `[m,now + b1]` to $\mathbf{x}$(queue), and `[m,now + b2]` to $\mathbf{y}$(queue) where b1 $\leq$ b2.

If `TimedChannel(b1, M)` performs a `receive(m)` action, and the state changes from $\mathbf{x}$ to $\mathbf{x}'$ then we need to show that `receive(m)` is also enabled in $\mathbf{y}$ and that there is an execution fragment with the required properties that ends in a state $\mathbf{y}'$ such that $\mathbf{x}'\ R\ \mathbf{y}'$. In order to show that `receive(m)` is enabled in $\mathbf{y}$, we use the hypothesis that $\mathbf{x}\ R\ \mathbf{y}$, which implies that the first element of $\mathbf{y}$(queue) is of the form `[m,u]` for some u. The execution fragment $\wp(\mathbf{y})$ `receive(m)` $\wp(\mathbf{y}')$ of `TimedChannel(b1, M)` can be shown to satisfy the required conditions.

For the third property, we consider a closed trajectory τ of `TimedChannel(b1, M)` with $\tau.\mathit{fstate} = \mathbf{x}$ and show that there exists a closed execution fragment β of the automaton `TimedChannel(b2, M)` with $\beta.\mathit{fstate} = \mathbf{y}$, $\mathit{trace}(\beta) = \mathit{trace}(\tau)$, and $\tau.\mathit{lstate} = \beta.\mathit{lstate}$. It is easy to check that the trajectory τ' of `TimedChannel(b2, M)` with $\tau'.\mathit{fstate} = \mathbf{y}$ and $\tau'.\mathit{ltime} = \tau.\mathit{ltime}$ satisfies the required conditions.

Example 4.27 (Time-bounded channel that keeps all messages). In this example we define a variant of `TimedChannel` from Example 4.1 called `TimedChannel2`. The main difference between `TimedChannel` and `TimedChannel2` is that the message queue in `TimedChannel2` is implemented using a finite sequence of (message, delivery deadline) pairs queue and a pointer ptr that points to the next element that is to be delivered. Hence, the internal variables of TimedChannel2 consist of queue, now and ptr. The variable ptr initially has value 1, which indicates that it is pointing to the first element in the sequence. A send(m) action causes messages and deadlines to be added to the sequence as in TimedChannel. A receive(m) causes ptr to be incremented to make it point to the next element in the sequence instead of removing the first element. The stops when predicate tests if there is a packet in the queue with index greater than or equal to ptr and deadline equal to now. The automaton TimedChannel can be viewed as an optimized implementation of TimedChannel2.

We define below a forward simulation R from TimedChannel to TimedChannel2. If $\mathbf{x}$ is a state of TimedChannel and $\mathbf{y}$ is a state of TimedChannel2, then $\mathbf{x}\ R\ \mathbf{y}$ provided that the following conditions are satisfied:

1. $\mathbf{x}(\texttt{now}) = \mathbf{y}(\texttt{now})$;

2. $\mathbf{x}(\texttt{queue}) = \mathbf{y}(\texttt{queue})(\mathbf{y}(\texttt{ptr}) \ldots |\mathbf{y}(\texttt{queue})|)$.

Here, we assume the sequence representation of queues and use the subsequence notation from Chapter 2 to denote the part of the queue that starts with the index ptr and ends with the index $\mathbf{y}(\texttt{queue})$.

Example 4.28 (Clock synchronization). In this example, we define a forward simulation from ClockSync(u,r:Real, i:Index) of Fig. 4.7 to an automaton that sends multiples of u. The specification of this automaton, which is called SendVal is given in Fig. 4.8. We assume that the Index types in both automata are identical. The variable counter keeps track of which multiple of u is to be sent next, and variable now contains the current time. The automaton parameter r is used in the precondition of the send and the stopping condition of the trajectory definition, to enforce bounds on the times of occurrence of send.

The following predicate defines a forward simulation R from automaton ClockSync() to automaton SendVal:

$$\texttt{now} * (1 - \texttt{r}) \leq \texttt{physclock} \leq \texttt{now} * (1 + \texttt{r}) \ \wedge\ \texttt{counter} * \texttt{u} = \texttt{nextsend} \geq \texttt{physclock}.$$

Whereas automaton ClockSync(u,r:Real, i:Index) is more intuitive as a specification, automaton SendVal is easier for analysis purposes, since its continuous dynamics is simpler.

4.6.2 REFINEMENTS

A *refinement* is a simple, special case of a forward simulation, often used in practice (see, for instance, [105, 110]), in which the relation between states of $\mathcal{A}$ and $\mathcal{B}$ is a partial function.

Let $\mathcal{A}$ and $\mathcal{B}$ be comparable TAs. A *refinement* from $\mathcal{A}$ to $\mathcal{B}$ is a partial function F from $Q_{\mathcal{A}}$ to $Q_{\mathcal{B}}$, satisfying the following conditions, for all states $\mathbf{x}_{\mathcal{A}}$ and $\mathbf{x}_{\mathcal{B}}$ of $\mathcal{A}$ and $\mathcal{B}$, respectively.

```
automaton SendVal(u, r: Real, i: Index) where u > 0 ∧ (0 ≤ r < 1)
  signature
    external send(m: Real),
             receive(m: Real, j: Index, const i: Index) where j ≠ i
  states
    counter: discrete Real := 0,
    now: Real := 0
  transitions
    external send(m, i)
      pre
        m = counter * u ∧ counter * u / (1 + r) ≤ now
      eff
        counter := counter + 1
    external receive(m, j, i)
  trajectories
    stop when
      now = counter * u / (1 - r)
    evolve
      d(now) = 1
```

Figure 4.8: Clock synchronization.

1. If $\mathbf{x}_{\mathcal{A}} \in \Theta_{\mathcal{A}}$ then $\mathbf{x}_{\mathcal{A}} \in dom(F)$ and $F(\mathbf{x}_{\mathcal{A}}) \in \Theta_{\mathcal{B}}$.

2. If α is an execution fragment of $\mathcal{A}$ consisting of one action surrounded by two point trajectories and $\alpha.fstate \in dom(F)$, then $\alpha.lstate \in dom(F)$ and $\mathcal{B}$ has a closed execution fragment β with $\beta.fstate = F(\alpha.fstate)$, $trace(\beta) = trace(\alpha)$, and $\beta.lstate = F(\alpha.lstate)$.

3. If α is an execution fragment of $\mathcal{A}$ consisting of a single closed trajectory and $\alpha.fstate \in dom(F)$, then $\alpha.lstate \in dom(F)$ and $\mathcal{B}$ has a closed execution fragment β with $\beta.fstate = F(\alpha.fstate)$, $trace(\beta) = trace(\alpha)$, and $\beta.lstate = F(\alpha.lstate)$.

Note that, by a trivial inductive argument, the set of states for which F is defined contains all the reachable states of $\mathcal{A}$ (and is thus an invariant of this automaton).

Theorem 4.29 *Let $\mathcal{A}$ and $\mathcal{B}$ be two TAs and suppose $R \subseteq Q_{\mathcal{A}} \times Q_{\mathcal{B}}$. Then R is a refinement from $\mathcal{A}$ to $\mathcal{B}$ if and only if R is a forward simulation from $\mathcal{A}$ to $\mathcal{B}$ and R is a partial function.*

The following theorem states a basic sanity property of refinements, namely closure under composition.

Theorem 4.30 *Let $\mathcal{A}$, $\mathcal{B}$, and $\mathcal{C}$ be comparable TAs. If R_1 is a refinement from $\mathcal{A}$ to $\mathcal{B}$ and R_2 is a refinement from $\mathcal{B}$ to $\mathcal{C}$, then $R_2 \circ R_1$ is a refinement from $\mathcal{A}$ to $\mathcal{C}$.*

A *weak isomorphism* from $\mathcal{A}$ to $\mathcal{B}$ is a refinement F from $\mathcal{A}$ to $\mathcal{B}$ such that F^{-1} is a refinement from $\mathcal{B}$ to $\mathcal{A}$. We say that two automata $\mathcal{A}$ and $\mathcal{B}$ are *weakly isomorphic*, if there exists an isomorphism from $\mathcal{A}$ to $\mathcal{B}$ (or, equivalently from $\mathcal{B}$ to $\mathcal{A}$).

Example 4.31 (Refinements). In Example 4.26 we established a forward simulation between two instances of the TA in Fig. 4.1, `TimedChannel(b1, M)` and `TimedChannel(b2, M)` with `b1` $\leq$ `b2`. It is not hard see that there also exists a refinement from `TimedChannel(b1, M)` to `TimedChannel(b2, M)`: just add `b2` $-$ `b1` to the deadline of each packet in the queue.

In Example 4.28 we defined a forward simulation from automaton `ClockSync(u,r:Real, i:Index)` to automaton `SendVal`. In this case, however, there does not exist a refinement from `ClockSync(u,r:Real, i:Index)` to `SendVal` if `r` > 0. The proof is by contradiction. Suppose that F is a refinement from `ClockSync(u,r:Real, i:Index)` to `SendVal`. Then F maps the initial state of `ClockSync(u,r:Real, i:Index)` to the initial state of `SendVal`. Since `send` actions can be simulated, the state `s0` of `ClockSync(u,r:Real, i:Index)` with `nextsend` $=$ `u` and `physclock` $= 0$ is mapped by F to the state of `SendVal` with `counter` $= 1$ and `now` $= 0$. Consider an outgoing trajectory of `s0` with positive limit time to a state `s1` in which the physical clock runs maximally fast, and a trajectory with the same limit time to a state `s2` in which the physical clock runs maximally slow. Since `r` > 0, `s1` and `s2` are distinct. By the transfer property for trajectories, both `s1` and `s2` are mapped onto the same state of `SendVal`. Now observe that there exists a trajectory with positive limit time from `s2` to `s1`. This trajectory can not be simulated in `SendVal`, since in this automaton there are no nontrivial trajectories from a state to itself. Contradiction.

4.6.3 BACKWARD SIMULATIONS

Let $\mathcal{A}$ and $\mathcal{B}$ be comparable TAs. A *backward simulation* from $\mathcal{A}$ to $\mathcal{B}$ is a total relation $R \subseteq Q_{\mathcal{A}} \times Q_{\mathcal{B}}$ satisfying the following conditions, for all states $\mathbf{x}_{\mathcal{A}}$ and $\mathbf{x}_{\mathcal{B}}$ of $\mathcal{A}$ and $\mathcal{B}$, respectively:

1. If $\mathbf{x}_{\mathcal{A}} \in \Theta_{\mathcal{A}}$ and $\mathbf{x}_{\mathcal{A}}\ R\ \mathbf{x}_{\mathcal{B}}$ then $\mathbf{x}_{\mathcal{B}} \in \Theta_{\mathcal{B}}$.

2. If $\mathbf{x}_{\mathcal{A}}\ R\ \mathbf{x}_{\mathcal{B}}$ and α is an execution fragment of $\mathcal{A}$ with $\alpha.lstate = \mathbf{x}_{\mathcal{A}}$, consisting of one discrete action surrounded by two point trajectories, then $\mathcal{B}$ has a closed execution fragment β with $\beta.lstate = \mathbf{x}_{\mathcal{B}}$, $trace(\beta) = trace(\alpha)$, and $\alpha.fstate\ R\ \beta.fstate$.

3. If $\mathbf{x}_{\mathcal{A}}\ R\ \mathbf{x}_{\mathcal{B}}$ and α is an execution fragment of $\mathcal{A}$ with $\alpha.lstate = \mathbf{x}_{\mathcal{A}}$, consisting of one trajectory, then $\mathcal{B}$ has a closed execution fragment β with $\beta.lstate = \mathbf{x}_{\mathcal{B}}$, $trace(\beta) = trace(\alpha)$, and $\alpha.fstate\ R\ \beta.fstate$.

Backward simulations are closed under relational composition, and hence induce a preorder between timed automata.

Theorem 4.32 *Let $\mathcal{A}$, $\mathcal{B}$, and $\mathcal{C}$ be comparable TAs. If R_1 is a backward simulation from $\mathcal{A}$ to $\mathcal{B}$ and R_2 is a backward simulation $\mathcal{B}$ to $\mathcal{C}$, then $R_2 \circ R_1$ is a backward simulation from $\mathcal{A}$ to $\mathcal{C}$.*

Theorem 4.33 *Let $\mathcal{A}$ and $\mathcal{B}$ be comparable TAs and let R be a backward simulation from $\mathcal{A}$ to $\mathcal{B}$. Let $\mathbf{x}_{\mathcal{A}}$ and $\mathbf{x}_{\mathcal{B}}$ be states of $\mathcal{A}$ and $\mathcal{B}$, respectively, such that $\mathbf{x}_{\mathcal{A}}\ R\ \mathbf{x}_{\mathcal{B}}$. Let β be the trace of a closed execution fragment of $\mathcal{A}$ from $\mathbf{y}_{\mathcal{A}}$ with last state $\mathbf{x}_{\mathcal{A}}$. Then there exists $\mathbf{y}_{\mathcal{B}}$ such that β is also the trace of a closed execution fragment of $\mathcal{B}$ from $\mathbf{y}_{\mathcal{B}}$ with last state $\mathbf{x}_{\mathcal{B}}$ and $\mathbf{y}_{\mathcal{A}}\ R\ \mathbf{y}_{\mathcal{B}}$.*

Proof. Fix some R, $\mathbf{x}_A$, $\mathbf{x}_B$, and β satisfying the conditions in the statement of the theorem. Let $\alpha \in \mathit{frags}_{\mathcal{A}}(\mathbf{y}_{\mathcal{A}})$ for some state $\mathbf{y}_{\mathcal{A}}$ of $\mathcal{A}$ with $\mathit{trace}(\alpha) = \beta$ and $\alpha.\mathit{lstate} = \mathbf{x}_{\mathcal{A}}$. By using the Axioms **T1** and **T2,** we can write α as the concatenation of a sequence of closed execution fragments, $\alpha = \alpha_0 \frown \alpha_1 \frown \ldots \alpha_n$, where each α_i is either a closed trajectory or an action surrounded by two point trajectories, $\alpha_i.\mathit{lstate} = \alpha_{i+1}.\mathit{fstate}$ for $0 \leq i \leq n-1$, and $\alpha_n.\mathit{lstate} = \mathbf{x}_{\mathcal{A}}$.

By using the definition of a backward simulation, working backwards from α_n, we can construct an execution fragment $\alpha' = \alpha'_0 \frown \alpha'_1 \frown \ldots \alpha'_n$ from a state $\mathbf{y}_{\mathcal{B}}$ of $\mathcal{B}$ such that (a) $\alpha'.\mathit{lstate} = \mathbf{x}_{\mathcal{B}}$, (b) for all i, $0 \leq i \leq n$, $\alpha_i.\mathit{fstate}\ R\ \alpha'_i.\mathit{fstate}$ and $\mathit{trace}(\alpha'_i) = \mathit{trace}(\alpha_i)$, (c) for all i, $0 \leq i \leq n-1$, $\alpha'_i.\mathit{lstate} = \alpha'_{i+1}.\mathit{fstate}$. Using Lemma 4.7, we can see that α' is an execution fragment of $\mathcal{B}$. By Lemma 3.9, $\mathit{trace}(\alpha) = \mathit{trace}(\alpha')$ as needed. □

The next corollary states that backward simulations constitute a sound technique for proving inclusion of closed traces between timed automata.

Corollary 4.34 *Let $\mathcal{A}$ and $\mathcal{B}$ be comparable TAs and let R be a backward simulation from $\mathcal{A}$ to $\mathcal{B}$. Then every closed trace of $\mathcal{A}$ is a trace of $\mathcal{B}$.*

Proof. Suppose R is a backward simulation from $\mathcal{A}$ to $\mathcal{B}$ and β is a closed trace of $\mathcal{A}$. Then $\beta = \mathit{trace}(\alpha)$ for some closed execution α of $\mathcal{A}$. Let $\mathbf{x}_{\mathcal{A}}$ and $\mathbf{y}_{\mathcal{A}}$ be the first and last states of α respectively. By the totality of relation R, there exists some state $\mathbf{y}_{\mathcal{B}}$ of $\mathcal{B}$ such that $\mathbf{y}_{\mathcal{A}}\ R\ \mathbf{y}_{\mathcal{B}}$. By Theorem 4.33, there exists $\mathbf{x}_{\mathcal{B}}$ of $\mathcal{B}$ such that β is the trace of a closed execution fragment of $\mathcal{B}$ from $\mathbf{x}_{\mathcal{B}}$ with last state $\mathbf{y}_{\mathcal{B}}$ and $\mathbf{x}_{\mathcal{A}}\ R\ \mathbf{x}_{\mathcal{B}}$. Property 1 of the definition of a backward simulation relation implies that $\mathbf{x}_{\mathcal{B}}$ is a start state of $\mathcal{B}$. It follows that $\beta \in \mathit{traces}_{\mathcal{B}}$, as needed. □

Image-finite backward simulations constitute a sound technique for proving inclusion of (all) traces between timed automata.

Theorem 4.35 *Let $\mathcal{A}$ and $\mathcal{B}$ be comparable TAs and let R be an image-finite backward simulation from $\mathcal{A}$ to $\mathcal{B}$. Then $\mathit{traces}_{\mathcal{A}} \subseteq \mathit{traces}_{\mathcal{B}}$.*

Proof. Let $\beta \in \mathit{traces}_{\mathcal{A}}$. If β is closed then Corollary 4.34 implies that β is a trace of $\mathcal{B}$. From now on we assume β is not closed.

Let $\alpha \in \mathit{execs}_{\mathcal{A}}$ with $\mathit{trace}(\alpha) = \beta$. Note that any such α is either an infinite sequence $\tau_0\ a_1\ \tau_1 \ldots$ or a finite sequence $\tau_0\ a_1\ \tau_1\ \ldots \tau_n$ where the final trajectory τ_n is right open. In either case, using the Axioms **T1** and **T2,** we can construct an infinite sequence $\alpha_0\,\alpha_1\ \ldots$ of closed execution fragments such that $\alpha = \alpha_0 \frown \alpha_1 \frown \ldots$ where α_0 is a point trajectory, each α_i is either a closed trajectory or an action surrounded by two point trajectories, and $\alpha_i.lstate = \alpha_{i+1}.fstate$ for each $i, 0 \leq i$.

We construct a directed graph G whose nodes are pairs $(\mathbf{x}, i)$ consisting of a state of $\mathcal{B}$ and an index such that $(\alpha_i.lstate, \mathbf{x}) \in R$. In G, there is an edge from $(\mathbf{x}, i)$ to $(\mathbf{x}', j)$ exactly if $j = i + 1$ and there is an $\alpha' \in frags_{\mathcal{B}}(\mathbf{x})$ with $trace(\alpha') = trace(\alpha_{i+1})$ such that $\alpha'.lstate = \mathbf{x}'$. By image-finiteness of R and the definition of the edge set, each node has finite outdegree. By using the definition of a backward simulation and the edge set of G, we can show that each node $(\mathbf{x}, i)$ is reachable from some root node $(\mathbf{z}, 0)$ for some start state $\mathbf{z}$ of $\mathcal{B}$. Since R is image-finite there are finitely many roots of G.

The directed graph G satisfies the hypotheses of Lemma 2.1, which implies that there is an infinite path in G starting from a root. An edge from a node $(\mathbf{x}, i)$ to $(\mathbf{x}', i + 1)$ along this infinite path corresponds to a closed execution fragment γ_{i+1} of $\mathcal{B}$ for $i, 0 \leq i$ such that $\gamma_{i+1}.fstate = \mathbf{x}$, $\gamma_{i+1}.lstate = \mathbf{x}'$ and $trace(\gamma_{i+1}) = trace(\alpha_{i+1})$. By Lemma 4.7, $\gamma = \gamma_1 \frown \gamma_2 \frown \ldots$ is an execution of $\mathcal{B}$ and by Lemma 3.9, $trace(\gamma) = trace(\gamma_1) \frown trace(\gamma_2) \ldots$. Since $trace(\gamma_{i+1}) = trace(\alpha_{i+1})$ for all i, $0 \leq i$, and α_0 is a point trajectory, by Lemma 3.9, we get $trace(\gamma) = trace(\alpha) = \beta$. □

Example 4.36 (A backward simulation relation). This example illustrates the difference between forward and backward simulations. We consider two automata $\mathcal{A}$ and $\mathcal{B}$ and show that a forward simulation from $\mathcal{A}$ to $\mathcal{B}$ does not exist while we exhibit a backward simulation from $\mathcal{A}$ to $\mathcal{B}$.

Let $\mathcal{A}$ and $\mathcal{B}$ be two comparable automata specified below. The trajectories consist of a set of point trajectories. This implies that the automaton does not allow time to pass — everything happens at time 0.

- $X_{\mathcal{A}} = \{stateA\}$ and $X_{\mathcal{B}} = \{stateB\}$ where:
  $stateA$ is a discrete variable with $type(stateA) = \{x_{\mathcal{A}}, y_{\mathcal{A}}, q_{\mathcal{A}}, s_{\mathcal{A}}\}$, and
  $stateB$ is a discrete variable with $type(stateB) = \{x_{\mathcal{B}}, y_{\mathcal{B}}, y'_{\mathcal{B}}, q_{\mathcal{B}}, s_{\mathcal{B}}\}$.

- $Q_{\mathcal{A}} = val(X_{\mathcal{A}})$ and $Q_{\mathcal{B}} = val(X_{\mathcal{B}})$. We write $\mathbf{x}_{\mathcal{A}}$ for the valuation that maps $stateA$ to $x_{\mathcal{A}}$, $\mathbf{y}_{\mathcal{A}}$ for the valuation that maps $stateA$ to $y_{\mathcal{A}}$, etc. Similarly, we write $\mathbf{x}_{\mathcal{B}}$ for the valuation that maps $stateB$ to $x_{\mathcal{B}}$, $\mathbf{y}_{\mathcal{B}}$ for the valuation that maps $stateB$ to $y_{\mathcal{B}}$, etc.

- $\Theta_{\mathcal{A}} = \{\mathbf{x}_{\mathcal{A}}\}$ and $\Theta_{\mathcal{B}} = \{\mathbf{x}_{\mathcal{B}}\}$.

- $E_{\mathcal{A}} = E_{\mathcal{B}} = \{a, b, c\}$ and $H_{\mathcal{A}} = H_{\mathcal{B}} = \emptyset$.

- $\mathcal{D}_{\mathcal{A}} = \{(\mathbf{x}_{\mathcal{A}}, a, \mathbf{y}_{\mathcal{A}}), (\mathbf{y}_{\mathcal{A}}, b, \mathbf{q}_{\mathcal{A}}), (\mathbf{y}_{\mathcal{A}}, c, \mathbf{s}_{\mathcal{A}})\}$, and
  $\mathcal{D}_{\mathcal{B}} = \{(\mathbf{x}_{\mathcal{B}}, a, \mathbf{y}_{\mathcal{B}}), (\mathbf{x}_{\mathcal{B}}, a, \mathbf{y}'_{\mathcal{B}}), (\mathbf{y}_{\mathcal{B}}, b, \mathbf{q}_{\mathcal{B}}), (\mathbf{y}'_{\mathcal{B}}, c, \mathbf{s}_{\mathcal{B}})\}$.

- $\mathcal{T}_{\mathcal{A}} = \{\wp(\mathbf{v}) \mid \mathbf{v} \in Q_{\mathcal{A}}\}$, and $\mathcal{T}_{\mathcal{B}} = \{\wp(\mathbf{v}) \mid \mathbf{v} \in Q_{\mathcal{B}}\}$.

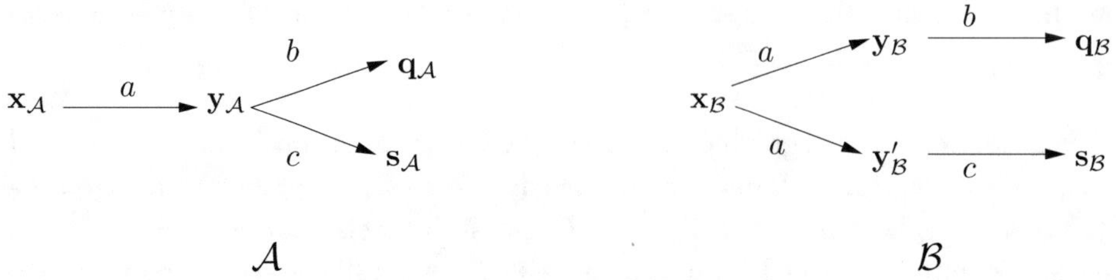

Figure 4.9: Difference between forward and backward simulations.

Figure 4.9 displays automata $\mathcal{A}$ and $\mathcal{B}$ as directed multigraphs. The nodes in the graph represent states and the edges represent discrete transitions where a label on an edge stands for the action involved in the transition.

An obvious candidate for a forward simulation from $\mathcal{A}$ to $\mathcal{B}$ is the relation

$$R = \{(\mathbf{x}_\mathcal{A}, \mathbf{x}_\mathcal{B}), (\mathbf{y}_\mathcal{A}, \mathbf{y}_\mathcal{B}), (\mathbf{y}_\mathcal{A}, \mathbf{y}'_\mathcal{B}), (\mathbf{q}_\mathcal{A}, \mathbf{q}_\mathcal{B}), (\mathbf{s}_\mathcal{A}, \mathbf{s}_\mathcal{B})\}.$$

However, observe that even though $\mathbf{y}_\mathcal{A}$ and $\mathbf{y}_\mathcal{B}$ are related by R, the execution fragment $\wp(\mathbf{y}_\mathcal{A})\ c\ \wp(\mathbf{s}_\mathcal{A})$ of $\mathcal{A}$ cannot be matched by any execution fragment of $\mathcal{B}$ starting with state $\mathbf{y}_\mathcal{B}$. Similarly, even though $\mathbf{y}_\mathcal{A}$ and $\mathbf{y}'_\mathcal{B}$ are related by R, the execution fragment $\wp(\mathbf{y}_\mathcal{A})\ b\ \wp(\mathbf{q}_\mathcal{A})$ of $\mathcal{A}$ cannot be matched by any execution fragment of $\mathcal{B}$ starting with $\mathbf{y}'_\mathcal{B}$. Therefore, R is not a forward simulation. In fact, there is no forward simulation relation from $\mathcal{A}$ to $\mathcal{B}$: there are finitely many possibilities for forward simulations from $\mathcal{A}$ to $\mathcal{B}$ and we see that none of them is a forward simulation by examining all the possibilities. The main reason for this is that while $\mathcal{A}$ makes the nondeterministic choice between performing b or c after performing a, $\mathcal{B}$ makes its choice earlier at the same time it performs a.

There is, however, a backward simulation from $\mathcal{A}$ to $\mathcal{B}$: the relation R defined above is a backward simulation.

4.6.4 HISTORY RELATIONS

A relation $R \subseteq Q_\mathcal{A} \times Q_\mathcal{B}$ is a *history relation* from $\mathcal{A}$ to $\mathcal{B}$ if R is a forward simulation from $\mathcal{A}$ to $\mathcal{B}$ and R^{-1} is a refinement from $\mathcal{B}$ to $\mathcal{A}$. History relations induce a preorder between timed automata.

An automaton $\mathcal{B}$ is obtained from an automaton $\mathcal{A}$ by *adding history variables* if there exists a set of variables X such that:

1. $X_\mathcal{B} = X_\mathcal{A} \cup X$ and $X_\mathcal{A} \cap X = \emptyset$;

2. $Q_\mathcal{B} \lceil X_\mathcal{A} \subseteq Q_\mathcal{A}$; and

3. relation $\{(\mathbf{x}, \mathbf{y}) \mid \mathbf{y} \in Q_\mathcal{B} \text{ and } \mathbf{y} \lceil X_\mathcal{A} = \mathbf{x}\}$ is a history relation from $\mathcal{A}$ to $\mathcal{B}$.

The method of adding history variables is typically used to make it possible to establish an implementation relationship using a refinement. If a refinement does not exist from a low-level automaton to a higher-level one, it can often be made to exist by adding history variables to the low-level automaton.

Example 4.37 (Adding history variables to obtain a refinement). We cannot show that `TimedChannel` is an implementation of `TimedChannel2` from Example 4.27 by using a refinement. This is because we have no way of specifying what the subsequence before the pointer should be in `TimedChannel2` when relating the states of the two automata. This example shows how we can add history variables to `TimedChannel` (actually, we add just one variable) to obtain a new automaton that is related to `TimedChannel2` by a refinement.

Let `log` be a discrete variable whose static type is the same as the static type of `queue` in `TimedChannel` and let the initial value of `log` be the empty sequence. We define a new automaton `TimedChannelH` whose set of variables consists of the variables of `TimedChannel` and the variable `log`. The rest of the definition of `TimedChannelH` is the same as `TimedChannel` except for the transition definition for `receive(m)`. A `receive(m)` event in `TimedChannelH` not only removes the first message from the message queue but also appends this message to the sequence contained in `log`.

Let X_1, X_2 be the set of variables and Q_1, Q_2 be the set of states of `TimedChannel` and `TimedChannelH`, respectively. It is easy to verify that the relation $\{(\mathbf{x}, \mathbf{y}) \mid \mathbf{y} \in Q_2 \text{ and } \mathbf{y} \lceil X_1 = \mathbf{x}\}$ is a history relation from `TimedChannel` to `TimedChannelH`. This means that `TimedChannelH` is obtained from `TimedChannel` by adding a history variable.

We now define a refinement F from `TimedChannelH` to `TimedChannel2` as follows. In our definition we assume the following conventions. Concatenation on the left corresponds to putting an element on the front of a queue. Recall also that we use juxtaposition for concatenation of sequences. If $\mathbf{x}$ is a state of `TimedChannelH` and $\mathbf{y}$ is a state of `TimedChannel2`, then $F(\mathbf{x}) = \mathbf{y}$ where:

1. $\mathbf{y}(\texttt{now}) = \mathbf{x}(\texttt{now})$;
2. $\mathbf{y}(\texttt{queue}) = \mathbf{x}(\texttt{log}) ^\frown \mathbf{x}(\texttt{queue})$;
3. $\mathbf{y}(\texttt{ptr}) = |\mathbf{x}(\texttt{log})| + 1$.

Whenever an automaton $\mathcal{B}$ is obtained from $\mathcal{A}$ by adding history variables, then there exists a history relation from $\mathcal{A}$ to $\mathcal{B}$ by definition. Theorem 4.38 states that the converse also holds, if weakly isomorphic automata are considered.

Theorem 4.38 *Let $\mathcal{A}$ and $\mathcal{B}$ be two comparable TAs. Suppose that there is a history relation from $\mathcal{A}$ to $\mathcal{B}$. Then, there exists a TA $\mathcal{C}$ that is weakly isomorphic to $\mathcal{B}$ and is obtained from $\mathcal{A}$ by adding history variables.*

Proof. Assume, without loss of generality, that $X_{\mathcal{A}}$ and $X_{\mathcal{B}}$ are disjoint. Let R be a history relation from $\mathcal{A}$ to $\mathcal{B}$. Define automaton $\mathcal{C}$ as follows:

- $X_{\mathcal{C}} = X_{\mathcal{A}} \cup X_{\mathcal{B}}$.
- $Q_{\mathcal{C}} = \{\mathbf{x} \in val(X_{\mathcal{C}}) \mid (\mathbf{x} \lceil X_{\mathcal{A}}, \mathbf{x} \lceil X_{\mathcal{B}}) \in R\}$.
- $\Theta_{\mathcal{C}} = \{\mathbf{x} \in Q_{\mathcal{C}} \mid \mathbf{x} \lceil X_{\mathcal{B}} \in \Theta_{\mathcal{B}}\}$.
- $E_{\mathcal{C}} = E_{\mathcal{B}}$ and $H_{\mathcal{C}} = H_{\mathcal{B}}$.
- $\mathbf{x} \xrightarrow{a}_{\mathcal{C}} \mathbf{y}$ if and only if $\mathbf{x} \lceil X_{\mathcal{B}} \xrightarrow{a}_{\mathcal{B}} \mathbf{y} \lceil X_{\mathcal{B}}$.
- $\mathcal{T}_{\mathcal{C}} = \{\tau \in trajs(Q_{\mathcal{C}}) \mid \tau \lceil X_{\mathcal{B}} \in \mathcal{T}_{\mathcal{B}}\}$.

Let $F : Q_{\mathcal{C}} \rightarrow Q_{\mathcal{B}}$ be the projection function such that $F(\mathbf{x}) = \mathbf{x} \lceil X_{\mathcal{B}}$ for all $\mathbf{x} \in Q_{\mathcal{C}}$. It is easy to check that F is a weak isomorphism from $\mathcal{C}$ to $\mathcal{B}$. We verify that $\mathcal{C}$ is obtained from $\mathcal{A}$ by adding history variables. Let $X_{\mathcal{B}}$ be the variable set X required in the definition of a history variable and let $R' = \{(\mathbf{x}, \mathbf{y}) \mid \mathbf{y} \in Q_{\mathcal{C}} \wedge \mathbf{y} \lceil X_{\mathcal{A}} = \mathbf{x}\}$. We need to show that R' is a history relation from $\mathcal{A}$ to $\mathcal{C}$.

1. R' is a forward simulation from $\mathcal{A}$ to $\mathcal{C}$.
   By definitions of the relations F, R' and the automaton $\mathcal{C}$, $R' = F^{-1} \circ R$. Since F^{-1} is a refinement from $\mathcal{B}$ to $\mathcal{C}$, by Theorem 4.29, we know that it is a forward simulation from $\mathcal{B}$ to $\mathcal{C}$. Since R is a forward simulation from $\mathcal{A}$ to $\mathcal{B}$, by Theorem 4.22 we have R' is a forward simulation from $\mathcal{A}$ to $\mathcal{C}$, as needed.

2. R'^{-1} is a refinement from $\mathcal{C}$ to $\mathcal{A}$.
   We use that $R'^{-1} = R^{-1} \circ F$. Since F is a refinement from $\mathcal{C}$ to $\mathcal{B}$ and R^{-1} is a refinement from $\mathcal{B}$ to $\mathcal{A}$, by Theorem 4.30, we have R'^{-1} is a refinement from $\mathcal{C}$ to $\mathcal{A}$, as needed.

□

In the untimed case, forward simulations are essentially the same as history relations (or variables) combined with refinements [85, Theorem 5.8]. Clearly, since history relations and refinements are both special cases of forward simulations, and since forward simulations compose, forward simulations are at least as powerful as arbitrary combinations of history relations and refinements. Conversely, if there is a forward simulation from $\mathcal{A}$ to $\mathcal{B}$ then there exists an automaton $\mathcal{C}$ with a history relation from $\mathcal{A}$ to $\mathcal{C}$ and a refinement from $\mathcal{C}$ to $\mathcal{B}$. In [87], a corresponding result is claimed for timed automata (Theorem 7.8), but the proof turns out to be flawed. Example 7.13 of [87] constitutes a counterexample to Theorem 7.8 of [87]. Below, we have translated the example to the setting of this monograph.

Example 4.39 (Forward simulations more powerful than combination history relations and refinements). Consider the automata A and B specified in Figure 4.10. The two automaton definitions

```
automaton A                              automaton B
  signature                                signature
    external a                               external a
  states                                   states
    init: Bool := true,                      init: Bool := true,
    now: Real := 0                           now: Real := 0
  transitions                              transitions
    external a                               external a
      pre                                      pre
        init ∧ rational(now)                     init ∧ integer(now)
      eff                                      eff
        init := false                            init := false
  trajectories                             trajectories
    evolve                                   evolve
      d(now) = 1                               d(now) > 0
```

Figure 4.10: The power of forward simulations.

are very similar. Whereas in A an a-action is enabled when init = true and the value of now is a rational number, in B an a-action is enabled when init = true and the value of now is an integer. Whereas automaton A has a perfect clock with rate 1, automaton B measures time with a clock that may run either too slow or too fast, in an arbitrary fashion.

It is easy to check that the predicate

$$\texttt{natural(B.now)} \wedge \texttt{A.init} = \texttt{B.init}$$

determines a forward simulation from A to B. However, there does not exists a timed automaton C with a history relation from A to C and a refinement from C to B. The proof is by contradiction: suppose C is such a timed automaton. Let $\mathbf{x}_0$ be a start state of C, let F be a history relation from A to C, and let R be a refinement from C to B. Then, by the start condition of a history relation, the start state $(0, \texttt{true})$ of A is related to $\mathbf{x}_0$ by F. By the start condition of a refinement, R maps $\mathbf{x}_0$ to the start state $(0, \texttt{true})$ of B. Since in A there is a trajectory with limit time 1 from $(0, \texttt{true})$ to $(1, \texttt{true})$, the transfer property for F gives that in C there is a trajectory τ with limit time 1 from $\mathbf{x}_0$ to some state $\mathbf{x}_1$ that is related by F to $(1, \texttt{true})$. Next, the transfer property for R gives that in B there is a trajectory with limit time 1 from $(0, \texttt{true})$ to state $R(\mathbf{x}_1) = (t, \texttt{true})$, for some $t > 0$. Since state $(1, \texttt{true})$ in A enables an a-action, $\mathbf{x}_1$ enables an execution fragment in which an a-action takes place within 0 time. Since $\mathbf{x}_1$ is mapped by R to $(t, \texttt{true})$, it follows by the transfer property for R that t in fact equals some natural number $n > 0$. By Axioms **T1** and **T2**, we can write τ as the concatenation $\tau_0\, \tau_1\, \cdots \tau_n$ of $n+1$ trajectories that all have limit time $\frac{1}{n+1}$. Using the fact that F is a history relation and the limit times of the trajectories τ_i are rational, we may infer that the last state of each trajectory τ_i enables an execution fragment in which an a-action takes place within 0 time. Using the fact that R is a refinement, we may infer that there is a trajectory in B from (0, `true`) to (n, `true`) on which there are at least $n+2$ states (including the first and last state) in which an a-action is enabled. This contradicts the fact that in B actions a are only enabled at integer times, which implies that there are only $n+1$ such states on any trajectory from (0, `true`) to (n, `true`).

4.6.5 PROPHECY RELATIONS

A relation $R \subseteq Q_{\mathcal{A}} \times Q_{\mathcal{B}}$ is a *prophecy relation* from $\mathcal{A}$ to $\mathcal{B}$ if R is a backward simulation from $\mathcal{A}$ to $\mathcal{B}$ and R^{-1} is a refinement from $\mathcal{B}$ to $\mathcal{A}$. Prophecy relations induce a preorder between timed automata.

An automaton $\mathcal{B}$ is obtained from an automaton $\mathcal{A}$ by *adding prophecy variables* if there exists a set of variables X such that:

1. $X_{\mathcal{B}} = X_{\mathcal{A}} \cup X$ and $X_{\mathcal{A}} \cap X = \emptyset$;
2. $Q_{\mathcal{B}} \lceil X_{\mathcal{A}} \subseteq Q_{\mathcal{A}}$; and
3. relation $\{(\mathbf{x}, \mathbf{y}) \mid \mathbf{y} \in Q_{\mathcal{B}} \text{ and } \mathbf{y} \lceil X_{\mathcal{A}} = \mathbf{x}\}$ is a prophecy relation from $\mathcal{A}$ to $\mathcal{B}$.

Example 4.40 (Adding prophecy variables to obtain a refinement). We consider adding a prophecy variable to the automaton $\mathcal{A}$ from Example 4.36. Let $\mathcal{C}$ be the automaton defined as follows.

- $X_{\mathcal{C}} = X_{\mathcal{A}} \cup \{v\}$ where v is a discrete variable with $type(v) = \{b, c\}$.
- $Q_{\mathcal{C}} = \{\mathbf{x}_{\mathcal{C}}, \mathbf{x}'_{\mathcal{C}}, \mathbf{y}_{\mathcal{C}}, \mathbf{y}'_{\mathcal{C}}, \mathbf{q}_{\mathcal{C}}, \mathbf{s}_{\mathcal{C}}\}$ such that

  $\mathbf{x}_{\mathcal{C}} \lceil X_{\mathcal{A}} = \mathbf{x}_{\mathcal{A}}$ and $\mathbf{x}_{\mathcal{C}}(v) = b$
  $\mathbf{x}'_{\mathcal{C}} \lceil X_{\mathcal{A}} = \mathbf{x}_{\mathcal{A}}$ and $\mathbf{x}'_{\mathcal{C}}(v) = c$
  $\mathbf{y}_{\mathcal{C}} \lceil X_{\mathcal{A}} = \mathbf{y}_{\mathcal{A}}$ and $\mathbf{y}_{\mathcal{C}}(v) = b$
  $\mathbf{y}'_{\mathcal{C}} \lceil X_{\mathcal{A}} = \mathbf{y}_{\mathcal{A}}$ and $\mathbf{y}'_{\mathcal{C}}(v) = c$
  $\mathbf{q}_{\mathcal{C}} \lceil X_{\mathcal{A}} = \mathbf{q}_{\mathcal{A}}$ and $\mathbf{q}_{\mathcal{C}}(v) = b$
  $\mathbf{s}_{\mathcal{C}} \lceil X_{\mathcal{A}} = \mathbf{s}_{\mathcal{A}}$ and $\mathbf{s}_{\mathcal{C}}(v) = c$
- $\Theta_{\mathcal{C}} = \{\mathbf{x}_{\mathcal{C}}, \mathbf{x}'_{\mathcal{C}}\}$.
- $E_{\mathcal{C}} = \{a, b, c\}$ and $H_{\mathcal{C}} = \emptyset$.
- $\mathcal{D}_{\mathcal{C}} = \{(\mathbf{x}_{\mathcal{C}}, a, \mathbf{y}_{\mathcal{C}}), (\mathbf{x}'_{\mathcal{C}}, a, \mathbf{y}'_{\mathcal{C}}), (\mathbf{y}_{\mathcal{C}}, b, \mathbf{q}_{\mathcal{C}}), (\mathbf{y}'_{\mathcal{C}}, c, \mathbf{s}_{\mathcal{C}})\}$.
- $\mathcal{T}_{\mathcal{C}} = \{\wp(\mathbf{v}) \mid \mathbf{v} \in Q_{\mathcal{C}}\}$.

Figure 4.11 displays automata $\mathcal{A}$ and $\mathcal{C}$ as directed multipgraphs.

Relation $R = \{(\mathbf{x}_{\mathcal{A}}, \mathbf{x}_{\mathcal{C}}), (\mathbf{x}_{\mathcal{A}}, \mathbf{x}'_{\mathcal{C}}), (\mathbf{y}_{\mathcal{A}}, \mathbf{y}_{\mathcal{C}}), (\mathbf{y}_{\mathcal{A}}, \mathbf{y}'_{\mathcal{C}}), (\mathbf{q}_{\mathcal{A}}, \mathbf{q}_{\mathcal{C}}), (\mathbf{s}_{\mathcal{A}}, \mathbf{s}_{\mathcal{C}})\}$ is a backward simulation from $\mathcal{A}$ to $\mathcal{C}$ and R^{-1} is a refinement. Therefore, $\mathcal{C}$ is obtained by adding a prophecy variable

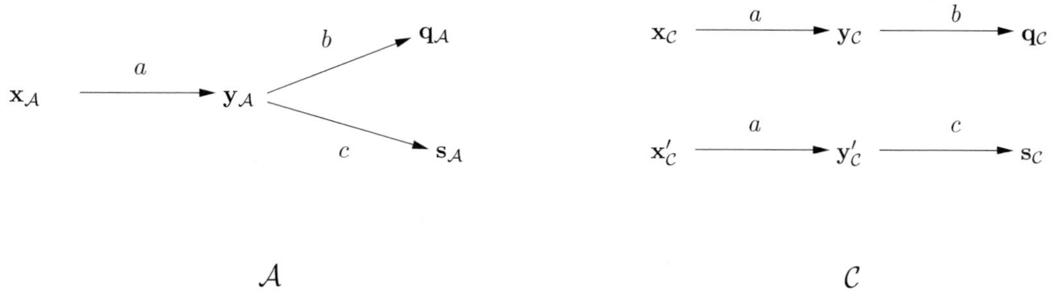

Figure 4.11: A prophecy variable.

to $\mathcal{A}$. Note that there is no refinement from $\mathcal{A}$ to $\mathcal{B}$ defined in Example 4.36. However, relation $F = \{(\mathbf{x}_\mathcal{C}, \mathbf{x}_\mathcal{B}), (\mathbf{x}'_\mathcal{C}, \mathbf{x}_\mathcal{B}), (\mathbf{y}_\mathcal{C}, \mathbf{y}_\mathcal{B}), (\mathbf{y}'_\mathcal{C}, \mathbf{y}'_\mathcal{B}), (\mathbf{q}_\mathcal{C}, \mathbf{q}_\mathcal{B}), (\mathbf{s}_\mathcal{C}, \mathbf{s}_\mathcal{B})\}$ is a refinement from $\mathcal{C}$ to $\mathcal{B}$.

Theorem 4.41 *Let $\mathcal{A}$ and $\mathcal{B}$ be two comparable TAs such that $V_\mathcal{A}$ and $V_\mathcal{B}$ are disjoint. Suppose that there is a prophecy relation from $\mathcal{A}$ to $\mathcal{B}$. Then, there exists an automaton $\mathcal{C}$ that is isomorphic to $\mathcal{B}$ and is obtained from $\mathcal{A}$ by adding prophecy variables.*

Proof. The proof is analogous to the proof of Theorem 4.38. We assume a backward simulation relation R instead of a forward simulation relation. We construct the automaton $\mathcal{C}$ as in Theorem 4.38 and verify that it is obtained from $\mathcal{A}$ by adding a prophecy variable. □

CHAPTER 5

Operations on Timed Automata

In this chapter we introduce three kinds of operations on timed automata: parallel composition, hiding, and adding lower and upper bounds for tasks.

5.1 COMPOSITION

The composition operation for timed automata allows an automaton representing a complex system to be constructed by composing automata representing individual system components. Our composition operation identifies external actions with the same name in different component automata. When any component automaton performs a discrete step involving an action a, so do all component automata that have a as an external action. The composition operator for timed automata is simpler than it is for general hybrid automata since all the variables in a timed automaton are internal.[1] All the proofs of this section are as in [79], with simplifications due to the absence of external variables.

5.1.1 DEFINITIONS AND BASIC RESULTS

Formally, we say that timed automata $\mathcal{A}_1$ and $\mathcal{A}_2$ are *compatible* if $H_1 \cap A_2 = H_2 \cap A_1 = \emptyset$ and $X_1 \cap X_2 = \emptyset$. If $\mathcal{A}_1$ and $\mathcal{A}_2$ are compatible then their *composition* $\mathcal{A}_1 \| \mathcal{A}_2$ is defined to be the structure $\mathcal{A} = (X, Q, \Theta, E, H, \mathcal{D}, \mathcal{T})$ where

- $X = X_1 \cup X_2$;
- $Q = \{\mathbf{x} \in val(X) \mid \mathbf{x} \lceil X_i \in Q_i, i \in \{1, 2\}\}$;
- $\Theta = \{\mathbf{x} \in Q \mid \mathbf{x} \lceil X_i \in \Theta_i, i \in \{1, 2\}\}$;
- $E = E_1 \cup E_2$ and $H = H_1 \cup H_2$;
- For each $\mathbf{x}, \mathbf{x}' \in Q$ and each $a \in A$, $\mathbf{x} \xrightarrow{a}_{\mathcal{A}} \mathbf{x}'$ iff for $i \in \{1, 2\}$, either (1) $a \in A_i$ and $\mathbf{x} \lceil X_i \xrightarrow{a}_i \mathbf{x}' \lceil X_i$, or (2) $a \notin A_i$ and $\mathbf{x} \lceil X_i = \mathbf{x}' \lceil X_i$;
- $\mathcal{T} \subseteq trajs(Q)$ is given by $\tau \in \mathcal{T} \Leftrightarrow \tau \downarrow X_i \in \mathcal{T}_i, i \in \{1, 2\}$.

Theorem 5.1 *If $\mathcal{A}_1$ and $\mathcal{A}_2$ are compatible timed automata then $\mathcal{A}_1 \| \mathcal{A}_2$ is a timed automaton.*

[1]The composition operation for general hybrid automata requires external variables to be identified as well as external actions. When any component automaton follows a particular trajectory for an external variable v, then so do all component automata of which v is an external variable.

The following "projection lemma" says that execution fragments of a composition of timed automata project to give executions fragments of the component automata. Moreover, certain properties of the fragments of the composition imply, or are implied by, similar properties for the component fragments.

Lemma 5.2 *Let $\mathcal{A} = \mathcal{A}_1 \| \mathcal{A}_2$ and let α be an execution fragment of $\mathcal{A}$. Then $\alpha \lceil (A_1, X_1)$ and $\alpha \lceil (A_2, X_2)$ are execution fragments of $\mathcal{A}_1$ and $\mathcal{A}_2$, respectively. Furthermore:*

1. *α is time-bounded iff both $\alpha \lceil (A_1, X_1)$ and $\alpha \lceil (A_2, X_2)$ are time-bounded;*
2. *α is admissible iff both $\alpha \lceil (A_1, X_1)$ and $\alpha \lceil (A_2, X_2)$ are admissible;*
3. *α is closed iff both $\alpha \lceil (A_1, X_1)$ and $\alpha \lceil (A_2, X_2)$ are closed;*
4. *α is nonZeno iff both $\alpha \lceil (A_1, X_1)$ and $\alpha \lceil (A_2, X_2)$ are nonZeno;*
5. *α is an execution iff both $\alpha \lceil (A_1, X_1)$ and $\alpha \lceil (A_2, X_2)$ are executions.*

The following lemma says that we obtain the same result for an execution fragment α of a composition if we first extract the trace and then restrict to one of the components, or if we first restrict to the component and then take the trace.

Lemma 5.3 *Let $\mathcal{A} = \mathcal{A}_1 \| \mathcal{A}_2$, and let α be an execution fragment of $\mathcal{A}$. Then, for $i \in \{1, 2\}$, $trace(\alpha) \lceil (E_i, \emptyset) = trace(\alpha \lceil (A_i, X_i))$.*

Proof. Straightforward, using the definition of *trace*() and Lemma 3.10. □

The following two theorems are fundamental results that relate the set of traces of a composed automaton to the sets of traces of its components. Theorem 5.4 is due to Gilbert [37][Lemma 11.14.1]. The proof closely follows the proof of Theorem 5.7 in [79].

Theorem 5.4 *Let $\mathcal{A} = \mathcal{A}_1 \| \mathcal{A}_2$. Let α_i be an execution fragment of $\mathcal{A}_i$, $i \in \{1, 2\}$. Let β be an $(E, \emptyset)$-sequence, where E is the set of external actions of $\mathcal{A}$. Suppose that $\beta \lceil (E_i, \emptyset) = trace(\alpha_i)$, $i \in \{1, 2\}$. Then there exists an execution fragment α of $\mathcal{A}$ such that $trace(\alpha) = \beta$ and $\alpha_i = \alpha \lceil (A_i, X_i)$, $i \in \{1, 2\}$.*

Theorem 5.5 *Let $\mathcal{A} = \mathcal{A}_1 \| \mathcal{A}_2$ and let E be the set of external actions of $\mathcal{A}$. Then $traces_{\mathcal{A}}$ is exactly the set of $(E, \emptyset)$-sequences whose restrictions to $\mathcal{A}_1$ and $\mathcal{A}_2$ are traces of $\mathcal{A}_1$ and $\mathcal{A}_2$, respectively. That is, $traces_{\mathcal{A}} = \{\beta \mid \beta$ is an $(E, \emptyset)$-sequence and $\beta \lceil (E_i, \emptyset) \in traces_{\mathcal{A}_i}, i \in \{1, 2\}\}$.*

Proof. We prove both inclusions.

Suppose that $\beta \in traces_{\mathcal{A}}$. Then by definition β is an $(E, \emptyset)$-sequence. Let α be an execution of $\mathcal{A}$ with $trace(\alpha) = \beta$. Then, by Lemma 5.2, $\alpha \lceil (A_i, X_i)$ is an execution of $\mathcal{A}_i$, and, by Lemma 5.3, $\beta \lceil (E_i, \emptyset) = trace(\alpha \lceil (A_i, X_i))$. Hence $\beta \lceil (E_i, \emptyset) \in traces_{\mathcal{A}_i}$.

For the other inclusion, suppose β is an $(E, \emptyset)$-sequence and $\beta \lceil (E_i, \emptyset) \in traces_{\mathcal{A}_i}, i \in \{1, 2\}$. Then there exist execution fragments α_i of $\mathcal{A}_i$ such that $trace(\alpha_i) = \beta \lceil (E_i, \emptyset)$. Hence, by Theorem 5.4, there exists an execution fragment α of $\mathcal{A}$ with $trace(\alpha) = \beta$. This implies $\beta \in traces_{\mathcal{A}}$, as required. □

These basic results about composition can be extended to arbitrary finite numbers of components instead of just two.

Notation: The compatibility conditions for composition require the set of internal variables of each automaton to be disjoint from the set of internal variables of all the other automata in the composition. We use a general scheme to disambiguate the internal variables of components in order to avoid possible name clashes that can violate the compatibility conditions. If $\mathcal{A}$ is the name of an automaton and v is an internal variable of $\mathcal{A}$, then we refer to this variable as $\mathcal{A}.v$ in the composite automaton. But if no confusion is possible, we write v rather than $\mathcal{A}.v$.

Example 5.6 (Periodic sending process with timeouts). Let $\mathcal{C}$ be the composition of three automata from Examples 4.1, 4.2, and 4.4:

$$\mathcal{C} = \texttt{PeriodicSend} \parallel \texttt{TimedChannel} \parallel \texttt{Timeout}$$

where $\texttt{M} = \{\texttt{m1}, \ldots, \texttt{mn}\}$ and $\texttt{b} + \texttt{u1} < \texttt{u2}$. In a setting where $\texttt{b} < \texttt{u1}$, the following sequence is a trace of $\mathcal{C}$:

$$\alpha = \overline{\texttt{u1}}\ \texttt{send(m1)}\ \overline{\texttt{b}}\ \texttt{receive(m1)}\ \overline{\texttt{u1} - \texttt{b}}\ \texttt{send(m2)}\ \overline{\texttt{b}}\ \texttt{receive(m2)}\ \overline{\texttt{u1} - \texttt{b}}\ \ldots$$

where $\bar{t}$ denotes the trace with as domain $[0, t]$ and as range the set consisting of the function with the empty domain. The following invariant states that $\mathcal{C}$ never performs a `timeout` action.

Invariant 4 *In any reachable state* $\mathbf{x}$ *of* $\mathcal{C}$, $\mathbf{x}(\texttt{suspected}) = \texttt{false}$.

In order to prove this invariant we can use auxiliary invariants for the component automata, such as the one established in Example 4.15, and an auxiliary global invariant such as the one below, which establishes the fact that every message is delivered before the variable `Timeout.clock` reaches the point at which a `timeout` action occurs.

Invariant 5 *In any reachable state* $\mathbf{x}$ *of* $\mathcal{C}$*:*

1. *if* $\mathbf{x}(\texttt{queue})$ *is not empty then there is a packet* $\texttt{p}$ *such that* $\texttt{p} \in \mathbf{x}(\texttt{queue})$ *and* $\texttt{p.deadline} - \mathbf{x}(\texttt{now}) < \texttt{u2} - \mathbf{x}(\texttt{Timeout.clock})$*;*

2. *if* $\mathbf{x}(\texttt{queue})$ *is empty then*
$\texttt{u1} - \mathbf{x}(\texttt{PeriodicSend.clock}) + \texttt{b} < \texttt{u2} - \mathbf{x}(\texttt{Timeout.clock})$.

Example 5.7 (Periodic sending process with failures and timeouts). In this example, we consider a composite automaton defined exactly like the one in Example 5.6 except that the automaton `PeriodicSend` is replaced with `PeriodicSend2`, the periodic sending process with failures. Let $\mathcal{C}$ = `PeriodicSend2` || `TimedChannel` || `Timeout`. The following sequence is a trace of $\mathcal{C}$:

$$\overline{\texttt{u1}}\ \texttt{send(m1)}\ \overline{\texttt{b}}\ \texttt{receive(m1)}\ \overline{\texttt{b}}\ \texttt{fail}\ \overline{\texttt{u2} - \texttt{b}}\ \texttt{timeout}\ \overline{\infty}.$$

According to this sample trace, the first message sent by the periodic sending process is received exactly b time units after it is sent. The periodic sending process fails $2 \times$ b time units after sending its first message. The timeout process performs a `timeout` since no second message arrives within the next u2 time units after the receipt of the first message.

The following invariant states that a `timeout` performed by $\mathcal{C}$ can be used to conclude that the sender process has failed. We assume again that `b + u1 < u2`.

Invariant 6 *In any reachable state* $\mathbf{x}$ *of* $\mathcal{C}$,

$$\mathbf{x}(\texttt{Timeout.suspected}) \Rightarrow \mathbf{x}(\texttt{PeriodicSend2.failed}).$$

The automaton $\mathcal{C}$ is guaranteed to perform a `timeout` to signal the failure of a process, within a specified amount of time after the occurrence of a fail event. The following is a formal statement of this property.

Let α be an admissible execution of $\mathcal{C}$ in which a `fail` event occurs. Let `t` be the point in time at which the first `fail` event occurs in α. Then a `timeout` event occurs in α in the interval [`t + u2 - u1`, `t + b + u2`].

Example 5.8 (Clock synchronization). In this example, we consider the composition of three clock synchronization automata with six time-bounded channel automata. A graphical representation of the composite automaton is given in Fig. 5.1. The abbreviation CS_i represents the automaton `ClockSync(u, r, i)` from Example 4.6. The abbreviation $TC_{i,j}$ represents the automaton `TimedChannel` from Example 4.1, the time-bounded channel with maximum delay b, but with the `send(m)` and `receive(m)` actions renamed to `send(m,i)` and `receive(m,i,j)`, respectively, to enable communication of real-valued messages from `ClockSync(u, r, i)` to `ClockSync(u, r, j)`. Let

$$\mathcal{C} = CS_1 \parallel CS_2 \parallel CS_3 \parallel TC_{1,2} \parallel TC_{2,1} \parallel TC_{1,3} \parallel TC_{3,1} \parallel TC_{2,3} \parallel TC_{3,2}.$$

A physical clock diverges from real time at the largest rate when it evolves with rate (`1 + r`) or (`1 - r`). For example, if a physical clock evolves with rate `1 + r`, then at time t, its value is $t \times$ `(1 + r)`. Hence, the largest possible difference between a physical clock and the real time is ($t \times$ r). This property is stated by the invariant below.

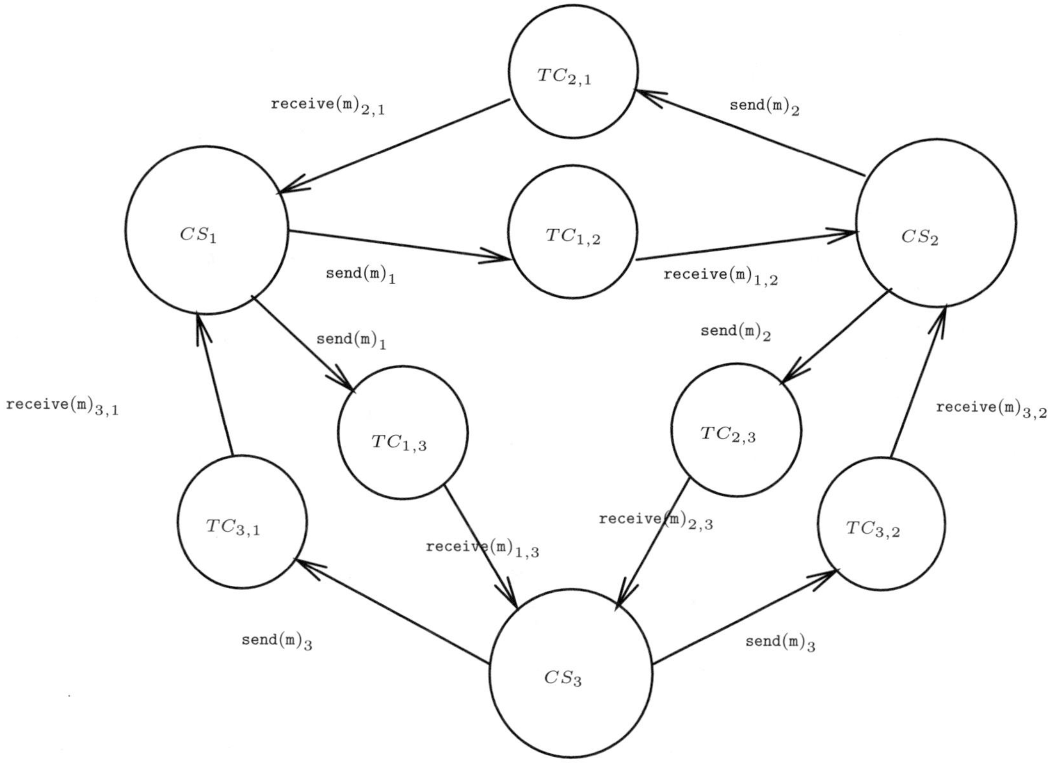

Figure 5.1: Clock synchronization network.

Invariant 7 *In any reachable state* $\mathbf{x}$ *of* $\mathcal{C}$, *at any time* $t \in \mathsf{T}$, *for any* $i \in \{1, 2, 3\}$, $|\mathbf{x}(CS_i.\texttt{physclock}) - t| \leq t \times \texttt{r}$.

Two physical clocks in $\mathcal{C}$ diverge at the largest rate when one evolves with rate (`1 + r`) and the other with (`1 - r`). It follows from Invariant 7 that, at any time t the largest possible difference between the physical clock values for two processes is $2 \times t \times \texttt{r}$. This property is formalized by the following invariant.

Invariant 8 *In any reachable state* $\mathbf{x}$ *of* $\mathcal{C}$, *at any time* $t \in \mathsf{T}$, *for any* $i, j \in \{1, 2, 3\}$, $|\mathbf{x}(CS_i.\texttt{physclock}) - \mathbf{x}(CS_j.\texttt{physclock})| \leq 2 \times t \times \texttt{r}$.

The following invariant states that in any reachable state there exists a process j such that the logical clock of each other process in the system is smaller than or equal to the physical clock of j. This follows from the definition of a logical clock and the fact that physical clocks always increase.

Invariant 9 *In any reachable state* $\mathbf{x}$ *of* $\mathcal{C}$, *there exists* $j \in \{1, 2, 3\}$ *such that for all* $i \in \{1, 2, 3\}$, $\mathbf{x}(CS_i.\texttt{logclock}) \leq \mathbf{x}(CS_j.\texttt{physclock})$.

The following invariant states that in any reachable state there exists a process j such that the logical clock of each other process in the system is larger than or equal to the physical clock of j. This follows from the definition of a logical clock.

Invariant 10 *In any reachable state* $\mathbf{x}$ *of* C*, there exists* $j \in \{1, 2, 3\}$ *such that for all* $i \in \{1, 2, 3\}$, $\mathbf{x}(CS_i.\texttt{logclock}) \geq \mathbf{x}(CS_j.\texttt{physclock})$.

Invariants 9 and 9 together are called *validity* properties. They express the condition that all the logical clocks remain in an envelope bounded by the maximum and minimum physical clock values in the system. The following invariant formalizes the property that all the logical clocks at a given time lie within the envelope formed by the largest and the smallest physical clock values in the system. It follows from Invariants 7, 9, and 10 that any point in this envelope can diverge from real time t by at most $t \times \texttt{r}$ time units.

Invariant 11 *In any reachable state* $\mathbf{x}$ *of* C*, at any time* $t \in \mathsf{T}$*, for any* $i \in \{1, 2, 3\}$, $|\mathbf{x}(CS_i.\texttt{logclock}) - t| \leq t \times \texttt{r}$.

Finally, we state a property about the *agreement* of logical clocks in C. It says that the difference between two logical clocks is always bounded by a constant (which depends on the message-sending interval and the bounds on clock drift and message delay).

Invariant 12 *In any reachable state* $\mathbf{x}$ *of* C*, for all* $i, j \in \{1, 2, 3\}$,
$|\mathbf{x}(CS_i.\texttt{logclock}) - \mathbf{x}(CS_j.\texttt{logclock})| \leq \texttt{u} + (\texttt{b} \times (1 + \texttt{r}))$.

To see why Invariant 12 holds, fix j to be a process with the largest physical clock in $\mathbf{x}$, and fix i to be any other process. Let v_j, v_i be the logical clock values of j and i, respectively, in state $\mathbf{x}$. Note that v_j is also the physical clock value of j in $\mathbf{x}$. By Invariant 9, we know that $v_i \leq v_j$. To show Invariant 12, it suffices to show that $v_j - v_i \leq \texttt{u} + (\texttt{b} \times (1 + \texttt{r}))$.

Let α be a finite execution that leads to state $\mathbf{x}$. There are two cases to consider.

1. Some message sent by j arrives at i in α.
   Consider the last such message and let v_1 be the value that it contains. Let v_2 be the newly adjusted logical clock value of i immediately after the message arrives. We know that $v_i \geq v_2 \geq v_1$.

   If j sends a later message to i in α, then it sends the next later message when its physical clock has value $v_1 + \texttt{u}$. By assumption, this message does not arrive at i. Therefore, the real time that elapses after sending it must be at most $\texttt{b}$. It follows that the physical clock increase of j since sending this message is at most $\texttt{b} \times (1 + \texttt{r})$ and so $v_j \leq v_1 + \texttt{u} + \texttt{b} \times (1 + \texttt{r})$. On the other hand, if j does not send a later message to i in α, then $v_j \leq v_1 + \texttt{u}$. In either case, we have $v_j \leq v_1 + \texttt{u} + \texttt{b} \times (1 + \texttt{r})$. Since $v_i \geq v_1$, we have $v_j - v_i \leq \texttt{u} + \texttt{b} \times (1 + \texttt{r})$, as needed for Invariant 12.

2. No message sent by j arrives at i in α.
   Since the first send occurs at time 0 and $\texttt{b}$ is the largest possible communication delay, the

fact that i has not received the first message sent by j at time 0 implies that $t \leq \mathtt{b}$. Since both clocks start at 0, we have $v_j \leq \mathtt{b} \times (1+\mathtt{r})$ and $v_i \geq 0$. Therefore, $v_j - v_i \leq \mathtt{u} + \mathtt{b} \times (1+\mathtt{r})$, which suffices for Invariant 12.

5.1.2 SUBSTITUTIVITY RESULTS

Theorem 5.5, which relates the set of traces of a composed automaton to the set of traces of component automata, is fundamental for compositional reasoning. We now introduce another important class of results, *substitutivity* results, that are useful for decomposing verification of composite automata. These results are best understood by viewing one of the components of a composition as the system and the other as the environment with which the system interacts.

The following result states that if a TA $\mathcal{A}_1$ can be shown to implement another one $\mathcal{A}_2$, with no assumptions about their environments, then $\mathcal{A}_1$ can be shown to implement $\mathcal{A}_2$ in a given environment $\mathcal{B}$.

Theorem 5.9 *Suppose $\mathcal{A}_1$, $\mathcal{A}_2$, and $\mathcal{B}$ are TAs, $\mathcal{A}_1$ and $\mathcal{A}_2$ are comparable, and each of $\mathcal{A}_1$ and $\mathcal{A}_2$ is compatible with $\mathcal{B}$. If $\mathcal{A}_1 \leq \mathcal{A}_2$ then $\mathcal{A}_1 \| \mathcal{B} \leq \mathcal{A}_2 \| \mathcal{B}$.*

Commutativity of the composition operation together with repeated application of Theorem 5.9 gives the following corollary.

Corollary 5.10 *Suppose $\mathcal{A}_1$, $\mathcal{A}_2$, $\mathcal{B}_1$, and $\mathcal{B}_2$ are TAs, $\mathcal{A}_1$ and $\mathcal{A}_2$ are comparable, $\mathcal{B}_1$ and $\mathcal{B}_2$ are comparable, and each of $\mathcal{A}_1$ and $\mathcal{A}_2$ is compatible with each of $\mathcal{B}_1$ and $\mathcal{B}_2$. If $\mathcal{A}_1 \leq \mathcal{A}_2$ and $\mathcal{B}_1 \leq \mathcal{B}_2$ then $\mathcal{A}_1 \| \mathcal{B}_1 \leq \mathcal{A}_2 \| \mathcal{B}_2$.*

We can strengthen Corollary 5.10 slightly by the following corollary: if $\mathcal{A}_1$ implements $\mathcal{A}_2$ in an environment $\mathcal{B}_2$, then $\mathcal{A}_1$ composed with an environment that is more restrictive than $\mathcal{B}_2$ (whose set of external behaviors is smaller than that of $\mathcal{B}_2$), implements $\mathcal{A}_2$ composed with $\mathcal{B}_2$.

Corollary 5.11 *Suppose $\mathcal{A}_1$, $\mathcal{A}_2$, $\mathcal{B}_1$, and $\mathcal{B}_2$ are TAs, $\mathcal{A}_1$ and $\mathcal{A}_2$ are comparable, $\mathcal{B}_1$ and $\mathcal{B}_2$ are comparable, and each of $\mathcal{A}_1$ and $\mathcal{A}_2$ is compatible with each of $\mathcal{B}_1$ and $\mathcal{B}_2$. If $\mathcal{A}_1 \| \mathcal{B}_2 \leq \mathcal{A}_2 \| \mathcal{B}_2$ and $\mathcal{B}_1 \leq \mathcal{B}_2$ then $\mathcal{A}_1 \| \mathcal{B}_1 \leq \mathcal{A}_2 \| \mathcal{B}_2$.*

Proof. Let $\beta \in traces_{\mathcal{A}_1 \| \mathcal{B}_1}$. By Theorem 5.5, $\beta \lceil (E_{\mathcal{A}_1}, \emptyset) \in traces_{\mathcal{A}_1}$ and $\beta \lceil (E_{\mathcal{B}_1}, \emptyset) \in traces_{\mathcal{B}_1}$. Since $\mathcal{B}_1 \leq \mathcal{B}_2$, $\beta \lceil (E_{\mathcal{B}_1}, \emptyset) \in traces_{\mathcal{B}_2}$. Since $\mathcal{B}_1$ and $\mathcal{B}_2$ have the same external actions, it follows that $\beta \lceil (E_{\mathcal{B}_2}, \emptyset) \in traces_{\mathcal{B}_2}$. We have $\beta \lceil (E_{\mathcal{A}_1}, \emptyset) \in traces_{\mathcal{A}_1}$ and $\beta \lceil (E_{\mathcal{B}_2}, \emptyset) \in traces_{\mathcal{B}_2}$. By Theorem 5.5, $\beta \in traces_{\mathcal{A}_1 \| \mathcal{B}_2}$. Since $\mathcal{A}_1 \| \mathcal{B}_2 \leq \mathcal{A}_2 \| \mathcal{B}_2$ by assumption, $\beta \in traces_{\mathcal{A}_2 \| \mathcal{B}_2}$, as needed. □

The following corollary assumes that $\mathcal{A}_1$ implements $\mathcal{A}_2$ in an auxiliary context $\mathcal{B}_3$ and symmetrically, that $\mathcal{B}_1$ implements $\mathcal{B}_2$ in an auxiliary context $\mathcal{A}_3$. $\mathcal{A}_3$, and $\mathcal{B}_3$ might express weaker constraints than $\mathcal{A}_2$ and $\mathcal{B}_2$, for instance, just their safety restrictions. The corollary further assumes that $\mathcal{A}_1 \| \mathcal{B}_1$ implements $\mathcal{A}_3 \| \mathcal{B}_3$—a fact that might be easy to show if the constraints expressed by $\mathcal{A}_3$ and $\mathcal{B}_3$ are sufficiently weak. The conclusion, as before, is that $\mathcal{A}_1 \| \mathcal{B}_1$ implements $\mathcal{A}_2 \| \mathcal{B}_2$.

Corollary 5.12 *Suppose $\mathcal{A}_1$, $\mathcal{A}_2$, $\mathcal{A}_3$, $\mathcal{B}_1$, $\mathcal{B}_2$, and $\mathcal{B}_3$ are TAs such that $\mathcal{A}_1$, $\mathcal{A}_2$, and $\mathcal{A}_3$ have the same external actions, $\mathcal{B}_1$, $\mathcal{B}_2$, and $\mathcal{B}_3$ have the same external actions, and $\mathcal{A}_i$ is compatible with $\mathcal{B}_j$ for $i, j \in \{1, 2, 3\}$. Suppose further that:*

1. *$\mathcal{A}_1 \| \mathcal{B}_1 \leq \mathcal{A}_3 \| \mathcal{B}_3$;*
2. *$\mathcal{A}_1 \| \mathcal{B}_3 \leq \mathcal{A}_2 \| \mathcal{B}_3$ and $\mathcal{A}_3 \| \mathcal{B}_1 \leq \mathcal{A}_3 \| \mathcal{B}_2$.*

Then $\mathcal{A}_1 \| \mathcal{B}_1 \leq \mathcal{A}_2 \| \mathcal{B}_2$.

Proof. Let β be a trace of $\mathcal{A}_1 \| \mathcal{B}_1$. By projection using Theorem 5.5, $\beta \lceil (E_{\mathcal{A}_1}, \emptyset) \in traces_{\mathcal{A}_1}$ and $\beta \lceil (E_{\mathcal{B}_1}, \emptyset) \in traces_{\mathcal{B}_1}$. Since $\mathcal{A}_1 \| \mathcal{B}_1 \leq \mathcal{A}_3 \| \mathcal{B}_3$, we know that $\beta \in traces_{\mathcal{A}_3 \| \mathcal{B}_3}$. By projection using Theorem 5.5, $\beta \lceil (E_{\mathcal{A}_3}, \emptyset) \in traces_{\mathcal{A}_3}$ and $\beta \lceil (E_{\mathcal{B}_3}, \emptyset) \in traces_{\mathcal{B}_3}$. By pasting using Theorem 5.5, we have $\beta \in traces_{\mathcal{A}_1 \| \mathcal{B}_3}$ and $\beta \in traces_{\mathcal{A}_3 \| \mathcal{B}_1}$. By Assumption 2, we get $\beta \in traces_{\mathcal{A}_2 \| \mathcal{B}_3}$ and $\beta \in traces_{\mathcal{A}_3 \| \mathcal{B}_2}$. Then, by projection using Theorem 5.5, $\beta \lceil (E_{\mathcal{A}_2}, \emptyset) \in traces_{\mathcal{A}_2}$ and $\beta \lceil (E_{\mathcal{B}_2}, \emptyset) \in traces_{\mathcal{B}_2}$. Finally, by pasting using Theorem 5.5, we have $\beta \in traces_{\mathcal{A}_2 \| \mathcal{B}_2}$, as needed. □

For other preorders, we also get substitutivity results, for example:

Theorem 5.13 *Suppose $\mathcal{A}_1$, $\mathcal{A}_2$, and $\mathcal{B}$ are TAs, $\mathcal{A}_1$ and $\mathcal{A}_2$ have the same external actions, and each of $\mathcal{A}_1$ and $\mathcal{A}_2$ is compatible with $\mathcal{B}$.*

1. *If every closed trace of $\mathcal{A}_1$ is a trace of $\mathcal{A}_2$ then every closed trace of $\mathcal{A}_1 \| \mathcal{B}$ is a trace of $\mathcal{A}_2 \| \mathcal{B}$.*
2. *If every admissible trace of $\mathcal{A}_1$ is a trace of $\mathcal{A}_2$ then every admissible trace of $\mathcal{A}_1 \| \mathcal{B}$ is a trace of $\mathcal{A}_2 \| \mathcal{B}$.*
3. *If every nonZeno trace of $\mathcal{A}_1$ is a trace of $\mathcal{A}_2$ then every nonZeno trace of $\mathcal{A}_1 \| \mathcal{B}$ is a trace of $\mathcal{A}_2 \| \mathcal{B}$.*

Example 5.14 (A counterexample for a desirable substitutivity theorem).

Suppose $\mathcal{A}_1$ and $\mathcal{A}_2$ have the same external actions, $\mathcal{B}_1$ and $\mathcal{B}_2$ have the same external actions, and that each of $\mathcal{A}_1$ and $\mathcal{A}_2$ is compatible with each of $\mathcal{B}_1$ and $\mathcal{B}_2$. If we view $\mathcal{A}_2$ and $\mathcal{B}_2$ as specifications and want to prove that $\mathcal{A}_1 \| \mathcal{B}_1 \leq \mathcal{A}_2 \| \mathcal{B}_2$, it would be useful to have a theorem that says if $\mathcal{A}_1 \| \mathcal{B}_2 \leq \mathcal{A}_2 \| \mathcal{B}_2$ and $\mathcal{A}_2 \| \mathcal{B}_1 \leq \mathcal{A}_2 \| \mathcal{B}_2$ then $\mathcal{A}_1 \| \mathcal{B}_1 \leq \mathcal{A}_2 \| \mathcal{B}_2$. That is, if $\mathcal{A}_1$ implements $\mathcal{A}_2$ in the context of $\mathcal{B}_2$ and $\mathcal{B}_1$ implements $\mathcal{B}_2$ in the context of $\mathcal{A}_2$, we would like to conclude that

```
automaton CatchUpA
  signature
    external a, b
  states
    counta: Nat := 0, countb: Nat := 0,
    now: Real := 0, next: discrete Real := 0
  transitions
    external a
      pre
        (counta ≤ countb)
          ∧ (now = next)
      eff
        counta := counta + 1;
        next := now + 1
    external b
      eff
      countb := countb + 1;
      next := now + 1
  trajectories
    stop when
      now = next
    evolve
      d(now) = 1
```

```
automaton CatchUpB
  signature
    external a, b
  states
    counta: Nat := 0, countb: Nat := 0,
    now: Real := 0, next: discrete Real := 0
  transitions
    external a
      eff
        counta := counta + 1
        next := now + 1
    external b
      pre
        (countb + 1) ≤ counta
          ∧ now = next
      eff
        countb := countb + 1;
        next := now + 1
  trajectories
    stop when
      now = next
    evolve
      d(now) = 1
```

Figure 5.2: CatchUpA and CatchUpB.

```
automaton BoundedAlternateA
  signature
    external a, b
  states
    myturn: Bool := true,
    maxout: Nat
  transitions
    external a                          external b
      pre                                 eff
        myturn ∧ (maxout > 0)           myturn := true
      eff
        myturn := false;
        maxout := maxout - 1
```

```
automaton BoundedAlternateB
  signature
    external a, b
  states
    myturn: Bool := false,
    maxout: Nat
  transitions
    external a                          external b
      eff                                 pre
        myturn := true                      myturn ∧ (maxout > 0)
                                          eff
                                            myturn := false;
                                            maxout := maxout - 1
```

Figure 5.3: `BoundedAlternateA` and `BoundedAlternateB`.

$\mathcal{A}_1 \| \mathcal{B}_1$ implements $\mathcal{A}_2 \| \mathcal{B}_2$. We show by means of a counterexample that it is impossible to prove such a theorem. The problem arises with the infinite behaviors of $A_1 \| \mathcal{B}_2$.

As examples for $\mathcal{A}_1$, $\mathcal{B}_1$, $\mathcal{A}_2$, and $\mathcal{B}_2$, consider, respectively, the automata `CatchUpA`, `CatchUpB`, `BoundedAlternateA`, `BoundedAlternateB` in Figs. 5.2 and 5.3. All automata have the same set of actions, consisting of the external actions `a` and `b`. `CatchUpA` can perform an arbitrary number of `b` actions, and can perform an `a` provided that `counta` $\leq$ `countb` and one time unit has elapsed since the occurrence of the last action. `CatchUpA` allows `counta` to increase to one more than `countb`. `CatchUpB` can perform an arbitrary number of `a` actions, and can perform a `b` provided that `counta` is at least one more than `countb`. `CatchUpB` allows `countb` to reach `counta`.

`BoundedAlternateA` has an infinite number of start states, each giving a different finite bound on the number of `a` actions it can perform. Similarly, `BoundedAlternateB` has an infinite number of start states, each giving a different finite bound on the number of `b` actions it can perform. Note that the absence of trajectory definitions in the specifications of these automata imply that they are timing-independent. That is, there is no constraint on the timing of actions.

The automata `CatchUpA` and `CatchUpB` strictly alternate `a`'s and `b`'s until a maximum count is reached, when put in the context of, respectively, `BoundedAlternateA` and `BoundedAlternateB`. Hence, on the one hand

$$(\texttt{CatchUpA}\|\texttt{BoundedAlternateB}) \leq (\texttt{BoundedAlternateA}\|\texttt{BoundedAlternateB}),$$

and

$$(\texttt{BoundedAlternateA}\|\texttt{CatchUpB}) \leq (\texttt{BoundedAlternateA}\|\texttt{BoundedAlternateB}).$$

On the other hand, $(\texttt{CatchUpA}\|\texttt{CatchUpB})$ can perform an infinite sequence of alternating `a` and `b` actions, which is not allowed allowed by $(\texttt{BoundedAlternateA}\|\texttt{BoundedAlternateB})$. Hence, $(\texttt{CatchUpA}\|\texttt{CatchUpB})$ does not implement $(\texttt{BoundedAlternateA}\|\texttt{BoundedAlternateB})$.

In Chapter 8, we revisit the substitutivity issue and prove Theorem 8.8, a variant of the desirable theorem considered in the above example, by assuming certain conditions on the environments $\mathcal{A}_2$ and $\mathcal{B}_2$.

5.2 HIDING

We now define an operation that "hides" external actions of a timed automaton by reclassifying them as internal actions. This prevents them from being used for further communication and means that they are no longer included in traces. The operation is parametrized by a set of external actions:

If $\mathcal{A}$ is a timed automaton and $E \subseteq E_{\mathcal{A}}$, then $\mathsf{ActHide}(E, \mathcal{A})$ is the structure $\mathcal{B}$ that is equal to $\mathcal{A}$ except that $E_{\mathcal{B}} = E_{\mathcal{A}} - E$ and $H_{\mathcal{B}} = H_{\mathcal{A}} \cup E$. It is immediate from the definitions that hiding is a well-defined operation on TAs.

Lemma 5.15 *If $E \subseteq E_{\mathcal{A}}$ then $\mathsf{ActHide}(E, \mathcal{A})$ is a TA.*

The following lemma characterizes the traces of the automaton that results from applying a hiding operation.

Lemma 5.16 *If $\mathcal{A}$ is a TA and $E \subseteq E_{\mathcal{A}}$ then $traces_{\mathsf{ActHide}(E,\mathcal{A})} = \{\beta \lceil (E_{\mathcal{A}} - E, \emptyset) \mid \beta \in traces_{\mathcal{A}}\}$.*

Using Lemma 5.16, it is straightforward to establish that the hiding operation respects the implementation relation.

Theorem 5.17 *Suppose $\mathcal{A}$ and $\mathcal{B}$ are TAs with $\mathcal{A} \leq \mathcal{B}$, and suppose $E \subseteq E_{\mathcal{A}}$. Then $\mathsf{ActHide}(E, \mathcal{A}) \leq \mathsf{ActHide}(E, \mathcal{B})$.*

Example 5.18 (Clock and manager). Consider a simple system consisting of a "clock" and a "manager". The clock ticks once every [c1, c2] time units and the manager issues a "grant" within b time units after counting $k > 0$ ticks. We assume $0 \leq b < c1 \leq c2$. The problem is to prove upper and lower bounds on the time between successive grant actions.

Figure 5.4 gives a formal specification of the clock in terms of the TA Clock(c1, c2) and the manager in terms of the TA Manager(k, b). The full system with the tick actions hidden can be defined by

$$\texttt{System} = \mathsf{ActHide}(\{\texttt{tick}\}, \texttt{Clock} \| \texttt{Manager}).$$

Consider the automaton Specification displayed in Fig. 5.5. This automaton is equal to Clock, except for some renamings. We claim that the manager issues a grant once every $[c1 * k - b, c2 * k + b]$ time units. An equivalent formulation of this claim is:

$$\texttt{System} \leq \texttt{Specification}(c1 * k - b, c2 * k + b).$$

In order to prove the claim, one may first establish that the predicate

$$\texttt{Inv} \triangleq 0 \leq x \leq c2 \wedge (\texttt{count} = 0 \Rightarrow x = y \leq b) \wedge 0 \leq \texttt{count} \leq k$$

defines an invariant of System, and use this to verify that the conjunction of Inv and

$$c1 * (k - \texttt{count}) - b \leq z - x \leq c2 * (k - \texttt{count})$$

defines a forward simulation from System to Specification$(c1 * k - b, c2 * k + b)$.

5.3 EXTENDING TIMED AUTOMATA WITH BOUNDS

In this section, we define a new class of automata, "TA with bounds" where the basic definition of a timed automaton is extended with the notion of a task and a pair of bounds (a lower and an upper bound) for each task. We then define an operation that transforms a given TA with bounds to another TA. This operation supports specifying a system by thinking in terms of tasks and bounds as in the timed automata of Merritt *et al.* [91] and the phase transition systems of Maler *et al.* [88].

In defining the operation for extending timed automata with bounds, we restrict attention to a class of automata where the enabling and disabling of actions during trajectories follow certain rules. Specifically, our operation is defined on automata in which each action is enabled or disabled throughout an entire trajectory, or becomes enabled once during a trajectory and remains so until the end of that trajectory. The given restrictions ensure that the result of applying the operation to a TA is another TA and that the resulting TA satisfies the restrictions.

Let $\mathcal{A}$ be a TA, C a set of actions of $\mathcal{A}$, and $\mathcal{T}$ the set of trajectories of $\mathcal{A}$. We say that $\mathcal{T}$ is *well-formed* with respect to C if for each $\tau \in \mathcal{T}$ and for each $t \in dom(\tau)$ both of the following conditions hold:

```
automaton Clock(c1, c2: Real) where 0 < c1 ∧ c1 ≤ c2
  signature
    external tick
  states
    x: Real := 0
  transitions
    external tick
      pre
        x ≥ c1
      eff
        x := 0
  trajectories
    stop when
      x = c2
    evolve
      d(x) = 1
```

```
automaton Manager(k: Int, b: Real) where  b > 0 ∧ k > 0
  signature
    external tick, grant
  states
    y: Real := 0,
    count : Int := k
  transitions
    external tick
      eff
        count := count - 1;
        if count = 0 then y := 0
     external grant
       pre
         count = 0
       eff
         count := k
  trajectories
    stop when
      count = 0 ∧ y = b
    evolve
      d(y) = 1
```

Figure 5.4: Automata Clock and Manager.

1. (Stability) If C is enabled in $\tau(t)$ then for all $t' \in dom(\tau)$ with $t < t'$, C is enabled in $\tau(t')$.
2. (Left-closedness) If C is not enabled in $\tau(t)$ then there exists a $t' \in dom(\tau)$ with $t < t'$ such that C is not enabled in $\tau(t')$.

```
automaton Specification(lb, ub: Real) where 0 < lb ∧ lb ≤ ub
  signature
    external grant
  states
    z: Real := 0
  transitions
    external grant
      pre
        z ≥ lb
      eff
        z := 0
  trajectories
    stop when
      z = ub
    evolve
      d(z) = 1
```

Figure 5.5: Automaton `Specification`.

A *TA with bounds*, $\mathcal{A} = (\mathcal{B}, C, l, u)$ consists of:

- A timed automaton $\mathcal{B} = (X, Q, \Theta, E, H, \mathcal{D}, \mathcal{T})$.
- A set $C \subseteq E \cup H$ of actions called a *task*; we assume that $\mathcal{T}$ is well-formed with respect to C.
- A lower time bound $l \in \mathsf{R}^{\geq 0}$ and an upper time bound $u \in \mathsf{R}^{\geq 0} \cup \{\infty\}$ with $l \leq u$.

Lower and upper bounds are used to specify how much time is allowed to pass between the enabling and the performance of an action. If l is the lower bound for a task C, then an action in C must remain enabled at least for l time units before being performed. If u is the upper bound for a task C, then an action in C can remain enabled at most u time units without being performed: it must either be performed or become disabled within u time units.

We now define an operation Extend, which transforms a TA $\mathcal{A}$ with bounds to another TA $\mathcal{A}'$ that incorporates the new bounds, in addition to the timing constraints already present in $\mathcal{A}$. Let $\mathcal{A} = (\mathcal{B}, C, l, u)$ be a TA with bounds where $\mathcal{B} = (X, Q, \Theta, E, H, \mathcal{D}, \mathcal{T})$. Then $\mathsf{Extend}(\mathcal{A})$ is the TA $\mathcal{A}' = (X', Q', \Theta', E', H', \mathcal{D}', \mathcal{T}')$ where

- $X' = X \cup \{now, first, last\}$ where:
  1. $now, first$, and $last$ are new variables that do not appear in X.
  2. now is an analog variable such that $type(now) = \mathsf{R}$.
  3. $first$ and $last$ are discrete variables where $type(first) = \mathsf{R}$ and $type(last) = \mathsf{R} \cup \{\infty\}$.
- $Q' = \{\mathbf{x} \in val(X') \mid \mathbf{x} \lceil X \in Q\}$.

- Θ' consists of all the states $\mathbf{x} \in Q'$ that satisfy the following conditions:

  1. $\mathbf{x} \lceil X \in \Theta$.
  2. $\mathbf{x}(now) = 0$.
  3. $\mathbf{x}(\mathit{first}) = \begin{cases} l & \text{if } C \text{ is enabled in } \mathbf{x} \lceil X, \\ 0 & \text{otherwise.} \end{cases}$

     $\mathbf{x}(\mathit{last}) = \begin{cases} u & \text{if } C \text{ is enabled in } \mathbf{x} \lceil X, \\ \infty & \text{otherwise.} \end{cases}$

- $E' = E$ and $H' = H$. We write $A' \triangleq E' \cup H'$.

- If $a \in A'$ then $(\mathbf{x}, a, \mathbf{x}') \in \mathcal{D}'$ exactly if all of the following conditions hold:

  1. $(\mathbf{x} \lceil X) \xrightarrow{a}_{\mathcal{A}} (\mathbf{x}' \lceil X)$.
  2. $\mathbf{x}'(now) = \mathbf{x}(now)$.
  3. (a) If $a \in C$, then $\mathbf{x}(\mathit{first}) \leq \mathbf{x}(now)$.

     (b) If C is enabled both in $\mathbf{x} \lceil X$ and $\mathbf{x}' \lceil X$ and $a \notin C$, then $\mathbf{x}(\mathit{first}) = \mathbf{x}'(\mathit{first})$ and $\mathbf{x}(\mathit{last}) = \mathbf{x}'(\mathit{last})$.

     (c) If C is enabled in $\mathbf{x}' \lceil X$ and either C is not enabled in $\mathbf{x} \lceil X$ or $a \in C$, then $\mathbf{x}'(\mathit{first}) = \mathbf{x}(now) + l$ and $\mathbf{x}'(\mathit{last}) = \mathbf{x}(now) + u$.

     (d) If C is not enabled in $\mathbf{x}' \lceil X$, then $\mathbf{x}'(\mathit{first}) = 0$ and $\mathbf{x}'(\mathit{last}) = \infty$.

- $\mathcal{T}'$ is a set that consists of all $\tau \in \mathit{trajs}(Q')$ that satisfy the following conditions:

  1. $(\tau \downarrow X) \in \mathcal{T}$.
  2. $d(now) = 1$.
  3. (a) If for all $t \in \mathit{dom}(\tau)$, C is enabled in $\tau \downarrow X(t)$ then *first* and *last* are constant throughout τ.

     (b) If for all $t \in \mathit{dom}(\tau)$, C is disabled in $\tau \downarrow X(t)$ then *first* and *last* are constant throughout τ.

     (c) If for all $t' \in [0, t)$, C is disabled in $\tau(t')$ and for all $t' \in \mathit{dom}(\tau) - [0, t)$, C is enabled in $\tau(t')$ then

        i. *first* and *last* are constant in $[0, t)$.

        ii. $\tau(t)(\mathit{first}) = \tau(t)(now) + l$ and $\tau(t)(\mathit{last}) = \tau(t)(now) + u$.

        iii. *first* and *last* are constant in $\mathit{dom}(\tau) - [0, t)$.

     (d) $now \leq \mathit{last}$.

The transformation is based on the idea of augmenting the state of the original automaton with a variable to represent current time (now) and the earliest time (first) and the latest time (last)

a task can be performed. All these variables represent time in absolute terms. Item 3(a) in the definition of $\mathcal{D}'$ expresses the new lower bound constraint and Item 3(d) in the definition of $\mathcal{T}'$ the new upper bound constraint.

Let $\mathcal{A}$ be a TA with bounds $(\mathcal{B}, C, l, u)$. In a start state $\mathbf{x}$ of $\mathsf{Extend}(\mathcal{A})$, the variables *first* and *last* are initialized to l and u, respectively, if C is enabled in $\mathbf{x}$. If C is not enabled in $\mathbf{x}$, then *first* is set to 0 and *last* is set to ∞. Items 3(c) in the definition of $\mathcal{D}'$ and 3(c) in the definition of $\mathcal{T}'$ show how the variables *first* and *last* are updated. When C becomes newly enabled by a discrete transition or when a C action leads to a state in which C is enabled, *first* is set to $now + l$ and *last* is set to $now + u$. The variables *first* and *last* are updated similarly when C becomes newly enabled in the course of a trajectory.

Theorem 5.19 *Suppose that $\mathcal{A} = (\mathcal{B}, C, l, u)$ is a TA with bounds. Then* $\mathsf{Extend}(\mathcal{A})$ *is a TA with a set of trajectories that is well formed with respect to C.*

Proof. The proof follows from the definitions of TA and the operation Extend. Step 3(a) in the definition of $\mathcal{D}'$ adds a new lower bound constraint, which makes enabling start at some particular time. Step 3(b) in the definition of $\mathcal{T}'$, adds a new upper bound constraint, which stops trajectories at a particular time and which does not add any enabling or disabling to trajectories. □

In the rest of this section, we sometimes speak of variables, states and traces of a TA with bounds. If $\mathcal{A} = (\mathcal{B}, C, l, u)$ is a TA with bounds, variables, states and traces of $\mathcal{A}$ refer to, respectively, the states and the traces of the underlying automaton $\mathcal{B}$.

Theorem 5.20 *Suppose $\mathcal{A}$ is a TA with bounds. Then $traces_{\mathsf{Extend}(\mathcal{A})} \subseteq traces_{\mathcal{A}}$.*

Proof. Let $F : Q' \to Q$ be defined as follows: $F(\mathbf{x}) = \mathbf{x} \lceil X$ where X is the set of internal variables of $\mathcal{A}$. It is easy to check that F is a refinement from $\mathsf{Extend}(\mathcal{A})$ to $\mathcal{A}$. By Theorem 4.29 and Corollary 4.25, we conclude that $traces_{\mathsf{Extend}(\mathcal{A})} \subseteq traces_{\mathcal{A}}$. □

Lemma 5.21 *Suppose that $\mathcal{A} = (\mathcal{B}, C, l, u)$ is a TA with bounds. For any reachable state $\mathbf{x}$ of* $\mathsf{Extend}(\mathcal{A})$, *if C is enabled in $\mathbf{x} \lceil X$ in $\mathcal{A}$, then $\mathbf{x}(last) \le \mathbf{x}(now) + u$.*

Proof. Consider a closed execution α of $\mathsf{Extend}(\mathcal{A})$. Using Axioms **T1** and **T2** for trajectories, we can write α as a concatenation of closed execution fragments $\alpha_0 \frown \alpha_1 \frown \ldots \alpha_k$ where α_0 is a point trajectory, and each α_i for $i \ge 1$ is either a trajectory or a discrete action surrounded by two point trajectories such that for all $0 \le i \le k-1$, $\alpha_i.lstate = \alpha_{i+1}.fstate$. We prove the invariant by induction on the length k of the sequence of execution fragments.

For the base case, suppose that C is enabled in $\alpha_0.fstate \lceil X$. Since α is an execution, we know that $\alpha_0.fstate$ is a start state of $\mathsf{Extend}(\mathcal{A})$. By definition of $\mathsf{Extend}(\mathcal{A})$, $\alpha_0.fstate(last) = u$. Since $\alpha_0.fstate(now) = 0$, $\alpha_0.fstate(last) \le \alpha_0.fstate(now) + u$, as required.

For the inductive step, we assume that the property is true for the sequence $\alpha_0 \frown \alpha_1 \frown \dots \alpha_k$ and show that it is true in the sequence α_{k+1} in $\alpha_0 \frown \alpha_1 \frown \dots \alpha_k \frown \alpha_{k+1}$. There are two cases to consider depending on whether α_{k+1} is a discrete action surrounded by two point trajectories or a trajectory.

1. α_{k+1} is an action a surrounded by two point trajectories $\wp(\mathbf{y})$ and $\wp(\mathbf{y}')$. Suppose that C is enabled in $\mathbf{y}' \lceil X$ in $\mathcal{A}$. There are two subcases to consider:
   (a) C is enabled in $\mathbf{y} \lceil X$ and $a \notin C$.
   Then, $\mathbf{y}'(last) = \mathbf{y}(last)$ and $\mathbf{y}'(now) = \mathbf{y}(now)$. By inductive hypothesis, $\mathbf{y}(last) \leq \mathbf{y}(now) + u$. Therefore, $\mathbf{y}'(last) \leq \mathbf{y}'(now) + u$, as needed.
   (b) C is disabled in $\mathbf{y} \lceil X$ or $a \in C$.
   Then, by definition of $\mathsf{Extend}(\mathcal{A})$, $\mathbf{y}'(last) = \mathbf{y}'(now) + u$, which suffices.
2. α_{k+1} is a trajectory.
   Suppose that C is enabled in $\alpha_{k+1}.lstate \lceil X$ in $\mathcal{A}$. There are two subcases to consider:
   (a) C is enabled in $\alpha_{k+1}.fstate \lceil X$ in $\mathcal{A}$.
   By inductive hypothesis $\alpha_{k+1}.fstate(last) \leq \alpha_{k+1}.fstate(now) + u$. By the well-formedness assumption, we know that C must be enabled throughout α_{k+1} and by definition of $\mathsf{Extend}(\mathcal{A})$ *last* is constant throughout α_{k+1}. Since the value of *now* increases, it is easy to see that $\alpha_{k+1}.lstate(last) \leq \alpha_{k+1}.lstate(now) + u$.
   (b) C is disabled in $\alpha_{k+1}.fstate \lceil X$ in $\mathcal{A}$.
   Then, since it is enabled in $\alpha_{k+1}.lstate \lceil X$ by the well-formedness assumption, it becomes enabled at some point t in the domain of α_{k+1} and remains enabled thereafter. Therefore, $\alpha_{k+1}(t)(last) = \alpha_{k+1}(t)(now) + u$, by definition of $\mathsf{Extend}(\mathcal{A})$. Since *last* remains constant after it is set and the value of *now* increases, $\alpha_{k+1}.lstate(last) \leq \alpha_{k+1}.lstate(now) + u$ holds.

□

The theorem below shows that the executions of an automaton obtained by applying the transformation Extend to a TA with bounds respect the time bounds specified by the lower bound l and the upper bound u.

Theorem 5.22 *Let $\mathcal{A} = (\mathcal{B}, C, l, u)$ be a TA with bounds. Then:*

1. *There does not exist a closed execution fragment α of $\mathsf{Extend}(\mathcal{A})$ from a reachable state, where $\alpha.ltime > u$, C is enabled in $\mathcal{A}$ in all the states of $\alpha \lceil (A, X)$ and no action in C occurs in α.*
2. *There does not exist a closed execution fragment α of $\mathsf{Extend}(\mathcal{A})$ from a reachable state, where $\alpha.ltime < l$, such that C is not enabled in $\mathcal{A}$ in the first state of $\alpha \lceil (A, X)$ and an action in C occurs in α.*

Proof. 1. Suppose, for the sake of contradiction, that there exists a closed execution fragment $\alpha = \tau_0\ a_1\tau_1\ a_2 \ldots\ \tau_n$ of $\mathsf{Extend}(\mathcal{A})$ from a reachable state, where $\alpha.ltime > u$, C is enabled in $\mathcal{A}$ in all the states of $\alpha \lceil (A, X)$ and none of the a_i in α is in C. By definition of trajectories for $\mathsf{Extend}(\mathcal{A})$ it must be the case that $\alpha.lstate(now) \leq \alpha.lstate(last)$.

Since C is enabled in $\mathcal{A}$ in all states in α, by Lemma 5.21 we have $\alpha.fstate(last) \leq \alpha.fstate(now) + u$. By definition of $\mathsf{Extend}(\mathcal{A})$, *last* remains constant throughout α; therefore, $\alpha.lstate(last) = \alpha.fstate(last)$. Since $\alpha.fstate(last) \leq \alpha.fstate(now) + u$, it follows that $\alpha.lstate(last) \leq \alpha.fstate(now) + u$. By definition of α, we have $\alpha.lstate(now) = \alpha.fstate(now) + \alpha.ltime$. It follows that $\alpha.fstate(now) + \alpha.ltime \leq \alpha.fstate(now) + u$. This implies $\alpha.ltime \leq u$. But this gives us the needed contradiction since $\alpha.ltime > u$.

2. We assume that α is a closed execution fragment of $\mathsf{Extend}(\mathcal{A})$ from a reachable state where $\alpha.ltime < l$, such that C is not enabled in $\mathcal{A}$ in the first state of α and an action in C occurs in α. Let $(\mathbf{x}, a, \mathbf{x}')$ be the first discrete transition of $\mathsf{Extend}(\mathcal{A})$ in α such that $a \in C$. We show that the condition $\mathbf{x}(first) \leq \mathbf{x}(now)$, which has to hold for the discrete transition to occur, cannot be true, hence arrive at a contradiction.

By Theorem 5.19, the set of trajectories of $\mathsf{Extend}(\mathcal{A})$ is well formed with respect to C. Therefore, C can become enabled by either a discrete transition or during a trajectory, and remains enabled until the occurrence of $(\mathbf{x}, a, \mathbf{x}')$.

(a) C becomes enabled by a discrete transition and remains enabled in $\mathcal{A}$ until the occurrence of $(\mathbf{x}, a, \mathbf{x}')$.
Let $(\mathbf{y}, b, \mathbf{y}')$ be the discrete transition of $\mathcal{A}$ that enables C. By item $3(c)$ in the definition of $\mathcal{D}'$ we know that *first* is set to $\mathbf{y}(now) + l$ when C becomes enabled. By item $3(b)$ in the definition of $\mathcal{D}'$ and $3(a)$ in the definition of $\mathcal{T}'$, we know that it remains constant so that $\mathbf{x}(first) = \mathbf{y}(now) + l$. Since $(\mathbf{x}, a, \mathbf{x}')$ is a discrete transition of $\mathsf{Extend}(\mathcal{A})$, it must be the case that $\mathbf{x}(first) \leq \mathbf{x}(now)$. Since $\mathbf{x}(now) \leq \mathbf{y}(now) + \alpha.ltime$ and $\mathbf{x}(first) = \mathbf{y}(now) + l$ it follows that $\mathbf{y}(now) + l \leq \mathbf{y}(now) + \alpha.ltime$. But we know by assumption that $\alpha.ltime < l$ which gives the needed contradiction.

(b) C becomes enabled at some point in the course of a trajectory τ and remains enabled in $\mathcal{A}$ until the occurrence of $(\mathbf{x}, a, \mathbf{x}')$.
Let $\mathbf{y}$ be a state in the range of τ where C becomes enabled. By item $3(c)$ in the definition of $\mathcal{T}'$ we know that *first* is set to $\mathbf{y}(now) + l$ when C becomes enabled and it remains constant in τ so that $\mathbf{x}(first) = \mathbf{y}(now) + l$. By item $3(b)$ in the definition of $\mathcal{D}'$ and $3(a)$ in the definition of $\mathcal{T}'$, we know that *first* remains constant until the occurrence of $(\mathbf{x}, a, \mathbf{x}')$. Since $(\mathbf{x}, a, \mathbf{x}')$ is a discrete transition of $\mathsf{Extend}(\mathcal{A})$, it must be the case that $\mathbf{x}(first) \leq \mathbf{x}(now)$. Since $\mathbf{x}(now) \leq \mathbf{y}(now) + \alpha.ltime$ and $\mathbf{x}(first) = \mathbf{y}(now) + l$ it follows that $\mathbf{y}(now) + l \leq \mathbf{y}(now) + \alpha.ltime$. But we know by assumption that $\alpha.ltime < l$ which gives the needed contradiction.

□

Example 5.23 (Fischer's algorithm specified using tasks and bounds). In Example 4.5 we presented the specification of Fischer's mutual exclusion algorithm as a TA. This example illustrates an alternative way of specifying the same algorithm by using a TA with bounds.

Recall that, formally, we define a TA with bounds as a TA augmented with a single task along with lower and upper bounds for that task. The automaton in Fig. 5.6 is, however, augmented with a set of tasks and bounds (we omit from the figure those transition definitions that are the same as in Example 4.5). This is for notational convenience and the automaton in Fig. 5.6 should be viewed as the automaton representing the cumulative result of adding in successive steps two tasks for each index. We assume that Extend is applied once for each task. That is, we start with the timing-independent version of `FischerME`, apply Extend to the automaton augmented with the task {`set(i)`} to add the lower bound 0 and the upper bound `u_set`, then apply Extend to the resulting automaton augmented with {`check(i)`} to add the lower bound `l_check` and the upper bound ∞. Such two successive applications are allowed since the result of the first application of Extend satisfies the the well-formedness conditions for the set of trajectories.

The result of these successive applications yields an automaton similar to the one in Example 4.5. The only difference is that the mechanical application of the transformation would reset the value of `firstcheck[i]` to 0 as an effect of `check(i)` while we do not reset `firstcheck[i]` explicitly in Example 4.5, when it becomes disabled. This is because we make use of the facts that the value of `firstcheck[i]` is used only in determining whether `check(i)` is enabled and that `check(i)` becomes enabled only in the poststate of `set(i)` which also sets the value of `firstcheck[i]`. Note that this discrepancy does not give rise to any difference in the behaviors of the two automata.

```
type Index = enumeration of p1, p2, p3, p4

type PcValue =  enumeration of rem, test, set, check,
                                leavetry, crit, reset, leaveexit

automaton FischerME(u_set, l_check: Real)
 where u_set ≥ 0 ∧ l_check ≥0 ∧ u_set < l_check
 signature
  external try(i:Index), crit(i:Index), exit(i:Index), rem(i:Index)
  internal test(i:Index), set(i:Index),
           check(i:Index), reset(i:Index)
 states
    x: Null[Index] := nil,
    pc: Array[Index, PcValue] := constant(rem)
 transitions
    internal test(i)
       pre
         pc[i] = test
       eff
         if x = nil then
            pc[i] := set
    internal set(i)
       pre
         pc[i] = set
       eff
         x := embed(i);
         pc[i] := check
    internal check(i)
       pre
         pc[i] = check
       eff
         if x = embed(i) then pc[i] := leavetry
         else pc[i] := test
 tasks
     set = {set(i)} for i: Index; check = {check(i)} for i: Index

 bounds
     set = [0, u_set]; check = [l_check, infty]
```

Figure 5.6: Fischer's mutual exclusion algorithm with bounds.

CHAPTER 6

Properties for Timed Automata

In this chapter, we define the notion of a *property* for hybrid sequences and define some common types of properties, in particular, *safety* and *liveness* properties. We define what it means for a timed automaton to satisfy a property, and present results that capture common proof methods for showing that automata satisfy properties.

6.1 PROPERTIES FOR HYBRID SEQUENCES

Common types of properties considered for systems include *safety properties* and *liveness properties* [3, 9]. These notions are usually defined in a setting in which the behavior of a system consists of a set of infinite sequences. A property is then a set of infinite sequences. However, the behavior of a TA, that is, its executions and traces, encompasses both finite and infinite sequences. It is natural to say that a TA *satisfies* a certain property if all its executions (or traces) are contained in the property. Therefore, we consider properties that may contain both finite and infinite sequences, and adjust the definitions of safety and liveness accordingly.

For any set A of actions and set V of variables, we define an (A, V)*-property* P to be any set of (A, V)-sequences. We define an (A, V)-property P to be a *safety property* provided that it is closed under prefix and limits of hybrid sequences. In other words, if a hybrid sequence satisfies a safety property P, then so do all its prefixes, and if all the executions in a chain of successive extensions satisfy P, then so does the limit of the chain. Safety properties are generally used to represent requirements that should be maintained by a system throughout its execution.

Example 6.1 (Safety property). For any A and V, the set of all (A, V)-sequences in which all valuations are equal is a safety property.

Example 6.2 (Always properties). Any set (property) of valuations can be used to define a safety property, as follows. Let I be any set of valuations of a set V of variables, and let A be any set of actions. Then define $always(I, A)$ to be the (A, V)-property consisting of all (A, V)-sequences in which all valuations are in I. It is immediate that $always(I, A)$ is a safety property. In this way, invariants that are formulated in terms of automaton states can be regarded as safety properties.

Example 6.3 (Timed automata executions and traces). For any TA $\mathcal{A}$, its set of executions, $execs_{\mathcal{A}}$, is a safety property. However, the set of traces $traces_{\mathcal{A}}$ need not be a safety property. For example, $\mathcal{A}$

could be defined to choose an integer k nondeterministically, and then perform an external action beep at integer times $0, 1, 2, \ldots, k$. The limiting sequence in which beep is performed infinitely many times, at all nonnegative integer times, is not in $traces_{\mathcal{A}}$.

Any (A, V)-property P can be weakened to a safety property. Define *safe*(P) to be the (A, V)-property that is obtained by taking the limit-closure of the prefix-closure of P. Then we can prove the following two lemmas.

Lemma 6.4 *Let P be an (A, V)-property and let α be a closed (A, V)-sequence in safe(P). Then α is a prefix of some element of P.*

Proof. Let Q be the prefix closure of P, and let R be the limit-closure of Q. Since $\alpha \in R$, there exists a chain $\alpha_0, \alpha_1, \alpha_2, \cdots$ of elements of Q with limit α. By Lemma 3.6, α is compact, and thus there is some α_j such that $\alpha \leq \alpha_j$. Since $\alpha_j \in Q$, there exists some $\beta \in P$ such that $\alpha_j \leq \beta$. Hence, α is a prefix of element β of P. □

Lemma 6.5 *For any (A, V)-property P, safe(P) is a safety property.*

Proof. Let Q be the prefix closure of P, and let R be the limit-closure of Q. We prove that $R =$ *safe*(P) is a safety property.

First, we show that R is closed under prefixes. Let $\alpha \in R$ and let $\beta \leq \alpha$. We must prove $\beta \in R$. Since $\alpha \in R$, there exists a chain $\alpha_0, \alpha_1, \alpha_2, \cdots$ of elements of Q with limit α. There exists a chain $\beta_0, \beta_1, \beta_2, \cdots$ of closed (A, V)-sequences with limit β. Fix an index i. Since $\beta_i \leq \beta$ and $\beta \leq \alpha$, we have $\beta_i \leq \alpha$. By Lemma 3.6, β_i is compact, and thus there is some α_j such that $\beta_i \leq \alpha_j$. Since $\alpha_j \in Q$ and Q is (trivially) prefix-closed, $\beta_i \in Q$. Since i was chosen arbitrarily, this implies $\beta \in R$.

Next, we show that R is limit-closed. Suppose that α is the limit of a chain $\alpha_0, \alpha_1, \alpha_2, \cdots$ of elements of R. We must prove that $\alpha \in R$. There exists a chain $\beta_0, \beta_1, \beta_2, \cdots$ of closed (A, V)-sequences with limit α. Fix an index i. By Lemma 3.6, β_i is compact, and thus there is some α_j such that $\beta_i \leq \alpha_j$. Since $\alpha_j \in R$ and R is closed under prefixes, $\beta_i \in R$. Hence, by Lemma 6.4, β_i is a prefix of an element of P, that is, $\beta_i \in Q$. Since i was chosen arbitrarily, this implies $\alpha \in R$, as required. □

We now turn to liveness properties. We define an (A, V)-property P to be a *liveness property* if, for every closed (A, V)-sequence α, P contains both α and an admissible extension of α, that is, $\mathsf{C}(A, V) \subseteq P$, and $\forall \alpha \in \mathsf{C}(A, V)\ \exists \beta \in P : \alpha \leq \beta \wedge \beta \in \mathsf{A}(A, V)$.

Liveness properties are commonly used to represent system requirements that should hold "eventually", or "infinitely often". In order for liveness properties to exist, we need a nontriviality assumption on the dynamic types of variables. If, for instance, the dynamic type of some variable only contains point trajectories, then there is no way in which we can extend closed hybrid sequences to admissible hybrid sequences. Therefore, we assume, in the rest of this section, that for any $v \in \mathsf{V}$ and for any value $c \in type(v)$, there exists a function $f \in dtype(v)$ whose domain is $[0, \infty)$ and with $f(0) = c$. Observe that, in combination with the fact that dynamic types are closed under time shift and concatenation, the nontriviality assumption implies that any closed hybrid sequence has an admissible extension.

Example 6.6 (Liveness properties). Fix a set of actions A containing action a, and a variable set V. Then the union of the set $\mathsf{C}(A, V)$ with the set of all (A, V)-sequences that contain at least one occurrence of a is a liveness property. The set of all (A, V)-sequences that do not contain any occurrence of a is not a liveness property, because this set does not include $\mathsf{C}(A, V)$. The union of $\mathsf{C}(A, V)$ with the set of (A, V)-sequences that contain infinitely many occurrences of a is a liveness property. The set of all (A, V)-sequences that contain finitely many occurrences of a is also a liveness property, since any closed (A, V)-sequence contains only finitely many occurrences of a, and has an admissible extension with only finitely many occurrences of a. Note that we need the dynamic type nontriviality assumption to assert the existence of the required admissible executions, in all three cases above.

Our definitions yield the following results, stated formally, as Theorems 6.7 and 6.8: (1) the classes of safety and liveness properties are (essentially) disjoint; and (2) every property satisfying certain basic closure conditions can be expressed as the intersection of a safety and a liveness property. The first theorem says that the only property that can be both a safety and a liveness property is the set of all (A, V)-sequences.

Theorem 6.7 *Let P be an (A, V)-property. If P is both a safety property and a liveness property, then P is the set of all (A, V)-sequences.*

Proof. Suppose that P is both a safety and a liveness property. Let α be any (A, V)-sequence; we show $\alpha \in P$. By Lemma 3.6, α can be expressed as the limit of a chain of closed (A, V)-sequences $\alpha_0, \alpha_1, \alpha_2, \ldots$. Since P is a liveness property, it follows that for every $i \geq 0$, $\alpha_i \in P$. But since P is a safety property, the limit of this chain, which is α, must also be in P. □

The second theorem says that any property that satisfies certain basic closure conditions can be expressed as the intersection of a safety property and a liveness property. This means that one can, in principle, specify any such property by listing a collection of safety and liveness requirements. In other frameworks, for instance those of [3, 9], *any* property can be expressed as the intersection of a safety and a liveness property, whereas we require two closure conditions. This is due to the fact that in our setting properties may also contain finite sequences. The closure conditions constrain the finite behaviors within a property.

Theorem 6.8 *Let P be a prefix-closed (A, V)-property such that any closed sequence in P has an admissible extension in P. Then there exist a safety property S and a liveness property L such that $P = S \cap L$.*

Proof. Let $S = \mathit{safe}(P)$ and let

$$L = P \cup \mathsf{C}(A, V) \cup \{\beta \in \mathsf{A}(A, V) \mid \exists \alpha \in \mathsf{C}(A, V) - P : \alpha \leq \beta\}$$

Lemma 6.5 implies that S is a safety property. We claim that L is a liveness property. L contains all closed sequences, by construction. Now fix any closed sequence β, and argue that L contains an admissible extension of β. If $\beta \in P$ then, by the closure conditions on P, it has an admissible extension in P, and hence in L. If $\beta \notin P$ then, by definition of L, an admissible extension of β is included in L. Note that the existence of this extension depends on the dynamic type nontriviality assumption.

From the definitions it is obvious that $P \subseteq S \cap L$. We claim that $S \cap L \subseteq P$. For contradiction, consider $\alpha \in (S \cap L) - P$. If α is closed then, since $\alpha \in \mathit{safe}(P)$, Lemma 6.4 and the fact that P is prefix-closed imply $\alpha \in P$, and we are done. So assume that α is not closed. Since $\alpha \in L - P$, α is an admissible extension of some $\beta \in \mathsf{C}(A, V) - P$. But since $\alpha \in S$ and P is prefix-closed, α is also the limit of a chain $\alpha_0, \alpha_1, \ldots$ of sequences in P. This implies that there exists some index j such that $\beta \leq \alpha_j$. But then, by prefix closure of P, $\beta \in P$. Contradiction. □

Example 6.9 (Expressing a property as an intersection of safety and liveness properties). Let P be the set of $(\{\mathtt{a}, \mathtt{b}\}, \emptyset)$-sequences whose action subsequences are strictly alternating as and bs, and are either finite and time-bounded, or else infinite and admissible (that is, admissible with infinitely many action occurrences). Thus, we are ruling out both infinite time-bounded sequences and finite admissible sequences (admissible sequences with finitely many action occurrences). It is easy to check that P is prefix-closed and that any closed sequence in P has an admissible extension in P.

Let S be the set of $(\{\mathtt{a}, \mathtt{b}\}, \emptyset)$-sequences whose action subsequences are strictly alternating as and bs. This includes all the sequences in P, plus the alternating infinite time-bounded sequences and the alternating finite admissible sequences. Clearly, S is closed under prefix and limits, and hence a safety property.

Let L' be the prefix closure of the set of all infinite and admissible $(\{\mathtt{a}, \mathtt{b}\}, \emptyset)$-sequences. Then, clearly, L' is a liveness property and $P = S \cap L'$.

The decomposition of a property into a safety and a liveness property is not unique. Since $S = \mathit{safe}(P)$, the definition of S is in agreement with the construction in the proof of Theorem 6.8. The set L', however, is larger than the liveness property L constructed in the proof of Theorem 6.8. This construction defines L to be the union of P and $\mathsf{C}(A, V)$ and the set of admissible $(\{\mathtt{a}, \mathtt{b}\}, \emptyset)$-sequences with an alternation error. Observe that $L \subset L'$ since L' also contains the open and time-bounded $(\{\mathtt{a}, \mathtt{b}\}, \emptyset)$-sequences with an alternation error. Nevertheless, according to the proof of Theorem 6.8, also L is a liveness property and $P = S \cap L$.

6.2 PROPERTIES FOR TIMED AUTOMATA

Now we define what it means for an automaton to satisfy a property. Consider a TA $\mathcal{A}$ and an (A, X)-property P, where A and X are the actions and variables of $\mathcal{A}$. Then we say that $\mathcal{A}$ *satisfies* P provided that $execs_{\mathcal{A}} \subseteq P$, that is, every execution of $\mathcal{A}$ is in P.

Sometimes we are interested in showing that an automaton satisfies a property of its traces, rather than of its executions. Thus, consider an $(E, \emptyset)$ property P, where E is the set of external actions of $\mathcal{A}$. Then we say that $\mathcal{A}$ *trace-satisfies* P provided that $traces_{\mathcal{A}} \subseteq P$.

For safety properties, we have the following three-way equivalence. The second and third conditions can be regarded as sufficient conditions for showing that $\mathcal{A}$ satisfies S. Lemma 6.10 assumes that $\mathcal{A}$ is feasible, the definition of which is given in Section 4.4.

Lemma 6.10 *Suppose that $\mathcal{A}$ is a feasible TA, and S is an (A, X)-safety property, where A and X are the actions and variables of $\mathcal{A}$. The following three statements are equivalent.*

1. *$\mathcal{A}$ satisfies S.*
2. *Every admissible execution of $\mathcal{A}$ is in S.*
3. *Every closed execution of $\mathcal{A}$ is in S.*

Proof. Obviously, Condition 1 implies both Conditions 2 and 3. We show that Condition 2 implies Condition 3 and Condition 3 implies Condition 1.

- 2 implies 3: Fix any closed execution α. Since $\mathcal{A}$ is feasible, α can be extended to an admissible execution α', which must be in S by Condition 2. Since S is prefix-closed, $\alpha \in S$, as needed.
- 3 implies 1: Fix any execution α. Then α is the limit of a sequence of closed executions, each of which must be in S by Condition 3. Since S is limit-closed, $\alpha \in S$, as needed.

□

A consequence of Lemma 6.10 is that, in order to prove that a TA $\mathcal{A}$ satisfies an (A, X)-safety-property S, it is enough to prove S for all closed executions of $\mathcal{A}$. This is typically done by induction on the i-length of the closed execution sequences (after strengthening the inductive hypothesis as needed). Such inductions have two types of inductive steps: for discrete transitions and for trajectories. A similar result to Lemma 6.10 holds for trace-satisfaction.

Lemma 6.11 *Suppose that $\mathcal{A}$ is a feasible TA, and S is an $(E, \emptyset)$-safety property, where E is the set of external actions of $\mathcal{A}$. The following three statements are equivalent.*

1. *$\mathcal{A}$ trace-satisfies S.*

2. *Every admissible trace of $\mathcal{A}$ is in S.*

3. *Every closed trace of $\mathcal{A}$ is in S.*

Now we consider the relationship between safety properties and invariants, as defined in Section 4.3. It follows directly from the definitions that I is an invariant of automaton $\mathcal{A}$ exactly if $\mathcal{A}$ satisfies the corresponding property *always*(I, A), as defined in Example 6.2.

Lemma 6.12 *Let $\mathcal{A}$ be a TA with variable set X, and let I be a set of valuations of X. Then I is an invariant of $\mathcal{A}$ if and only if $\mathcal{A}$ satisfies the safety property always(I, A).*

Lemma 6.12 is of little use when one has to prove an invariant. For proving invariants it is better to use the methods described in Section 4.3. Methods for proving liveness properties for timed automata are less standardized than those for proving safety properties. In untimed settings, formal temporal logic methods are often used [65]. In timed settings, "eventual" properties and "infinitely often" properties are more commonly sharpened into time bound properties, which are expressed as safety properties and proved using safety proof techniques [49].

Example 6.13 (Formulating an eventual property as a safety property). Consider the liveness property L consisting of sequences α such that either α is finite and time-bounded, or α contains at least one occurrence of a. Also, consider the safety property S consisting of all sequences α such that either $\alpha.ltime \leq t$ or α contains at least one occurrence of a by time t.

Note that S does not quite imply L, because S allows the case where α is an infinite sequence with $\alpha.ltime \leq t$ that contains no a, whereas L does not. However, we can say that, if α is in S and α is not an infinite sequence with $\alpha.ltime \leq t$, then $\alpha \in L$. So, for example, for an automaton $\mathcal{A}$ having no infinite, time-bounded executions (executions with finite *ltime*), if we show that all executions of $\mathcal{A}$ satisfy S, then we know that they all satisfy L.

6.3 IMPLEMENTATION

The following theorem relating implementation and properties is immediate.

Theorem 6.14 *Let $\mathcal{A}$ and $\mathcal{B}$ be TAs with the same set E of external actions, and let P be any $(E, \emptyset)$-property. If $\mathcal{A} \leq \mathcal{B}$ (that is, if $traces_{\mathcal{A}} \subseteq traces_{\mathcal{B}}$) and $\mathcal{B}$ trace-satisfies P, then $\mathcal{A}$ trace-satisfies P.*

Theorem 6.14 provides a simple proof method for showing that an automaton $\mathcal{A}$ trace-satisfies a property P: show that $\mathcal{A}$ implements some other automaton $\mathcal{B}$ and show that $\mathcal{B}$ satisfies P.

6.4 OPERATIONS

In this section, we define composition of properties and give some basic results about when a composition of automata satisfies a composition of properties. Suppose P_i is an (A_i, V_i)-property, $i \in \{1, 2\}$. Then define $P_1 \| P_2$ to be the $(A_1 \cup A_2, V_1 \cup V_2)$-property containing exactly those sequences α such that $\alpha \lceil (A_i, V_i) \in P_i, i \in \{1, 2\}$.

Theorem 6.15 *Let P_i be an (A_i, V_i)-property, $i \in \{1, 2\}$. If P_1 and P_2 are safety properties, then $P_1 \| P_2$ is a safety property.*

The following theorem gives a simple sufficient condition for a composition of TA to implement a composition of properties.

Theorem 6.16 *Let $\mathcal{A}_1$ and $\mathcal{A}_2$ be compatible TAs and let P_i be an (A_i, X_i)-property, $i \in \{1, 2\}$, where A_i and X_i are the sets of actions and states of $\mathcal{A}_i$. Suppose $\mathcal{A}_i$ satisfies P_i, $i \in \{1, 2\}$. Then $\mathcal{A}_1 \| \mathcal{A}_2$ satisfies $P_1 \| P_2$.*

Proof. Let $\alpha \in execs_{\mathcal{A}_1 \| \mathcal{A}_2}$. By Lemma 5.2, $\alpha \lceil (A_i, X_i) \in execs_{\mathcal{A}_i}, i \in \{1, 2\}$. Since $\mathcal{A}_i$ satisfies P_i, we have that $\alpha \lceil (A_i, X_i) \in P_i$, for $i \in \{1, 2\}$. Therefore, $\alpha \in P_1 \| P_2$. □

A similar result holds for traces.

Theorem 6.17 *Let $\mathcal{A}_1$ and $\mathcal{A}_2$ be compatible TAs and let P_i be an $(E_i, \emptyset)$-property, $i \in \{1, 2\}$, where E_i is the set of external actions of $\mathcal{A}_i$. Suppose $\mathcal{A}_i$ trace-satisfies P_i, $i \in \{1, 2\}$. Then $\mathcal{A}_1 \| \mathcal{A}_2$ trace-satisfies $P_1 \| P_2$.*

Theorems 6.16 and 6.17 provide basic proof methods for showing that a composed system satisfies composed properties. We can also obtain slightly stronger results, such as the following two trace-satisfaction theorems, which are analogous to Corollaries 5.11 and 5.12. The first theorem says that $\mathcal{A}_1 \| \mathcal{A}_2$ trace-satisfies $P_1 \| P_2$ provided that $\mathcal{A}_2$ trace-satisfies P_2, and every trace of $\mathcal{A}_1$ consistent with property P_2 also has property P_1.

Theorem 6.18 *Let $\mathcal{A}_1$ and $\mathcal{A}_2$ be compatible TAs and let P_i be an $(E_i, \emptyset)$-property, $i \in \{1, 2\}$. Suppose $\mathcal{A}_2$ trace-satisfies P_2. Suppose that every trace β of $\mathcal{A}_1$ such that $\beta \lceil (E_2, \emptyset) \in P_2$ is in P_1. Then $\mathcal{A}_1 \| \mathcal{A}_2$ trace-satisfies $P_1 \| P_2$.*

Example 6.19 (Compositional proof of property satisfaction). Let $\mathcal{A}_2$ be a TA with one external action a. $\mathcal{A}_2$ is allowed to perform a only at integer times, and at most once at each integer time. It does not force any a events to occur, and lets time pass without constraint. Let P_2 be the set of $(\{\mathsf{a}\}, \emptyset)$-sequences in which, by any finite time, there are only finitely many occurrences of a. Clearly, $\mathcal{A}_2$ trace-satisfies P_2.

Let $\mathcal{A}_1$ be a timed automaton with two external actions, a and b. $\mathcal{A}_1$ is allowed to perform any number of a events, at any time. It can perform b at any time, but only if it has previously performed a at the same time with no intervening b. $\mathcal{A}_1$ also lets time pass unconstrained. Let P_1 be the set of $(\{a, b\}, \emptyset)$-sequences in which, by any finite time, there are only finitely many occurrences of b. Then every trace β of $\mathcal{A}_1$ such that $\beta \lceil (E_2, \emptyset) \in P_2$ is in P_1.

It follows from Theorem 6.18 that $\mathcal{A}_1 \| \mathcal{A}_2$ trace-satisfies $P_1 \| P_2$, which means that the composition of the two automata guarantees that, by any finite time, there are only finitely many occurrences of a and only finitely many occurrences of b.

The second theorem incorporates auxiliary properties. It says that $\mathcal{A}_1 \| \mathcal{A}_2$ trace-satisfies $P_1 \| P_2$ provided that, for some auxiliary properties Q_1 and Q_2, $\mathcal{A}_1 \| \mathcal{A}_2$ trace-satisfies $Q_1 \| Q_2$, every trace of $\mathcal{A}_1$ consistent with property Q_2 also has property P_1, and every trace of $\mathcal{A}_2$ consistent with property Q_1 also has property P_2.

Theorem 6.20 *Let $\mathcal{A}_1$ and $\mathcal{A}_2$ be compatible TAs and let P_i and Q_i be $(E_i, \emptyset)$-properties, $i \in \{1, 2\}$. Suppose that:*

1. *$\mathcal{A}_1 \| \mathcal{A}_2$ trace-satisfies $Q_1 \| Q_2$.*
2. *Every trace β of $\mathcal{A}_1$ such that $\beta \lceil (E_1, \emptyset) \in Q_2$ is in P_1, and every trace β of $\mathcal{A}_2$ such that $\beta \lceil (E_2, \emptyset) \in Q_1$ is in P_2.*

Then, $\mathcal{A}_1 \| \mathcal{A}_2$ trace-satisfies $P_1 \| P_2$.

We close this chapter with a trace-satisfaction result for hiding.

Theorem 6.21 *Let $\mathcal{A}$ be a TA, let P be an $(E_{\mathcal{A}}, \emptyset)$-property, and let $E \subseteq E_{\mathcal{A}}$. Suppose that $\mathcal{A}$ trace-satisfies P. Then $\mathsf{ActHide}(E, \mathcal{A})$ trace-satisfies the property $P \lceil (E_{\mathcal{A}} - E, \emptyset) = \{\beta \lceil (E_{\mathcal{A}} - E, \emptyset) \mid \beta \in P\}$.*

CHAPTER 7

Timed I/O Automata

In this chapter we refine the timed automaton model of Chapter 4 by distinguishing between input and output actions. Typically, an interaction between a system and its environment is modeled by using output and input actions to represent, respectively, the external events under the control of the system and the environment. We extend the results on simulation relations and composition from Chapters 4 and 5 to this new setting. We also introduce special kinds of timed I/O automata: I/O feasible, progressive, and receptive TIOAs.

7.1 DEFINITION OF TIMED I/O AUTOMATA

A *timed I/O automaton (TIOA)* $\mathcal{A}$ is a tuple $(\mathcal{B}, I, O)$ where:

- $\mathcal{B} = (X, Q, \Theta, E, H, \mathcal{D}, \mathcal{T})$ is a TA.
- I and O partition E into *input* and *output actions*, respectively. Actions in $L \triangleq H \cup O$ are called *locally controlled*; as before, we write $A \triangleq E \cup H$.
- The following additional axioms are satisfied:

  E1 *(Input action enabling)*
  For every $\mathbf{x} \in Q$ and every $a \in I$, there exists $\mathbf{x}' \in Q$ such that $\mathbf{x} \xrightarrow{a} \mathbf{x}'$.

  E2 *(Time-passage enabling)*
  For every $\mathbf{x} \in Q$, there exists $\tau \in \mathcal{T}$ such that $\tau.\mathit{fstate} = \mathbf{x}$ and either

  1. $\tau.\mathit{ltime} = \infty$, or
  2. τ is closed and some $l \in L$ is enabled in $\tau.\mathit{lstate}$.

Input action enabling is the input enabling condition of ordinary I/O automata [84, 83, 76, 53, 54]; it says that a TIOA is able to perform an input action at any time. The time-passage enabling condition says that a TIOA either allows time to advance forever, or it allows time to advance for a while, up to a point where it is prepared to react with some locally controlled action. The condition ensures what is called time reactivity in [12] and timelock freedom in [14], that is, whenever time progress stops there exists at least one enabled transition. Because TIOAs have no external variables, **E1** and **E2** are slightly simpler than the corresponding axioms for HIOAs in [79].

Notation: As we did for TAs, we often denote the components of a TIOA $\mathcal{A}$ by $\mathcal{B}_{\mathcal{A}}$, $I_{\mathcal{A}}$, $O_{\mathcal{A}}$, $X_{\mathcal{A}}$, $Q_{\mathcal{A}}$, $\Theta_{\mathcal{A}}$, etc., and those of a TIOA $\mathcal{A}_i$ by H_i, I_i, O_i, X_i, Q_i, Θ_i, etc. We sometimes omit these subscripts, where no confusion is likely. We abuse notation slightly by referring to a TIOA $\mathcal{A}$ as a TA when we intend to refer to $\mathcal{B}_{\mathcal{A}}$.

Example 7.1 (TAs viewed as TIOAs). The automaton `TimedChannel` described in Example 4.1 can be turned into a TIOA by classifying the `send` actions as inputs, and the `receive` actions as outputs. Since there is no precondition for `send` actions, they are enabled in each state, so clearly the input enabling condition **E1** holds. It is also easy to see that Axiom **E2** holds: in each state either `queue` is nonempty, in which case a `receive` output action is enabled after a point trajectory, or `queue` is empty, in which case time can advance forever.

The automaton `ClockSync(u,r,i)` of Example 4.6 can be turned into a TIOA by classifying the `send` actions as outputs, and the `receive` actions as inputs. Axiom **E1** then holds trivially. Axiom **E2** holds since from each state either time can advance forever, or we have an outgoing trajectory (possibly of length 0) to a state in which `physclock` = `nextsend`, and from there a `send` output action is enabled.

7.2 EXECUTIONS AND TRACES

An *execution fragment*, *execution*, *trace fragment*, or *trace* of a TIOA $\mathcal{A}$ is defined to be an execution fragment, execution, trace fragment, or trace of the underlying TA $\mathcal{B}_{\mathcal{A}}$, respectively.

We say that an execution fragment of a TIOA is *locally-Zeno* if it is Zeno and contains infinitely many locally controlled actions, or equivalently, if it has finite limit time and contains infinitely many locally controlled actions.

7.3 SPECIAL KINDS OF TIMED I/O AUTOMATA

7.3.1 FEASIBLE AND I/O FEASIBLE TIOAS

A TIOA $\mathcal{A} = (\mathcal{B}, I, O)$ is defined to be *feasible* provided that its underlying TA $\mathcal{B}$ is feasible according to the definition given in Section 4.4: for every state $\mathbf{x}$ of $\mathcal{B}$, there exists an admissible execution fragment of $\mathcal{B}$ from $\mathbf{x}$. As noted in Section 4.4, feasibility is a basic requirement that any TA (or TIOA) should satisfy. I/O feasibility is a strengthened version of feasibility that take inputs into account. It says that the automaton is capable of providing some response from any state, for any sequence of input actions and any amount of intervening time-passage. In particular, it should allow time to pass to infinity if the environment does not submit any input actions. Formally, we define a TIOA to be *I/O feasible* provided that, for each state $\mathbf{x}$ and each $(I, \emptyset)$-sequence β, there is some execution fragment α from $\mathbf{x}$ such that $\alpha \lceil (I, \emptyset) = \beta$. That is, an I/O feasible TIOA accommodates arbitrary input actions occurring at arbitrary times. The given $(I, \emptyset)$-sequence β describes the inputs and the amounts of intervening times.

7.3.2 PROGRESSIVE TIOAS

A progressive TIOA never generates infinitely many locally controlled actions in finite time. Formally, a TIOA $\mathcal{A}$ is *progressive* if it has no locally-Zeno execution fragments. For reasons that will become clear later on in this section (see Theorem 7.6), we define progressiveness for execution fragments rather than for executions.

The following lemma says that any progressive TIOA is capable of advancing time forever.

Lemma 7.2 *Every progressive TIOA is feasible.*

Proof. Let $\mathcal{A}$ be a progressive TIOA and let $\mathbf{x}$ be a state of $\mathcal{A}$. Since $\mathcal{A}$ is a TIOA it satisfies Axiom **E2**. We construct an admissible execution fragment $\alpha = \alpha_0 \frown \alpha_1 \frown \alpha_2 \cdots$ from $\mathbf{x}$ as follows.

1. $\alpha_0 = \wp(\mathbf{x})$.
2. For each $i > 0$,
   (a) If there exists a trajectory τ from $\alpha_{i-1}.lstate$ such that $\tau.ltime = \infty$ then α_i is the final execution fragment in the sequence and $\alpha_i = \tau$.
   (b) Otherwise, let τ_i be a closed trajectory from $\alpha_{i-1}.lstate$ such that $l \in L$ is enabled in $\tau_i.lstate$. Define $\alpha_i = \tau_i \; l \; \tau_{i+1}$ where $\tau_{i+1} = \wp(\mathbf{y})$ and $\tau_i.lstate \xrightarrow{l} \mathbf{y}$.

The above construction either ends after finitely many stages such that the last trajectory of α is admissible, or goes through infinitely many stages such that α contains infinitely many local actions. In the former case, we know that α is admissible since it ends with an admissible trajectory. In the latter case, since $\mathcal{A}$ is progressive, the fact that α has infinitely many local actions implies that α is admissible, as needed. □

The following lemma says that a progressive TIOA is capable of allowing any amount of time to pass from any state.

Lemma 7.3 *Let $\mathcal{A}$ be a progressive TIOA, let $\mathbf{x}$ be a state of $\mathcal{A}$, and let $\tau \in trajs(\emptyset)$. Then there exists an execution fragment α of $\mathcal{A}$ such that $\alpha.fstate = \mathbf{x}$ and $\alpha \lceil (I, \emptyset) = \tau$.*

Proof. The result follows from the construction used in the proof of Lemma 7.2. Let α be an admissible execution fragment from $\mathbf{x}$ constructed as in the proof of Lemma 7.2. Let α' be a prefix of α such that $\alpha' \lceil (\emptyset, \emptyset) = \tau$. Since our construction uses no actions from I, we have $\alpha' \lceil (I, \emptyset) = \alpha' \lceil (\emptyset, \emptyset) = \tau$, as needed. □

The following theorem says that a progressive TIOA is capable not just of allowing arbitrary amounts of time to pass, but of allowing arbitrary input actions at arbitrary times.

Theorem 7.4 *Every progressive TIOA is I/O feasible.*

Proof. Let $\mathcal{A}$ be a progressive TIOA, let $\mathbf{x}$ be a state of $\mathcal{A}$, and let $\beta = \tau_0\, a_1\, \tau_1\, a_2\, \tau_2 \ldots$ be an $(I, \emptyset)$-sequence. We construct a finite or infinite sequence $\alpha_0\, \alpha_1\, \ldots$ of execution fragments such that:

1. $\alpha_0.\mathit{fstate} = \mathbf{x}$.

2. For each nonfinal index i, $\alpha_i.\mathit{lstate} = \alpha_{i+1}.\mathit{fstate}$.

3. For each i, $(\alpha_0 \frown \alpha_1 \frown \cdots \frown \alpha_i) \lceil (I, \emptyset) = \tau_0\, a_1\, \tau_1 \ldots \tau_i$.

The construction is carried out recursively. To define α_0, we start with $\mathbf{x}$ and use Lemma 7.3 to "span" the time interval of τ_0. For $i > 0$, we define α_i by starting with $\alpha_{i-1}.\mathit{lstate}$, using Axiom **E1** to perform the input action a_i and move to a new state and then using Lemma 7.3 to span τ_i.

Let $\alpha = \alpha_0 \frown \alpha_1 \frown \cdots$. By Lemma 3.8, α is an execution fragment of $\mathcal{A}$ from $\mathbf{x}$ such that $\alpha \lceil (I, \emptyset) = \beta$, as needed. □

7.3.3 RECEPTIVE TIMED I/O AUTOMATA

In this section, we define the notion of *receptiveness* for TIOAs. A TIOA will be defined to be receptive provided that it admits a *strategy* for resolving its nondeterministic choices that never generates infinitely many locally controlled actions in finite time. This notion has an important consequence: A receptive TIOA provides some response from any state, for any sequence of discrete input actions at any times. This implies that the automaton has a nontrivial set of execution fragments, in fact, it has execution fragments that accommodate any inputs from the environment. The automaton cannot simply stop at some point and refuse to allow time to elapse; it must allow time to pass to infinity if the environment does so. Previous studies of receptiveness properties include [24, 1, 107, 81]. The notion of receptiveness for TIOAs as discussed here is a special case of the same notion for HIOAs [79].

We build our definition of receptiveness on our earlier definition of progressive TIOAs. Namely, we define a *strategy* for resolving nondeterministic choices, and define receptiveness in terms of the existence of a progressive strategy.

We define a *strategy* for a TIOA $\mathcal{A}$ to be a TIOA $\mathcal{A}'$ that differs from $\mathcal{A}$ only in that $\mathcal{D}' \subseteq \mathcal{D}$ and $\mathcal{T}' \subseteq \mathcal{T}$. That is, we require:

- $\mathcal{D}' \subseteq \mathcal{D}$,

- $\mathcal{T}' \subseteq \mathcal{T}$,

- $X = X'$, $Q = Q'$, $\Theta = \Theta'$, $H = H'$, $I = I'$, and $O = O'$.

Our strategies are nondeterministic and memoryless. They provide a way of choosing some of the evolutions that are possible from each state $\mathbf{x}$ of $\mathcal{A}$. The fact that the state set Q' of $\mathcal{A}'$ is the same as the state set Q of $\mathcal{A}$ implies that $\mathcal{A}'$ chooses evolutions from every state of $\mathcal{A}$.

Our notion of strategy is very similar to the winning strategies defined by Maler, Pnueli, and Sifakis for certain games defined on Alur-Dill style timed automata [89]. The motivation for this work is the automatic synthesis of real-time controllers. Efficient algorithms for computing these strategies have recently been implemented in the tool Uppaal Tiga [17]. Notions of strategy have been used also in previous studies of receptiveness [24, 1, 107, 81]. However, in these earlier works, strategies are functions which, based on the full history, specify the next system move. Defining strategies using automata allows us to avoid introducing extra mathematical machinery.

Lemma 7.5 *If $\mathcal{A}'$ is a strategy for $\mathcal{A}$, then every execution fragment of $\mathcal{A}'$ is also an execution fragment of $\mathcal{A}$.*

We define a TIOA to be *receptive* if it has a progressive strategy. The following theorem says that any receptive TIOA can respond to any inputs from the environment.

Theorem 7.6 *Every receptive TIOA is I/O feasible.*

Proof. Immediate from the definitions, Theorem 7.4 and Lemma 7.5. □

Note that for this theorem to hold it is crucial that the progressive strategy $\mathcal{A}'$ for a receptive TIOA $\mathcal{A}$ is defined for *all* states of $\mathcal{A}'$, not just for the reachable ones. Even though $\mathcal{A}$ and $\mathcal{A}'$ have the same states, they may differ in their sets of reachable states. Thus, if we only have figured out what to do in the reachable states of $\mathcal{A}'$, there may be some reachable states of $\mathcal{A}$ for which no "strategy" has been defined.

Example 7.7 (Progressive and receptive TIOAs). The time-bounded channel automaton described in Example 4.1 is not progressive since it allows for an infinite execution in which `send` and `receive` actions alternate without any passage of time in between. The time-bounded channel automaton is receptive, however, as we may construct a progressive strategy for it by adding a condition `head(queue).deadline = now` to the precondition of the `receive` action. In this way we enforce that the channel operates maximally slow and messages are only delivered at their delivery deadline. The clock synchronization automaton of Example 4.6 is progressive (and therefore receptive) since it can only generate a locally controlled action each time its physical clock advances by `u` time units and the real time that elapses between two locally produced actions is at least `u` × `(1-r)` time units.

7.4 IMPLEMENTATION RELATIONSHIPS

Two TIOAs $\mathcal{A}_1$ and $\mathcal{A}_2$ are *comparable* if their inputs and outputs coincide, that is, if $I_1 = I_2$ and $O_1 = O_2$. If $\mathcal{A}_1$ and $\mathcal{A}_2$ are comparable, then $\mathcal{A}_1 \leq \mathcal{A}_2$ is defined to mean that the traces of $\mathcal{A}_1$ are included among those of $\mathcal{A}_2$: $\mathcal{A}_1 \leq \mathcal{A}_2 \triangleq \mathit{traces}_{\mathcal{A}_1} \subseteq \mathit{traces}_{\mathcal{A}_2}$.

Lemma 7.8 *Let $\mathcal{A}_1$, $\mathcal{A}_2$ be two comparable TIOAs and let $\mathcal{B}_1$, $\mathcal{B}_2$ be, respectively, the underlying TAs for $\mathcal{A}_1$ and $\mathcal{A}_2$. Then $\mathcal{B}_1$ and $\mathcal{B}_2$ are comparable and $\mathcal{A}_1 \leq \mathcal{A}_2$ iff $\mathcal{B}_1 \leq \mathcal{B}_2$.*

Proof. Immediate from the definitions. □

7.5 SIMULATION RELATIONS

The definition of forward simulation for TIOAs is the same as for TAs. Formally, if $\mathcal{A}_1 = (\mathcal{B}_1, I_1, O_1)$ and $\mathcal{A}_2 = (\mathcal{B}_2, I_2, O_2)$ are two comparable TIOAs, then a forward simulation from $\mathcal{A}_1$ to $\mathcal{A}_2$ is a forward simulation from $\mathcal{B}_1$ to $\mathcal{B}_2$.

Theorem 7.9 *If $\mathcal{A}_1$ and $\mathcal{A}_2$ are comparable TIOAs and there is a forward simulation from $\mathcal{A}_1$ to $\mathcal{A}_2$, then $\mathcal{A}_1 \leq \mathcal{A}_2$.*

The definitions and results about backward simulations, history and prophecy relations for timed automata from Chapter 4 carry over to timed automata with input and output distinction in a similar fashion.

CHAPTER 8

Operations on Timed I/O Automata

In this chapter, we define the operations of composition and hiding and present projection, pasting and substitutivity results for TIOAs. We revisit the special kinds of TIOAs introduced in Chapter 7 and show that the classes of progressive and receptive TIOAs closed under composition, while this is not true for the class of I/O feasible automata.

8.1 COMPOSITION

8.1.1 DEFINITIONS AND BASIC RESULTS

The definition of composition for TIOAs is based on the corresponding definition for TAs, but also takes the input/output structure into account. We require that precisely one component should "control" any given internal or output action. We say that TIOAs $\mathcal{A}_1$ and $\mathcal{A}_2$ are *compatible* if, for $i \neq j, X_i \cap X_j = H_i \cap A_j = O_i \cap O_j = \emptyset$. It is immediate that if two TIOAs are compatible, their underlying TAs are also compatible.

Lemma 8.1 *If $\mathcal{A}_1 = (\mathcal{B}_1, I_1, O_1)$ and $\mathcal{A}_2 = (\mathcal{B}_2, I_2, O_2)$ are compatible TIOAs, then $\mathcal{B}_1$ and $\mathcal{B}_2$ are compatible TAs.*

If $\mathcal{A}_1$ and $\mathcal{A}_2$ are compatible TIOAs then their *composition* $\mathcal{A}_1 \| \mathcal{A}_2$ is defined to be the tuple $\mathcal{A} = (\mathcal{B}, I, O)$ where:

- $\mathcal{B} = \mathcal{B}_1 \| \mathcal{B}_2$,
- $I = (I_1 \cup I_2) - (O_1 \cup O_2)$, and
- $O = O_1 \cup O_2$.

Thus, an external action of the composition is classified as an output if it is an output of one of the component automata, and otherwise it is classified as an input. The composition of compatible TIOAs is guaranteed to be a TIOA:

Theorem 8.2 *If $\mathcal{A}_1$ and $\mathcal{A}_2$ are compatible TIOAs then $\mathcal{A}_1 \| \mathcal{A}_2$ is a TIOA.*

Proof. The proof is straightforward except for showing that Axiom **E2** is satisfied by the composition. Let $\mathbf{x}$ be a state of $\mathcal{A}_1 \| \mathcal{A}_2$. We need to show the existence of a trajectory from $\mathbf{x}$ that satisfies **E2**.

By definition of $\mathcal{A}_1 \| \mathcal{A}_2$, $\mathbf{x} \lceil X_1$ is a state of $\mathcal{A}_1$ and $\mathbf{x} \lceil X_2$ is a state of $\mathcal{A}_2$. We know that both $\mathcal{A}_1$ and $\mathcal{A}_2$ satisfy **E2**. Let τ_1 be a trajectory of $\mathcal{A}_1$ with $\tau_1.\mathit{fstate} = \mathbf{x} \lceil X_1$ that satisfies **E2**, let τ_2 be a trajectory of $\mathcal{A}_2$ with $\tau_2.\mathit{fstate} = \mathbf{x} \lceil X_2$ that satisfies **E2**, and consider the following cases.

1. $\tau_1.\mathit{ltime} = \infty$ and $\tau_2.\mathit{ltime} = \infty$.
   Then, define τ such that $\tau \downarrow X_1 = \tau_1$ and $\tau \downarrow X_2 = \tau_2$.

2. $\tau_1.\mathit{ltime} = \infty$ and τ_2 is closed where some $l \in L_2$ is enabled in $\tau_2.\mathit{lstate}$.
   Then, define τ such that $\tau \downarrow X_1 = \tau_1 \lceil \mathit{dom}(\tau_2)$ and $\tau \downarrow X_2 = \tau_2$.

3. τ_1 is closed where some $l \in L_1$ is enabled in $\tau_1.\mathit{lstate}$ and $\tau_2.\mathit{ltime} = \infty$.
   Then, define τ such that $\tau \downarrow X_1 = \tau_1$ and $\tau \downarrow X_2 = \tau_2 \lceil \mathit{dom}(\tau_1)$.

4. τ_1 is closed where some $l \in L_1$ is enabled in $\tau_1.\mathit{lstate}$ and τ_2 is closed where some $l \in L_2$ is enabled in $\tau_2.\mathit{lstate}$.
   If $\mathit{dom}(\tau_1) \subseteq \mathit{dom}(\tau_2)$, then define τ such that $\tau \downarrow X_1 = \tau_1$ and $\tau \downarrow X_2 = \tau_2 \lceil \mathit{dom}(\tau_1)$. Otherwise, define τ such that $\tau \downarrow X_1 = \tau_1 \lceil \mathit{dom}(\tau_2)$ and $\tau \downarrow X_2 = \tau_2$.

In all the cases, τ is a trajectory of $\mathcal{A}_1 \| \mathcal{A}_2$ from $\mathbf{x}$, and either $\tau.\mathit{ltime} = \infty$ or τ is closed. Moreover, if τ is closed then in the last state one of the automata, say $\mathcal{A}_i$, enables a locally controlled action l. Since $\mathcal{A}_1$ and $\mathcal{A}_2$ are compatible, either l is not in the signature of the other automaton $\mathcal{A}_j$, or l is an input action of $\mathcal{A}_j$ which is enabled within any state of $\mathcal{A}_j$ by Axiom **E1**. In both cases, the last state of τ enables l in the composition $\mathcal{A}_1 \| \mathcal{A}_2$. This completes the proof that $\mathcal{A}_1 \| \mathcal{A}_2$ satisfies Axiom **E2**. □

Note that this theorem is stronger than the corresponding theorem [79, Theorem 6.12] for general HIOAs. Two HIOAs $\mathcal{A}_1$ and $\mathcal{A}_2$ are required to be "strongly compatible" for their composition to be a hybrid I/O automaton. This extra condition is needed to rule out dependencies among external variables that may prevent the component automata from evolving together. The absence of external variables in TIOA eliminates this kind of problematic behavior. Thus, for the timed case, we do not require the notion of strong compatibility that was needed for the hybrid case.

Composition of TIOAs satisfies the following projection and pasting results, which follow from the corresponding results for TAs (Theorems 5.4 and 5.5).

Theorem 8.3 *Let $\mathcal{A}_1$ and $\mathcal{A}_2$ be compatible TIOAs, and let $\mathcal{A} = \mathcal{A}_1 \| \mathcal{A}_2$. Let α_i be an execution fragment of $\mathcal{A}_i$, $i \in \{1, 2\}$.*
Let β be an $(E, \emptyset)$-sequence, where E is the set of external actions of $\mathcal{A}$. Suppose that $\beta \lceil (E_i, \emptyset) = \mathit{trace}(\alpha_i)$, $i \in \{1, 2\}$. Then there exists an execution fragment α of $\mathcal{A}$ such that $\mathit{trace}(\alpha) = \beta$ and $\alpha_i = \alpha \lceil (A_i, X_i)$, $i \in \{1, 2\}$.

Theorem 8.4 *Let $\mathcal{A}_1$ and $\mathcal{A}_2$ be compatible TIOAs, let $\mathcal{A} = \mathcal{A}_1 \| \mathcal{A}_2$, and let E be the set of external acions of $\mathcal{A}$. Then $traces_{\mathcal{A}}$ is exactly the set of $(E, \emptyset)$-sequences whose restrictions to $\mathcal{A}_1$ and $\mathcal{A}_2$ are traces of $\mathcal{A}_1$ and $\mathcal{A}_2$, respectively.*
That is, $traces_{\mathcal{A}} = \{\beta \mid \beta$ is an $(E, \emptyset)$-sequence and $\beta \lceil (E_i, \emptyset) \in traces_{\mathcal{A}_i}, i \in \{1, 2\}\}$.

8.1.2 SUBSTITUTIVITY RESULTS

The following theorem is analogous to Theorem 5.9 for TAs. It shows that the introduction of this distinction does not cause any changes to the substitutivity results we obtained for general TAs.

Theorem 8.5 *Suppose $\mathcal{A}_1$ and $\mathcal{A}_2$ are comparable TIOAs with $\mathcal{A}_1 \leq \mathcal{A}_2$. Suppose that $\mathcal{B}$ is a TIOA that is compatible with each of $\mathcal{A}_1$ and $\mathcal{A}_2$. Then $\mathcal{A}_1 \| \mathcal{B} \leq \mathcal{A}_2 \| \mathcal{B}$.*

The corollaries are analogous to Corollaries 5.10 and 5.11 of Theorem 5.9.

Corollary 8.6 *Suppose $\mathcal{A}_1$, $\mathcal{A}_2$, $\mathcal{B}_1$, and $\mathcal{B}_2$ are TIOAs, $\mathcal{A}_1$ and $\mathcal{A}_2$ are comparable, $\mathcal{B}_1$ and $\mathcal{B}_2$ are comparable, and each of $\mathcal{A}_1$ and $\mathcal{A}_2$ is compatible with each of $\mathcal{B}_1$ and $\mathcal{B}_2$. If $\mathcal{A}_1 \leq \mathcal{A}_2$ and $\mathcal{B}_1 \leq \mathcal{B}_2$ then $\mathcal{A}_1 \| \mathcal{B}_1 \leq \mathcal{A}_2 \| \mathcal{B}_2$.*

Corollary 8.7 *Suppose $\mathcal{A}_1$, $\mathcal{A}_2$, $\mathcal{B}_1$, and $\mathcal{B}_2$ are TIOAs, $\mathcal{A}_1$ and $\mathcal{A}_2$ are comparable, $\mathcal{B}_1$ and $\mathcal{B}_2$ are comparable, and each of $\mathcal{A}_1$ and $\mathcal{A}_2$ is compatible with each of $\mathcal{B}_1$ and $\mathcal{B}_2$. If $\mathcal{A}_1 \| \mathcal{B}_2 \leq \mathcal{A}_2 \| \mathcal{B}_2$ and $\mathcal{B}_1 \leq \mathcal{B}_2$ then $\mathcal{A}_1 \| \mathcal{B}_1 \leq \mathcal{A}_2 \| \mathcal{B}_2$.*

The basic substitutivity theorem, Theorem 8.5, is desirable for any formalism for interacting processes. For design purposes, it enables one to refine individual components without violating the correctness of the system as a whole. For verification purposes, it enables one to prove that a composite system satisfies its specification by proving that each component satisfies its specification, thereby breaking down the verification task into more manageable pieces. However, it might not always be possible or easy to show that each component $\mathcal{A}_1$ (resp. $\mathcal{B}_1$) satisfies its specification $\mathcal{A}_2$ (resp. $\mathcal{B}_2$) without using any assumptions about the environment of the component. *Assume-guarantee* style results [1, 2, 31, 48, 52, 101, 114, 115] are special kinds of substitutivity results that state what *guarantees* are expected from each component in an environment constrained by certain *assumptions*. Since the environment of each component consists of the other components in the system, assume-guarantee style results need to break the circular dependencies between the assumptions and guarantees for components. Below, we present two assume-guarantee style theorems, Theorem 8.8 and Corollary 8.9 taken from [55], which can be used for proving that a system specified as a composite automaton $\mathcal{A}_1 \| \mathcal{B}_1$ implements a specification represented by a composite automaton $\mathcal{A}_2 \| \mathcal{B}_2$.

The main idea behind Theorem 8.8 is to assume that $\mathcal{A}_1$ implements $\mathcal{A}_2$ in a context represented by $\mathcal{B}_2$, and symmetrically that $\mathcal{B}_1$ implements $\mathcal{B}_2$ in a context represented by $\mathcal{A}_2$ where $\mathcal{A}_2$

and $\mathcal{B}_2$ are automata whose trace sets are closed under limits. The requirement about limit-closure implies that $\mathcal{A}_2$ and $\mathcal{B}_2$ specify trace safety properties. Moreover, we assume that the trace sets of $\mathcal{A}_2$ and $\mathcal{B}_2$ are closed under time-extension. That is, the automata allow arbitrary time-passage. This is the most general assumption one could make to ensure that $\mathcal{A}_2 \| \mathcal{B}_2$ does not impose stronger constraints on time-passage than $\mathcal{A}_1 \| \mathcal{B}_1$. Recall that the definition of time extension of a hybrid sequence can be found in Section 3.4.1.

Theorem 8.8 *Suppose $\mathcal{A}_1$, $\mathcal{A}_2$, $\mathcal{B}_1$, $\mathcal{B}_2$ are TIOAs such that $\mathcal{A}_1$ and $\mathcal{A}_2$ are comparable, $\mathcal{B}_1$ and $\mathcal{B}_2$ are comparable, and each of $\mathcal{A}_1$ and $\mathcal{A}_2$ is compatible with each of $\mathcal{B}_1$ and $\mathcal{B}_2$. Suppose further that:*

1. *the sets $traces_{\mathcal{A}_2}$ and $traces_{\mathcal{B}_2}$ are closed under limits;*
2. *the sets $traces_{\mathcal{A}_2}$ and $traces_{\mathcal{B}_2}$ are closed under time-extension;*
3. *$\mathcal{A}_1 \| \mathcal{B}_2 \leq \mathcal{A}_2 \| \mathcal{B}_2$ and $\mathcal{A}_2 \| \mathcal{B}_1 \leq \mathcal{A}_2 \| \mathcal{B}_2$.*

Then, $\mathcal{A}_1 \| \mathcal{B}_1 \leq \mathcal{A}_2 \| \mathcal{B}_2$.

Proof. Let β be a closed trace of $\mathcal{A}_1 \| \mathcal{B}_1$. We first prove by induction on the i-length of β that β is also a trace of $\mathcal{A}_2 \| \mathcal{B}_2$.

For the base case, assume that β has i-length 1. Then β consists of a single point trajectory over the empty set of variables. Axiom **T0** in the definition of a TA implies that β is a trace of $\mathcal{A}_2 \| \mathcal{B}_2$, as needed.

For the inductive step we consider the following cases.

1. $\beta = \beta' \, a \, \tau$, where a is an output action of $\mathcal{A}_1$ and τ is a point trajectory.

   Then $\beta \lceil (E_{\mathcal{A}_1}, \emptyset) \in traces_{\mathcal{A}_1}$ by projection using Theorem 8.4. By inductive hypothesis, $\beta' \in traces_{\mathcal{A}_2 \| \mathcal{B}_2}$. So $\beta' \lceil (E_{\mathcal{B}_2}, \emptyset) \in traces_{\mathcal{B}_2}$, by projection using Theorem 8.4. Let α be an execution of $\mathcal{B}_2$ such that $trace(\alpha) = \beta' \lceil (E_{\mathcal{B}_2}, \emptyset)$. Since $\mathcal{A}_1$ and $\mathcal{B}_2$ are compatible TIOAs and a is an output action of $\mathcal{A}_1$, we know that either a is an input action of $\mathcal{B}_2$ or the action set of $\mathcal{B}_2$ does not contain a. In the former case, by the input-enabling axiom (**E1**) we know that there exists $\mathbf{x}'$ such that $(\alpha.lstate, a, \mathbf{x}')$ is a discrete transition of $\mathcal{B}_2$. It follows that $\beta \lceil (E_{\mathcal{B}_2}, \emptyset) \in traces_{\mathcal{B}_2}$. In the latter case, since $\beta \lceil (E_{\mathcal{B}_2}, \emptyset) = \beta' \lceil (E_{\mathcal{B}_2}, \emptyset)$ and $\beta' \lceil (E_{\mathcal{B}_2}, \emptyset) \in traces_{\mathcal{B}_2}$ we also get $\beta \lceil (E_{\mathcal{B}_2}, \emptyset) \in traces_{\mathcal{B}_2}$. By pasting using Theorem 8.4, $\beta \in traces_{\mathcal{A}_1 \| \mathcal{B}_2}$. Then by Assumption 3, $\beta \in traces_{\mathcal{A}_2 \| \mathcal{B}_2}$.

2. $\beta = \beta' \, b \, \tau$, where b is an output action of $\mathcal{B}_1$ and τ is a point trajectory.

   This case is symmetric with the previous one.

3. $\beta = \beta' \, c \, \tau$, where c is an input action of both $\mathcal{A}_1$ and $\mathcal{B}_1$ and τ is a point trajectory.

   By inductive hypothesis, $\beta' \in traces_{\mathcal{A}_2 \| \mathcal{B}_2}$. By projection using Theorem 8.4 we get $\beta' \lceil (E_{\mathcal{A}_2}, \emptyset) \in traces_{\mathcal{A}_2}$ and $\beta' \lceil (E_{\mathcal{B}_2}, \emptyset) \in traces_{\mathcal{B}_2}$. Let α be an execution of $\mathcal{A}_2$ such that

$trace(\alpha) = \beta' \lceil (E_{\mathcal{A}_2}, \emptyset)$. Since $\mathcal{A}_1$ and $\mathcal{A}_2$ are comparable and a is an input action of $\mathcal{A}_1$ we know that a is an input action of $\mathcal{A}_2$. By the input-enabling axiom (**E1**) we know that there exists $\mathbf{x}'$ such that $(\alpha'.lstate, a, \mathbf{x}')$ is a discrete transition of $\mathcal{A}_2$. It follows that $\beta \lceil (E_{\mathcal{A}_2}, \emptyset) \in traces_{\mathcal{A}_2}$. Similarly, let α' be an execution of $\mathcal{B}_2$ such that $trace(\alpha') = \beta' \lceil (E_{\mathcal{B}_2}, \emptyset)$. Since $\mathcal{B}_1$ and $\mathcal{B}_2$ are comparable and a is an input action of $\mathcal{B}_1$ we know that a is an input action of $\mathcal{B}_2$. By the input-enabling axiom (**E1**) we know that there exists $\mathbf{y}'$ such that $(\alpha'.lstate, a, \mathbf{y}')$ is a discrete transition of $\mathcal{B}_2$. It follows that $\beta \lceil (E_{\mathcal{B}_2}, \emptyset) \in traces_{\mathcal{B}_2}$. By pasting using Theorem 8.4, we get $\beta \in traces_{\mathcal{A}_2 \| \mathcal{B}_2}$.

4. $\beta = \beta' \, d \, \tau$, where d is an input action of $\mathcal{A}_1$ but not an action of $\mathcal{B}_1$ and τ is a point trajectory.

   By inductive hypothesis, $\beta' \in traces_{\mathcal{A}_2 \| \mathcal{B}_2}$. By projection using Theorem 8.4, we have $\beta' \lceil (E_{\mathcal{A}_2}, \emptyset) \in traces_{\mathcal{A}_2}$ and $\beta' \lceil (E_{\mathcal{B}_2}, \emptyset) \in traces_{\mathcal{B}_2}$. Let α be an execution of $\mathcal{A}_2$ such that $trace(\alpha) = \beta' \lceil (E_{\mathcal{A}_2}, \emptyset)$. Since $\mathcal{A}_1$ and $\mathcal{A}_2$ are comparable TIOAs and a is an input action of $\mathcal{A}_1$, a must be an input action of $\mathcal{A}_2$. By the input-enabling axiom (**E1**) we know that there exists $\mathbf{x}'$ such that $(\alpha.lstate, a, \mathbf{x}')$ is a discrete transition of $\mathcal{A}_2$. It follows that $\beta \lceil (E_{\mathcal{A}_2}, \emptyset) \in traces_{\mathcal{A}_2}$. Since $\mathcal{B}_1$ and $\mathcal{B}_2$ are comparable and a is not an action of $\mathcal{B}_1$, a cannot be an external action of $\mathcal{B}_2$. Therefore, $\beta \lceil (E_{\mathcal{B}_2}, \emptyset) = \beta' \lceil (E_{\mathcal{B}_2}, \emptyset)$. Since $\beta' \lceil (E_{\mathcal{B}_2}, \emptyset) \in traces_{\mathcal{B}_2}$ we get $\beta \lceil (E_{\mathcal{B}_2}, \emptyset) \in traces_{\mathcal{B}_2}$. By pasting using Theorem 8.4, we get $\beta \in traces_{\mathcal{A}_2 \| \mathcal{B}_2}$.

5. $\beta = \beta' e \tau$, where e is an input action of $\mathcal{B}_1$ but not an action of $\mathcal{A}_1$ and τ is a point trajectory.

   This case is symmetric with the previous one.

6. $\beta = \beta' \frown \beta''$, where β' ends with a point trajectory and β'' is a hybrid sequence consisting of a single trajectory τ.

   By inductive hypothesis, $\beta' \in traces_{\mathcal{A}_2 \| \mathcal{B}_2}$. By projection using Theorem 8.4, we get $\beta' \lceil (E_{\mathcal{A}_2}, \emptyset) \in traces_{\mathcal{A}_2}$ and $\beta' \lceil (E_{\mathcal{B}_2}, \emptyset) \in traces_{\mathcal{B}_2}$. By Assumption 2, we have $\beta' \lceil (E_{\mathcal{A}_2}, \emptyset) \frown \beta'' \lceil (E_{\mathcal{A}_2}, \emptyset) \in traces_{\mathcal{A}_2}$ and $\beta' \lceil (E_{\mathcal{B}_2}, \emptyset) \frown \beta'' \lceil (E_{\mathcal{B}_2}, \emptyset) \in traces_{\mathcal{B}_2}$. Then by pasting using Theorem 8.4, $\beta \in traces_{\mathcal{A}_2 \| \mathcal{B}_2}$, as needed.

We have thus shown that every closed trace of $\mathcal{A}_1 \| \mathcal{B}_1$ is a trace of $\mathcal{A}_2 \| \mathcal{B}_2$. Now consider any nonclosed trace β of $\mathcal{A}_1 \| \mathcal{B}_1$. This β can be written as the limit of a sequence $\beta_1 \, \beta_2 \, \cdots$ of closed traces of $\mathcal{A}_1 \| \mathcal{B}_1$. By the first part of the proof we know that each $\beta_i \in traces_{\mathcal{A}_2 \| \mathcal{B}_2}$, and by projection using Theorem 8.4 each $\beta_i \lceil (E_{\mathcal{A}_2}, \emptyset)$ is a closed trace of $\mathcal{A}_2$, and $\beta_i \lceil (E_{\mathcal{B}_2}, \emptyset)$ is a closed trace of $\mathcal{B}_2$. Since restriction is a continuous operation (Lemma 3.8), we know that $\beta \lceil (E_{\mathcal{A}_2}, \emptyset)$ is the limit of the $\beta_i \lceil (E_{\mathcal{A}_2}, \emptyset)$ and similarly $\beta \lceil (E_{\mathcal{B}_2}, \emptyset)$ is the limit of the $\beta_i \lceil (E_{\mathcal{B}_2}, \emptyset)$. Since the sets $traces_{\mathcal{A}_2}$ and $traces_{\mathcal{B}_2}$ are limit-closed by Assumption 1, we get $\beta \lceil (E_{\mathcal{A}_2}, \emptyset) \in traces_{\mathcal{A}_2}$ and $\beta \lceil (E_{\mathcal{B}_2}, \emptyset) \in traces_{\mathcal{B}_2}$. Finally, by pasting using Theorem 8.4, we get $\beta \in traces_{\mathcal{A}_2 \| \mathcal{B}_2}$. □

Note that automata with FIN and timing-independence (see Section 4.4 for definitions) constitute examples for context automata $\mathcal{A}_2$ and $\mathcal{B}_2$ that satisfy Assumptions 1 and 2. The property FIN implies Assumption 1 (Lemma 4.20) and timing-independence implies Assumption 2.

Theorem 8.8 has a corollary, Corollary 8.9 below, which can be used in the decomposition of proofs even when $\mathcal{A}_2$ and $\mathcal{B}_2$ neither admit arbitrary time-passage nor have limit-closed trace sets. The main idea behind this corollary is to assume that $\mathcal{A}_1$ implements $\mathcal{A}_2$ in a context $\mathcal{B}_3$ that is a variant of $\mathcal{B}_2$, and symmetrically that $\mathcal{B}_1$ implements $\mathcal{B}_2$ in a context $\mathcal{A}_3$ that is a variant of $\mathcal{A}_2$. That is, the correctness of implementation relationship between $\mathcal{A}_1$ and $\mathcal{A}_2$ does not depend on all the environment constraints, just on those expressed by $\mathcal{B}_3$ (symmetrically for $\mathcal{B}_1, \mathcal{B}_2$, and $\mathcal{A}_3$). In order to use this corollary to prove $\mathcal{A}_1 \| \mathcal{B}_1 \leq \mathcal{A}_2 \| \mathcal{B}_2$, one needs to be able to find appropriate variants of $\mathcal{A}_2$ and $\mathcal{B}_2$ that meet the required closure properties. This corollary prompts one to pin down what is essential about the behavior of the environment in proving the intended implementation relationship, and also allows one to avoid the unnecessary details of the environment in proofs.

Corollary 8.9 *Suppose* $\mathcal{A}_1, \mathcal{A}_2, \mathcal{A}_3, \mathcal{B}_1, \mathcal{B}_2, \mathcal{B}_3$ *are TIOAs such that* $\mathcal{A}_1, \mathcal{A}_2$, *and* $\mathcal{A}_3$ *are comparable,* $\mathcal{B}_1, \mathcal{B}_2$, *and* $\mathcal{B}_3$ *are comparable, and* $\mathcal{A}_i$ *is compatible with* $\mathcal{B}_j$ *for* $i, j \in \{1, 2, 3\}$. *Suppose further that:*

1. *the sets* $traces_{\mathcal{A}_3}$ *and* $traces_{\mathcal{B}_3}$ *are closed under limits;*
2. *the sets* $traces_{\mathcal{A}_3}$ *and* $traces_{\mathcal{B}_3}$ *are closed under time-extension;*
3. $\mathcal{A}_2 \| \mathcal{B}_3 \leq \mathcal{A}_3 \| \mathcal{B}_3$ *and* $\mathcal{A}_3 \| \mathcal{B}_2 \leq \mathcal{A}_3 \| \mathcal{B}_3$*;*
4. $\mathcal{A}_1 \| \mathcal{B}_3 \leq \mathcal{A}_2 \| \mathcal{B}_3$ *and* $\mathcal{A}_3 \| \mathcal{B}_1 \leq \mathcal{A}_3 \| \mathcal{B}_2$.

Then, $\mathcal{A}_1 \| \mathcal{B}_1 \leq \mathcal{A}_2 \| \mathcal{B}_2$.

Proof. Since $\mathcal{A}_1 \| \mathcal{B}_3 \leq \mathcal{A}_2 \| \mathcal{B}_3$ by Assumption 4, and $\mathcal{A}_2 \| \mathcal{B}_3 \leq \mathcal{A}_3 \| \mathcal{B}_3$ by Assumption 3, we get $\mathcal{A}_1 \| \mathcal{B}_3 \leq \mathcal{A}_3 \| \mathcal{B}_3$. Similarly, we have $\mathcal{A}_3 \| \mathcal{B}_1 \leq \mathcal{A}_3 \| \mathcal{B}_2 \leq \mathcal{A}_3 \| \mathcal{B}_3$. Since $\mathcal{A}_1 \| \mathcal{B}_3 \leq \mathcal{A}_3 \| \mathcal{B}_3$ and $\mathcal{A}_3 \| \mathcal{B}_1 \leq \mathcal{A}_3 \| \mathcal{B}_3$, by using Assumptions 1 and 2, and Theorem 8.8 we have $\mathcal{A}_1 \| \mathcal{B}_1 \leq \mathcal{A}_3 \| \mathcal{B}_3$. The result then follows from Corollary 5.12. □

Example 8.10 (Using environment assumptions to prove safety). This example illustrates that, in cases where specifications $\mathcal{A}_2$ and $\mathcal{B}_2$ satisfy certain closure properties, it is possible to decompose the proof of $\mathcal{A}_1 \| \mathcal{B}_1 \leq \mathcal{A}_2 \| \mathcal{B}_2$ by using Theorem 8.8, even if it is not the case that $\mathcal{A}_1 \leq \mathcal{A}_2$ or $\mathcal{B}_1 \leq \mathcal{B}_2$.

The automata `AlternateA` and `AlternateB` in Figure 8.1 are timing-independent automata in which no consecutive outputs occur without inputs happening in between. `AlternateA` and `AlternateB` perform a handshake, outputting an alternating sequence of `a` and `b` actions when they are composed. The automata `CatchUpA` and `CatchUpB` in Figure 5.2 are timing-dependent automata that do not necessarily alternate inputs and outputs as `AlternateA` and `AlternateB`. `CatchUpA` can perform an arbitrary number of `b` actions, and can perform an `a` provided that `counta` ≤ `countb`. It allows `counta` to increase to one more than `countb`. `CatchUpB` can perform an arbitrary number of `a` actions, and can perform a `b` provided that `counta` ≥ `countb + 1`. It allows `countb` to reach `counta`. Timing constraints require each output to occur exactly one time unit after the last action.

```
automaton AlternateA
  signature
    output a, input b
  states
    myturn: Bool := true
  transitions
    output a
      pre
        myturn
      eff
        myturn := false
    input b
      eff
        myturn := true
```

```
automaton AlternateB
  signature
    input a, output b
  states
    myturn: Bool := false
  transitions
    input a
      eff
        myturn := true
    output b
      pre
        myturn
      eff
        myturn := false
```

Figure 8.1: `AlternateA` and `AlternateB`.

`CatchUpA` and `CatchUpB` perform an alternating sequence of a actions and b actions when they are composed.

Suppose that we want to prove that `CatchUpA` $\|$ `CatchUpB` $\leq$ `AlternateA` $\|$ `AlternateB`. We cannot apply the basic substituvity theorem Theorem 8.5, in particular Corollary 8.6, since the assertions `CatchUpA` $\leq$ `AlternateA` and `CatchUpB` $\leq$ `AlternateB` are not true. Consider the trace $\overline{1}$ b $\overline{1}$ a $\overline{1}$ a $\overline{1}$ of `CatchUpA`. After having performed one b and one a, `CatchUpA` can perform another a. But, this is impossible for `AlternateA` which needs an input to enable the second a. `AlternateA` and `CatchUpA` behave similarly only when put in a context that imposes alternation.

It is easy to check that `AlternateA` and `AlternateB` satisfy the closure properties required by Assumptions 1 and 2 of Theorem 8.8 and, hence can be substituted for $\mathcal{A}_2$ and $\mathcal{B}_2$ respectively. Similarly, we can easily check that Assumption 3 is satisfied if we substitute `CatchUpA` for $\mathcal{A}_1$ and `CatchUpB` for $\mathcal{B}_1$.

Example 8.11 (Extracting essential environment assumptions with auxiliary automata). This example illustrates that it may be possible to decompose verification, using Corollary 8.9, in cases where Theorem 8.8 is not applicable. If the aim is to show $\mathcal{A}_1 \| \mathcal{B}_1 \leq \mathcal{A}_2 \| \mathcal{B}_2$ where $\mathcal{A}_2$ and $\mathcal{B}_2$ do not satisfy the assumptions of Theorem 8.8, then we find appropriate context automata $\mathcal{A}_3$ and $\mathcal{B}_3$ that abstract from those details of $\mathcal{A}_2$ and $\mathcal{B}_2$ that are not essential in proving $\mathcal{A}_1 \| \mathcal{B}_1 \leq \mathcal{A}_2 \| \mathcal{B}_2$.

```
signature
  output a, input b
states
  maxout: Nat, now: Real := 0, next: AugmentedReal := 0
transitions
  output a                             input b
    pre                                  eff
      (maxout > 0) ∧ (now = next)          if next = infty
    eff                                     then next := now + 1
      maxout := maxout - 1;
      next := infty
trajectories
  stop when
    now = next
  evolve
    d(now) = 1
```

```
signature
  input a, output b
states
  maxout: Nat, now: Real := 0, next: AugmentedReal := infty
transitions
  input a                          output b
    eff                              pre
      if next = infty                  (maxout > 0) ∧ (now = next)
       then next := now + 1          eff
                                       maxout := maxout - 1;
                                       next := infty
trajectories
  stop when
    now = next
  evolve
    d(now) = 1
```

Figure 8.2: `UseOldInputA` and `UseOldInputB`.

```
signature
  output a, input b
states
  maxout: Nat, now: Real := 0, next: AugmentedReal := 0
transitions
  output a                          input b
    pre                               eff
      (maxout > 0) ∧ (now = next)       next := now + 1
    eff
      maxout := maxout - 1;
      next := infty
trajectories
  stop when
    now = next
  evolve
    d(now) = 1
```

```
signature
  input a, output b
states
  maxout: Nat, now: Real := 0, next: AugmentedReal := infty
transitions
  input a                        output b
    eff                            pre
      next := now + 1                (maxout > 0) ∧ (now = next)
                                   eff
                                     maxout := maxout - 1;
                                     next := infty
trajectories
  stop when
    now = next
  evolve
    d(now) = 1
```

Figure 8.3: `UseNewInputA` and `UseNewInputB`.

Consider the automata `UseOldInputA` and `UseOldInputB` in Figure 8.2. `UseOldInputA` keeps track of the next time it is supposed to perform an output, which may be never (`infty`). The number of outputs that `UseOldInputA` can perform is bounded by a natural number. In the case of repeated `b` inputs, it is the oldest input that determines when the next output will occur. The automaton `UseOldInputB` is the same as `UseOldInputA` (inputs and outputs reversed) except that the `next` variable of `UseOldInputB` is set to `infty` initially. Note that `UseOldInputA` and `UseOldInputA` are not timing-independent and their trace sets are not limit-closed. For each automaton, there are infinitely many start states, one for each natural number. We can build an infinite chain of traces, where each element in the chain corresponds to an execution starting from a distinct start state. The limit of such a chain, which contains infinitely many outputs, cannot be a trace of `UseOldInputA` or `UseOldInputB` since the number of outputs they can perform is bounded by a natural number. The automaton `UseNewInputA` in Figure 8.3 behaves similarly to `UseOldInputA` except for the handling of inputs. In the case of repeated `b` inputs, it is the most recent input that determines when the next output will occur. The automaton `UseNewInputB` in Figure 8.3 is the same as `UseNewInputA` (inputs and outputs reversed) except that the `next` variable of `UseNewInputB` is set to `infty` initially. Suppose that we want to prove that:

$$\texttt{UseNewInputA} \| \texttt{UseNewInputB} \leq \texttt{UseOldInputA} \| \texttt{UseOldInputB}.$$

Theorem 8.8 is not applicable here because the high-level automata `UseOldInputA` and `UseOldInputB` do not satisfy the required closure properties. However, we can use Corollary 8.9 to decompose verification. It requires us to find auxiliary automata that are less restrictive than `UseOldInputA` and `UseOldInputB` but that are restrictive enough to express the constraints that should be satisfied by the environment, for `UseNewInputA` to implement `UseOldInputA` and for `UseNewInputB` to implement `UseOldInputB`.

The automata `AlternateA` and `AlternateB` in Figure 8.1 can be used as auxiliary automata in this example. They satisfy the closure properties required by Corollary 8.9 and impose alternation, which is the only additional condition to ensure the needed trace inclusion.

We can define a forward simulation relation from `UseNewInputA` $\|$ `UseNewInputB` to `UseOldInputA` $\|$ `UseOldInputB`, which is based on the equality of the `next` $=$ `infty` predicate of the implementation and the specification automata. The fact that this simulation relation only uses the predicate `next` $=$ `infty` reinforces the idea that the auxiliary contexts, which only keep track of their turn, capture exactly what is needed for the proof of `UseNewInputA` $\|$ `UseNewInputB` $\leq$ `UseOldInputA` $\|$ `UseOldInputB`. We can observe that a direct proof of this assertion would require one to deal with state variables such as `maxout` and `next` of both `UseOldInputA` and `UseOldInputB` which do not play any essential role in the proof. On the other hand, by decomposing the proof along the lines of Corollary 8.9 some of the unnecessary details can be avoided. Even though, this is a toy example with an easy proof it should not be hard to observe how this simplification would scale to large proofs.

8.1.3 COMPOSITION OF SPECIAL KINDS OF TIOAS

The following example illustrates that the set of I/O feasible TIOAs is not closed under composition:

Example 8.12 (Two I/O feasible TIOAs whose composition is not I/O feasible). Consider two I/O feasible TIOAs $\mathcal{A}$ and $\mathcal{B}$, where $O_{\mathcal{A}} = I_{\mathcal{B}} = \{a\}$ and $O_{\mathcal{B}} = I_{\mathcal{A}} = \{b\}$. Suppose that $\mathcal{A}$ performs its output a at time 0 and then waits, allowing time to pass, until it receives input b. If and when it receives b, it responds with output a without allowing any time to pass (and ignoring any inputs that occur before it has a chance to perform its output). On the other hand, $\mathcal{B}$ starts out waiting, allowing time to pass, until it receives input a. If and when it receives a, it responds with output b without allowing time to pass.

It is not difficult to see that $\mathcal{A}$ and $\mathcal{B}$ are individually I/O feasible. We claim that the composition $\mathcal{A}\|\mathcal{B}$ is not I/O feasible. To see this, consider the start state of $\mathcal{A}\|\mathcal{B}$ and the unique input sequence β with $\beta.\mathit{ltime} = \infty$; β simply allows time to pass to infinity. The composition $\mathcal{A}\|\mathcal{B}$ has no way of accommodating this input, since it will never allow time to pass beyond 0.

In contrast to this, the classes of progressive and receptive TIOAs are closed under composition:

Theorem 8.13 *If $\mathcal{A}_1$ and $\mathcal{A}_2$ are compatible progressive TIOAs, then their composition is also progressive.*

Proof. The proof is similar to the proof of Theorem 7.4 in [79]. The main idea behind the proof is that a Zeno execution of $\mathcal{A}_1 \| \mathcal{A}_2$ with infinitely many locally controlled actions contains infinitely many locally controlled actions of either $\mathcal{A}_1$ or $\mathcal{A}_2$. Suppose without loss of generality that the automaton that contributes infinitely many locally controlled actions is $\mathcal{A}_1$. Then the projection onto $\mathcal{A}_1$ violates progressiveness for $\mathcal{A}_1$. □

Theorem 8.14 *Let $\mathcal{A}_1$ and $\mathcal{A}_2$ be two compatible TIOAs with strategies $\mathcal{A}'_1$ and $\mathcal{A}'_2$, respectively. Then $\mathcal{A}'_1 \| \mathcal{A}'_2$ is a strategy for $\mathcal{A}_1 \| \mathcal{A}_2$.*

Proof. The proof is similar to the proof of Theorem 7.7 in [79]. Since $\mathcal{A}_1$ and $\mathcal{A}_2$ are compatible and a strategy for a TIOA has the same signature as this TIOA, $\mathcal{A}'_1$ and $\mathcal{A}'_2$ are also compatible. Hence, by Theorem 8.2, $\mathcal{A}'_1 \| \mathcal{A}'_2$ is a TIOA. Let $\mathcal{A}$ denote $\mathcal{A}_1 \| \mathcal{A}_2$ and let $\mathcal{A}'$ denote $\mathcal{A}'_1 \| \mathcal{A}'_2$. From the definition of composition and strategy, $\mathcal{A}'$ differs from $\mathcal{A}$ only in that $\mathcal{D}' \subseteq \mathcal{D}$ and $\mathcal{T}' \subseteq \mathcal{T}$. Then the definition of strategy implies that $\mathcal{A}'$ is a strategy for $\mathcal{A}$. □

Now, we can state the main result of this section, which follows easily from the previous two theorems. It shows that the class of receptive TIOAs is closed under composition.

Theorem 8.15 *Let $\mathcal{A}_1$ and $\mathcal{A}_2$ be compatible receptive TIOAs with progressive strategies $\mathcal{A}'_1$ and $\mathcal{A}'_2$, respectively. Then $\mathcal{A}_1 \| \mathcal{A}_2$ is a receptive TIOA with progressive strategy $\mathcal{A}'_1 \| \mathcal{A}'_2$.*

Example 8.16 (Composition of receptive TIOAs). Theorem 8.15 implies that the composition of clock synchronization automata with channel automata described in Example 5.8 (viewed as TIOAs as explained in Example 7.1) is receptive. Since by Theorem 7.6 any receptive TIOA is I/O feasible, we also have that it is I/O feasible.

Actually, the fact that the set of I/O feasible TIOAs is not closed under composition motivated the definition of the more restrictive class of receptive TIOAs. That is, receptiveness is a reasonable sufficient condition that implies I/O feasibility, and that also is preserved by composition.

The special case of the HIOA model, represented by the TIOA model, has simpler and stronger composition theorems than the general HIOA model. In particular, the main compositionality result for receptive HIOAs (Theorem 7.12 in [79]) has a more intricate proof than ours. It makes an assumption about the existence of strongly compatible strategies (discussed briefly at the end of Section 8.1.1) and needs an additional lemma that shows that if two HIOAs $\mathcal{A}_1$ and $\mathcal{A}_2$ have strongly compatible strategies $\mathcal{A}'_1$ and $\mathcal{A}'_2$, then $\mathcal{A}_1$ and $\mathcal{A}_2$ are also strongly compatible.

8.2 HIDING

We extend the definition of action hiding to any TIOA $\mathcal{A}$. For TIOAs, we consider hiding outputs only (but not inputs), by converting them to internal actions. Namely, if $\mathcal{A} = (\mathcal{B}, I, O)$ is a TIOA and $O' \subseteq O$, then

$$\mathsf{ActHide}(O', \mathcal{A}) \quad = \quad (\mathsf{ActHide}(O', \mathcal{B}), I, O - O').$$

It is immediate from the definitions that hiding is a well-defined operation on TIOAs.

Lemma 8.17 *If $\mathcal{A} = (\mathcal{B}, I, O)$ is a TIOA and $O' \subseteq O$ then $\mathsf{ActHide}(O', \mathcal{A})$ is a TIOA.*

Using the corresponding result for TAs (Theorem 5.17), it is straightforward to establish that the hiding operation on TIOAs respects the implementation relation.

Theorem 8.18 *Suppose $\mathcal{A}_1$ and $\mathcal{A}_2$ are comparable TIOAs with $\mathcal{A}_1 \leq \mathcal{A}_2$, and suppose $O \subseteq O_1$. Then $\mathsf{ActHide}(O, \mathcal{A}_1) \leq \mathsf{ActHide}(O, \mathcal{A}_2)$.*

CHAPTER 9

Conclusions and Future Work

In this book, we presented the TIOA mathematical framework for describing and analyzing the behavior of timed systems and timed distributed algorithms. The TIOA framework is a special case of the Hybrid I/O Automaton modeling framework [79].

Designers of real-time systems or timing-based algorithms can use the TIOA framework to describe their systems and to decompose them into manageable pieces. In particular, they can describe their systems at multiple levels of abstraction, establish implementation relationships among these levels, and decompose their systems into more primitive, interacting components. Many timed systems and timed distributed algorithms have already been modeled and analyzed using TIOA, including systems for vehicle and air-traffic control, communication, and mobile robotics, and algorithms for implementing atomic memory, synchronizing clocks, and implementing applications in mobile wireless networks.

Although the framework presented here provides only conceptual tools for modeling, and manual proof methods, it also is a natural basis for building computerized modeling and analysis tools. The Tempo language and toolset [51] provides basic tool support for TIOA.

The TIOA framework does not include any facilities for modeling probabilistic behavior. A probabilistic extension of TIOA, PTIOA, was recently developed by Mitra and co-workers [94, 95]. In PTIOA, randomness appears in the form of random choices of the target states of discrete transitions. As in other probabilistic models, subtleties arise because of the interplay between nondeterministic and probabilistic choice: in order to define probability distributions on executions and traces, some mechanism is needed for resolving the nondeterministic choices. PTIOA uses an oblivious scheduler mechanism. PTIOA includes facilities for composition and abstraction based on those in TIOA. The PTIOA framework borrows many ideas from an earlier Probabilistic Timed Automaton modeling framework of Segala [106].

The earliest version of this work [58] included additional material, such as: (a) notions of fairness for timed I/O automata, and results that state conditions under which the "fair" traces of one TIOA must be included among the fair traces of another; (b) a TIOA version of a region construction that is sometimes used for model-checking other types of timed automata models. We have not included this material here, since it has not yet been tested adequately on interesting examples.

A great deal of interesting future work remains. First, on the theoretical side, we would like to have a general, unified input/output automaton modeling framework, extending the TIOA Automaton framework, which incorporates timed, hybrid, and probabilistic behavior. The probabilistic behavior might include continuous random choice during trajectories, rather than just probabilistic choice during discrete transitions. Such a unified framework would allow system and algorithm designers to model systems with a combination of timing-dependent, hybrid, and probabilistic behavior. An example of an application domain that could benefit from such a general framework is robot motion coordination.

Second, and also theoretically, work remains in relating our framework formally to others that are comparable, such as [91, 107, 87, 86, 7, 88].

Third, many more systems and algorithms can be modeled and analyzed using TIOAs. Especially promising application domains include wireless networks, embedded systems, and mobile robotics. TIOAs are particularly useful for modeling mobile systems, because they provide natural facilities for modeling the behavior of physical system components (e.g., the motion of vehicles or robots), as well as that of the software.

Fourth, and finally, more and better tools for analyzing TIOA descriptions would be most welcome. The Tempo system uses a programmer-friendly plug-in architecture that should make it easy for a tool developer to integrate new analysis tools, with new capabilities, into the current basic system.

Bibliography

[1] M. Abadi and L. Lamport. Composing specifications. *ACM Transactions on Programming Languages and Systems*, 1(15):73–132, 1993. DOI: 10.1145/151646.151649 88, 89, 93

[2] M. Abadi and L. Lamport. Conjoining specifications. *ACM Transactions on Programming Languages and Systems*, 17(3):507–534, 1995. DOI: 10.1145/203095.201069 93

[3] B. Alpern and F. B. Schneider. Defining liveness. *Information Processing Letters*, 21:181–185, 1985. DOI: 10.1016/0020-0190(85)90056-0 77, 79

[4] R. Alur. *Techniques for Automatic Verification of Real-Time Systems*. PhD thesis, Stanford University, 1991. 6

[5] R. Alur. Timed automata. In *Proceedings of 11th International Conference on Computer-Aided Verification (CAV)*, volume 1633 of *Lecture Notes in Computer Science*, pages 8–22. Springer-Verlag, 1999. An earlier and longer version appears in NATO-ASI Summer School on Verification of Digital and Hybrid Systems, 1998. DOI: 10.1007/3-540-48683-6_3 5

[6] R. Alur, C. Courcoubetis, N. Halbwachs, T. A. Henzinger, P. H. Ho, X. Nicolin, A. Olivero, J. Sifakis, and Yovine S. The algorithmic analysis of hybrid systems. *Theoretical Computer Science*, 138:3–34, 1995. DOI: 10.1016/0304-3975(94)00202-T 5, 42

[7] R. Alur and D.L. Dill. A theory of timed automata. *Theoretical Computer Science*, 126:183–235, 1994. DOI: 10.1016/0304-3975(94)90010-8 4, 5, 104

[8] R. Alur, S. La Torre, and P. Madhusudan. Perturbed timed automata. In *Proceedings of the Eighth International Workshop on Hybrid Systems: Computation and Control (HSCC)*, Zurich, Zwitserland, volume 3414 of *Lecture Notes in Computer Science*, pages 70–85. Springer-Verlag, 2005. 5

[9] C. Baier and J.-P. Katoen. *Principles of Model Checking*. MIT Press, Cambridge, Massachusetts, 2008. 77, 79

[10] J. Berendsen, B. Gebremichael, F.W. Vaandrager, and M. Zhang. Formal specification and analysis of zeroconf using Uppaal. *ACM Transactions on Embedded Computing Systems*, 10(3), 2011. To appear. 6

[11] J. Berendsen and F.W. Vaandrager. Compositional abstraction in real-time model checking. In *Proceedings Sixth International Conference on Formal Modeling and Analysis of Timed*

Systems (FORMATS 2008), September 15-17, 2008, Saint-Malo, France, volume 5215 of *Lecture Notes in Computer Science*, pages 233–249. Springer Berlin / Heidelberg, 2008. Full version available as Technical Report ICIS–R07027, Radboud University Nijmegen, 2007. DOI: 10.1007/978-3-540-85778-5_17 6

[12] S. Bornot and J. Sifakis. An algebraic framework for urgency. *Information and Computation*, 163:172–202, 2000. DOI: 10.1006/inco.2000.2999 85

[13] P. Bouyer, C. Dufourd, E. Fleury, and A. Petit. Updatable timed automata. *Theor. Comput. Sci.*, 321(2-3):291–345, 2004. DOI: 10.1016/j.tcs.2004.04.003 5

[14] H. Bowman. Modelling timeouts without timelocks. In J.-P. Katoen, Ed., *ARTS'99, 5th International AMAST Workshop on Real-time and Probabilistic Systems*, volume 1601 of *Lecture Notes in Computer Science*, pages 334–353. Springer, May 1999. 85

[15] M. Bozga, S. Graf, Il. Ober, Iul. Ober, and J. Sifakis. The IF toolset. In *Proceedings of Formal Methods for the Design of Real-Time Systems*, volume 3185 of *Lecture Notes in Computer Science*, pages 237–267. Springer-Verlag, September 2004. DOI: 10.1007/978-3-540-30080-9_8 6

[16] M. Brown. Air traffic control using virtual stationary automata. Master of Engineering Thesis, Department of Electrical Engineering and Computer Science, Massachusetts Institute of Technology, Cambridge, MA, September 2007. 5

[17] F. Cassez, A. David, E. Fleury, K.G. Larsen, and D. Lime. Efficient on-the-fly algorithms for the analysis of timed games. In Martín Abadi and Luca de Alfaro, Eds., *CONCUR 2005 - Concurrency Theory, 16th International Conference, CONCUR 2005, San Francisco, CA, USA, August 23-26, 2005, Proceedings*, volume 3653 of *Lecture Notes in Computer Science*, pages 66–80. Springer, 2005. 6, 89

[18] F. Cassez and K.G. Larsen. The impressive power of stopwatches. In C. Palamidessi, Ed., *CONCUR 2000 - Concurrency Theory, 11th International Conference, University Park, PA, USA, August 22-25, 2000, Proceedings*, volume 1877 of *Lecture Notes in Computer Science*, pages 138–152. Springer, 2000. 5

[19] Gregory Chockler, Seth Gilbert, and Nancy Lynch. Virtual infrastructure for collision-prone wireless networks. In *Proceedings of the 27th Symposium on Principles of Distributed Computing (PODC 2008)*, pages 233–242, Toronto, Canada, August 2008. DOI: 10.1145/1400751.1400783 5

[20] Gregory Chockler, Nancy Lynch, Sayan Mitra, and Joshua Tauber. Proving atomicity: An assertional approach. In Pierre Fraigniaud, Ed., *Distributed Computing, 19th International Conference (DISC 2006), Cracow, Poland, September 2005*, volume 3724 of *Lecture Notes in Computer Science*, pages 152–168. Springer, 2005. 5

[21] Alexandre David, Kim G. Larsen, Axel Legay, Ulrik Nyman, and Andrzej Wasowski. Timed I/O automata: a complete specification theory for real-time systems. In Karl Henrik Johansson and Wang Yi, Eds., *Proceedings of the 13th ACM International Conference on Hybrid Systems: Computation and Control, HSCC 2010, Stockholm, Sweden, April 12-15, 2010*, pages 91–100. ACM, 2010. DOI: 10.1145/1755952 6

[22] C. Daws, A. Olivero, S. Tripakis, and S. Yovine. The tool Kronos. In *Proceedings of Hybrid Systems III, Verification and Control*, volume 1066 of *Lecture Notes in Computer Science*, pages 208–219. Springer-Verlag, 1996. DOI: 10.1007/BFb0020947 6

[23] R. DePrisco, B. Lampson, and Nancy Lynch. Revisiting the Paxos algorithm. In M. Mavronicolas and P. Tsigas, Eds., *Distributed Algorithms* Proceedings of the 11th International Workshop, WDAG'97, Saarbrücken, Germany, September 1997, volume 1320 of *Lecture Notes in Computer Science*, pages 111–125. Springer-Verlag, 1997. 4, 6, 7

[24] D. Dill. *Trace Theory for Automatic Hierarchical Verification of Speed-Independent Circuits*. ACM Distinguished Dissertations. MIT Press, Cambridge, MA, 1988. 88, 89

[25] Shlomi Dolev, Seth Gilbert, Limor Lahiani, Nancy Lynch, and Tina Nolte. Brief announcement: Virtual stationary automata for mobile networks. In *Proceedings of the 24th Annual ACM Symposium on Principles of Distributed Computing (PODC 2005)*, Las Vegas, NV, July 2005. DOI: 10.1145/1073814.1073876 5

[26] Shlomi Dolev, Limor Lahiani, Nancy Lynch, and Tina Nolte. Self-stabilizing mobile node location management and message routing. In Sebastien Tixeuil Ted Herman, Ed., *Self-Stabilizing Systems: Seventh International Symposium on Self-Stabilizing Systems (SSS 2005), Barcelona, Spain, October 26-27*, volume 3764 of *Lecture Notes in Computer Science*, pages 96–112. Springer, 2005. Also, Technical Report MIT-LCS-TR-999, MIT Computer Science and Artificial Intelligence Laboratory, Cambridge, MA, August 2005. 5

[27] Ekaterina Dolginova and Nancy Lynch. Safety verification for automated platoon maneuvers: A case study. In Oded Maler, Ed., *Hybrid and Real-Time Systems: International Workshop, (HART 1997), Grenoble, France, March 1997*, volume 1201 of *Lecture Notes in Computer Science*, pages 154–170. Springer-Verlag, 1997. 4

[28] Rui Fan, Indraneel Chakraborty, and Nancy Lynch. Clock synchronization for wireless networks. In Teruo Higashino, Ed., *Principles of Distributed Systems: 8th International Conference on Principles of Distributed Systems (OPODIS 2004), Grenoble, France, December 15-17, 2004*, volume 3544 of *Lecture Notes in Computer Science*, pages 400–414. Springer, 2005. 5

[29] Rui Fan, Ralph Droms, Nancy Griffeth, and Nancy Lynch. The DHCP failover protocol: A formal perspective. In *27th IFIP WG 6.1 International Conference on Formal Methods for Networked and Distributed Systems (FORTE 2007), Tallinn, Estonia, June 26-29,*

2007, volume 4574 of *Lecture Notes in Computer Science*, pages 211–226. Springer, 2007. DOI: 10.1007/978-3-540-73196-2_14 5

[30] Rui Fan and Nancy Lynch. Gradient clock synchronization. *Distributed Computing*, 18(4):255–266, November 2006. DOI: 10.1007/s00446-005-0135-6 5

[31] Goran Frehse. *Compositional Verification of Hybrid Systems using Simulation Relations*. PhD thesis, Radboud University Nijmegen, October 2005. 93

[32] S. Garland. TIOA user guide and reference manual, September 2005. Available through URL `http://theory.csail.mit.edu/tds/reflist.html`. 4, 25

[33] S. Garland, D. Kaynar, N. A. Lynch, J. Tauber, and M. Vaziri. TIOA tutorial, May 2005. Available through URL `http://theory.csail.mit.edu/tds/reflist.html`. 4, 25

[34] S. Garland and N. A. Lynch. Using I/O automata for developing distributed systems. In Gary T. Leavens and Murali Sitaraman, Ed., *Foundations of Component-Based Systems*, chapter 13, pages 285–312. Cambridge University Press, New York, 2000. 1

[35] S. Garland, Nancy Lynch, and M. Vaziri. *IOA: A Language for Specifying, Programming, and Validating Distributed Systems*. MIT Laboratory for Computer Science, Cambridge, MA, 2001. URL `http://theory.lcs.mit.edu/tds/ioa.html`. 4

[36] R. Gawlick, R. Segala, J. F. Søgaard-Andersen, and Nancy Lynch. Liveness in timed and untimed systems. In S. Abiteboul and E. Shamir, Eds., *Proceedings* 21th *ICALP*, Jerusalem, volume 820 of *Lecture Notes in Computer Science*. Springer-Verlag, 1994. A full version appears as MIT Technical Report number MIT/LCS/TR-587. 40

[37] Seth Gilbert. *Virtual Infrastructure for Wireless Ad Hoc Networks*. PhD thesis, Department of Electrical Engineering and Computer Science, Massachusetts Institute of Technology, Cambridge, MA, 2007. 58

[38] Seth Gilbert and Nancy Lynch. Brewer's conjecture and the feasibility of consistent, available, partition-tolerant web services. *ACM Sigact News*, 33(2):48–51, June 2002. DOI: 10.1145/564585.564601 5

[39] Seth Gilbert, Nancy Lynch, Sayan Mitra, and Tina Nolte. Self-stabilizing mobile robot formations with virtual nodes. In Sandeep S. Kulkarni and Andre Schiper, Eds., *Stabilization, Safety and Security of Distributed Systems, 10th International Symposium (SSS 2008), Detroit, Michigan, November 2008*, volume 5340 of *Lecture Notes in Computer Science*, pages 188–202. Springer, 2008. DOI: 10.1007/978-3-540-89335-6 5

[40] Seth Gilbert, Nancy Lynch, Sayan Mitra, and Tina Nolte. Self-stabilizing robot formations over unreliable networks. *ACM Transactions on Autonomous and Adaptive Systems*, 4(3), 2009. DOI: 10.1145/1552297.1552300 5

[41] Seth Gilbert, Nancy Lynch, and Alex Shvartsman. RAMBO II: Rapidly reconfigurable atomic memory for dynamic networks. In *International Conference on Dependable Systems and Networks (DSN 2003)*, pages 259–268, San Francisco, CA, June 2003. DOI: 10.1109/DSN.2003.1209936 5

[42] C. A. Gunter. *Semantics of Programming Languages: Structures and Techniques.* MIT Press, Cambridge, MA, 1992. 10

[43] Vida Uyen Ha. Verification of an attitude control system. Bachelor of Science and Master of Engineering, Department of Electrical Engineering and Computer Science, Massachusetts Institute of Technology, Cambridge, MA, May 2003. 4

[44] C. Heitmeyer and Nancy Lynch. The generalized railroad crossing: A case study in formal verification of a real-time system. In *Proceedings of the 15th IEEE Real-Time Systems Symposium*, pages 120–131, 1994. DOI: 10.1109/REAL.1994.342724 4

[45] M. Hennessy. *Algebraic Theory of Processes.* MIT Press, Cambridge, MA, 1988. 10

[46] T. Henzinger, X. Nicollin, J. Sifakis, and S. Yovine. Symbolic model-checking for real-time systems. *Information and Computation*, 111(2):193–244, 1994. DOI: 10.1006/inco.1994.1045 6

[47] T. A. Henzinger, P.-H. Ho, and H. Wong-Toi. HyTech: A Model Checker for Hybrid Systems. In O. Grumberg, Ed., em Proceedings of the 9th International Conference on Computer Aided Verification, volume 1254 of *Lecture Notes in Computer Science*, pages 460–463. Springer-Verlag, 1997. 6

[48] T. A. Henzinger, S. Qadeer, and S. K. Rajamani. Decomposing refinement proofs using assume-guarantee reasoning. In *Proceedings of the International Conference on Computer-Aided Design (ICCAD)*, pages 245–252. IEEE Computer Society Press, 2000. DOI: 10.1109/ICCAD.2000.896481 93

[49] T.A. Henzinger. Sooner is safer than later. *Information Processing Letters*, 43:135–141, 1992. DOI: 10.1016/0020-0190(92)90005-G 82

[50] Thomas A. Henzinger, Peter W. Kopke, Anuj Puri, and Pravin Varaiya. What's decidable about hybrid automata? *J. Comput. Syst. Sci.*, 57(1):94–124, 1998. DOI: 10.1006/jcss.1998.1581 5

[51] VeroModo Inc. `http://www.veromodo.com`. 4, 103

[52] C. B. Jones. Specification and design of parallel programs. In R. E. A. Mason, Ed., *Information Processing 83: Proceedings of the IFIP 9th World Congress*, pages 321–332. North-Holland, 1983. 93

[53] B. Jonsson. Modular verification of asynchronous networks. In *Proceedings of the* 6th *Annual ACM Symposium on Principles of Distributed Computing*, pages 152–166, August 1987. DOI: 10.1145/41840.41853 3, 85

[54] Bengt Jonsson. Compositional specification and verification of distributed systems. *ACM Trans. Program. Lang. Syst.*, 16(2):259–303, 1994. DOI: 10.1145/174662.174665 3, 85

[55] D. Kaynar and N. A. Lynch. Decomposing verification of timed I/O automata. In Y. Lakhnech and S. Yovine, Eds., *Proceedings Joint International Conferences on Formal Modelling and Analysis of Timed Systems, FORMATS 2004 and Formal Techniques in Real-Time and Fault-Tolerant Systems, FTRTFT 2004,* Grenoble, France, September 22-24, 2004, volume 3253 of *Lecture Notes in Computer Science*, pages 84–101. Springer, 2004. 93

[56] D. Kaynar, N. A. Lynch, S. Mitra, and S. Garland. The TIOA language, May 2005. Available through URL `http://theory.csail.mit.edu/tds/reflist.html`. 4, 25

[57] Dilsun K. Kaynar, Nancy Lynch, and Sayan Mitra. Specifying and proving timing properties with TIOA tools. In *Proceedings of the 5th IEEE International Real-Time Systems Symposium, Work in Progress Session (RTSS WIP)*, pages 96–99, Lisbon, Portugal, December 2004. 3, 4

[58] Dilsun K. Kaynar, Nancy Lynch, Roberto Segala, and Frits Vaandrager. The theory of timed I/O automata. Technical Report MIT-LCS-TR-917a, MIT Laboratory for Computer Science, 2004. Available online at `http://theory.csail.mit.edu/tds/reflist.html`. 7, 103

[59] Dilsun K. Kaynar, Nancy Lynch, Roberto Segala, and Frits Vaandrager. *The Theory of Timed I/O Automata.* Synthesis Lectures on Computer Science. Morgan-Claypool Publishers, May 2006. Also, revised and shortened version of Technical Report MIT-LCS-TR-917a (from 2004), MIT Laboratory for Computer Science, Cambridge, MA. DOI: 10.2200/S00006ED1V01Y200508CSL001 7

[60] D. E. Knuth. *Fundamental Algorithms*, volume 1 of *The Art of Computer Programming*. Addision-Wesley, Reading, MA, second edition, 1973. 11

[61] Fabian Kuhn, Thomas Locher, and Rotem Oshman. Gradient clock synchronization in dynamic networks. In *Proceedings of the ACM Symposium on Parallelism in Algorithms and Architectures (SPAA)*, Calgary, Alberta, Canada, August 2009. To appear. DOI: 10.1145/1583991.1584059 5

[62] Fabian Kuhn, Nancy Lynch, and Calvin Newport. The abstract MAC layer. Technical Report MIT-CSAIL-TR-2009-021, MIT CSAIL, Cambridge, MA, May 2009. Earlier version as Technical Report MIT-CSAIL-TR-2009-009, MIT CSAIL, Cambridge, MA, February 2009. 5

[63] Fabian Kuhn and Rotem Oshman. Gradient clock synchronization using reference broadcasts. Submitted for publication. DOI: 10.1007/978-3-642-10877-8_17 5

[64] Gerardo Lafferriere, George J. Pappas, and Sergio Yovine. A new class of decidable hybrid systems. In Frits W. Vaandrager and Jan H. van Schuppen, Eds., *Hybrid Systems: Computation and Control, Second International Workshop, HSCC'99, Berg en Dal, The Netherlands, March 29-31, 1999, Proceedings*, volume 1569 of *Lecture Notes in Computer Science*, pages 137–151. Springer, 1999. 5

[65] L. Lamport. The temporal logic of actions. *ACM Transactions on Programming Languages and Systems*, 16(3):872–923, May 1994. DOI: 10.1145/177492.177726 82

[66] K. G. Larsen, P. Pettersson, and W. Yi. Uppaal in a nutshell. *Journal of Software Tools for Technology Transfer*, 1–2:134–152, 1997. DOI: 10.1007/s100090050010 4, 5

[67] K. G. Larsen and W. Yi. Time abstracted bisimulation: Implicit specifications and decidability. In S.D. Brookes, M.G. Main, A. Melton, M.W. Mislove, and D.A. Schmidt, Eds., *Mathematical Foundations of Programming Semantics, 9th International Conference, New Orleans, LA, USA, April 7-10, 1993, Proceedings*, volume 802 of *Lecture Notes in Computer Science*, pages 160–176. Springer, 1993. 42

[68] C. Livadas, J. Lygeros, and N. A. Lynch. High-level modeling and analysis of TCAS. In *Proceedings of the 20th IEEE Real-Time Systems Symposium*, pages 115–125, 1999. DOI: 10.1109/REAL.1999.818833 4

[69] Carl Livadas and Idit Keidar. Caching-enhanced scalable reliable multicast. In *International Conference on Dependable Systems and Networks (DSN)*, pages 253–264, Florence, Italy, June-July 2004. DOI: 10.1109/DSN.2004.1311895 5

[70] Carl Livadas, John Lygeros, and Nancy Lynch. High-level modeling and analysis of the traffic alert and collision avoidance system (TCAS). *Proceedings of IEEE, Special Issue on Hybrid Systems: Theory and Applications*, 88(7):926–948, July 2000. DOI: 10.1109/5.871302 4

[71] Carolos Livadas, Idit Keidar, and Nancy A. Lynch. Designing a caching-based reliable multicast protocol. In *Proceedings of the International Conference on Dependable Systems and Networks (DSN 2001) Fast Abstracts Supplement*, pages B44–B45, Gothenburg, Sweden, July 2001. 5

[72] Carolos Livadas and Nancy A. Lynch. Formal verification of safety-critical hybrid systems. In S. Sastry and T.A. Henzinger, Eds., *Hybrid Systems: Computation and Control. First International Workshop (HSCC 1998), Berkeley, CA, USA, April, 1998*, volume 1386 of *Lecture Notes in Computer Science*, pages 253–272. Springer Verlag, 1998. 4

[73] Carolos Livadas and Nancy A. Lynch. A formal venture into reliable multicast territory. In Moshe Y. Vardi Doron Peled, Ed., em Formal Techniques for Networked and Distributed Systems: Proceedings of the 22nd IFIP WG 6.1 International Conference (FORTE 2002), Houston, Texas, USA, November 11-14, 2002, volume 2529 of *Lecture Notes in Computer Science*, pages 146–161. Springer, 2002. Also, Technical Report MIT-LCS-TR-868, MIT Laboratory for Computer Science, Cambridge, MA, November 2002. 5

[74] John Lygeros and Nancy Lynch. Strings of vehicles: Modeling and safety conditions. In S. Sastry and T.A. Henzinger, Eds., *Hybrid Systems: Computation and Control. First International Workshop (HSCC 1998), Berkeley, CA, USA, April, 1998*, volume 1386 of *Lecture Notes in Computer Science*, pages 273–288. Springer Verlag, 1998. 4

[75] N. A. Lynch and A. Shvartsman. RAMBO: A reconfigurable atomic memory service for dynamic networks. In D. Malkhi, Ed., *Distributed Computing, Proceedings of the 16th International Symposium on DIStributed Computing (DISC), Toulouse, France, October 2002*, volume 2508 of *Lecture Notes in Computer Science*, pages 173–190. Springer-Verlag, 2002. Also, Technical Report MIT-LCS-TR-856. 7

[76] Nancy Lynch. *Distributed Algorithms*. Morgan Kaufmann Publishers, Inc., San Fransisco, CA, 1996. 3, 85

[77] Nancy Lynch. A three-level analysis of a simple acceleration maneuver, with uncertainties. In *Real-Time Systems: Modeling, Design, and Applications*, volume 8 of *AMAST Series in Computing*. World Scientific Publishing Company, 2005. DOI: 10.1142/9789812708472_0016 4

[78] Nancy Lynch, Sayan Mitra, and Tina Nolte. Motion coordination using virtual nodes. In *Forty-Fourth IEEE Conference on Decision and Control and European Control Conference (CDC-ECC 2005)*, Seville, Spain, December 2005. DOI: 10.1109/CDC.2005.1582591 5

[79] Nancy Lynch, Roberto Segala, and Frits Vaandrager. Hybrid I/O automata. *Information and Computation*, 185(1):105–157, 2003. DOI: 10.1016/S0890-5401(03)00067-1 3, 13, 24, 57, 58, 85, 88, 92, 101, 102, 103

[80] Nancy Lynch, Roberto Segala, Frits Vaandrager, and H. B. Weinberg. Hybrid I/O automata. In R. Alur, T. A. Henzinger, and E. D. Sontag, Eds., *Hybrid Systems III*, volume 1066 of *Lecture Notes in Computer Science*, pages 496–510. Springer-Verlag, 1996. 40

[81] Nancy Lynch, Roberto Segala, Frits Vaandrager, and H. B. Weinberg. Hybrid I/O automata. Report CSI-R9907, Computing Science Institute, University of Nijmegen, April 1999. DOI: 10.1007/BFb0020971 40, 88, 89

[82] Nancy Lynch and Alex Shvartsman. RAMBO: A reconfigurable atomic memory service for dynamic networks. In D. Malkhi, Ed., *Distributed Computing: Proceedings of the 16th*

International Symposium on DIStributed Computing (DISC 2002), Toulouse, France, October 2002, volume 2508 of *Lecture Notes in Computer Science*, pages 173–190. Springer-Verlag, 2002. Also, Technical Report MIT-LCS-TR-856, MIT Laboratory for Computer Science, Cambridge, MA. 5

[83] Nancy Lynch and Mark Tuttle. Hierarchical correctness proofs for distributed algorithms. In *Proceedings of the 6th Annual ACM Symposium on Principles of Distributed Computing*, pages 137–151, August 1987. A full version is available as MIT Technical Report MIT/LCS/TR-387. DOI: 10.1145/41840.41852 3, 85

[84] Nancy Lynch and Mark Tuttle. An introduction to input/output automata. *CWI Quarterly*, 2(3):219–246, September 1989. 3, 85

[85] Nancy Lynch and Frits Vaandrager. Forward and backward simulations, I: Untimed systems. *Information and Computation*, 121(2):214–233, September 1995. DOI: 10.1006/inco.1995.1134 52

[86] Nancy Lynch and Frits Vaandrager. Action transducers and timed automata. *Formal Aspects of Computing*, 8(5):499–538, 1996. DOI: 10.1007/BF01211907 4, 24, 34, 40, 104

[87] Nancy Lynch and Frits Vaandrager. Forward and backward simulations — Part II: Timing-based systems. *Information and Computation*, 128(1):1–25, July 1996. DOI: 10.1006/inco.1996.0060 4, 52, 104

[88] O. Maler, Z. Manna, and A. Pnueli. From timed to hybrid systems. In J. W. de Bakker, C. Huizing, W. P. de Roever, and G. Rozenberg, Ed., *Proceedings REX Workshop on Real-Time: Theory in Practice,* Mook, The Netherlands, June 1991, volume 600 of *Lecture Notes in Computer Science*, pages 447–484. Springer-Verlag, 1992. 4, 6, 14, 68, 104

[89] O. Maler, A. Pnueli, and J. Sifakis. On the synthesis of discrete controllers for timed systems. In E.W. Mayr and C. Puech, Eds., *Proceedings STACS'95*, volume 900 of *Lecture Notes in Computer Science*, pages 229–242. Springer-Verlag, 1995. 89

[90] Z. Manna and A. Pnueli. *Temporal Verification of Reactive Systems: Safety.* Springer-Verlag, 1995. 36, 38

[91] M. Merritt, F. Modugno, and M. Tuttle. Time constrained automata. In J. C. M. Baeten and J. F. Groote, Eds., *Proceedings CONCUR 91,* Amsterdam, volume 527 of *Lecture Notes in Computer Science*, pages 408–423. Springer-Verlag, 1991. 4, 6, 68, 104

[92] R. Milner. *A Calculus of Communicating Systems*, volume 92 of *Lecture Notes in Computer Science*. Springer-Verlag, 1980. 5

[93] S. Mitra, Y. Wang, N. A. Lynch, and E. Feron. Safety verification of model helicopter controller using hybrid input/output automata. In O. Maler and A. Pnueli, Eds., *Proceedings of Hybrid Systems: Computation and Control,* Prague, the Czech Republic April 3-5, volume 2623 of *Lecture Notes in Computer Science*, pages 343–358, 2003. DOI: 10.1007/3-540-36580-X 25

[94] Sayan Mitra. *A Verification Framework for Ordinary and Probabilistic Hybrid Systems*. PhD thesis, Department of Electrical Engineering and Computer Science, Massachusetts Institute of Technology, Cambridge, MA, 2007. 103

[95] Sayan Mitra and Nancy Lynch. Trace-based semantics of probabilistic timed I/O automata. In Alberto Bemporad, Antonio Bicchi, and Giorgio C. Buttazzo, Eds., *Hybrid Systems: Computation and Control (HSCC 2007), Pisa, Italy, April 3-5, 2007*, volume 4416 of *Lecture Notes in Computer Science*, pages 718–722. Springer, 2007. 103

[96] Tina Nolte and Nancy Lynch. Self-stabilization and virtual node layer emulations. In Toshimitsu Masuzawa and Sebastien Tixeuil, Eds., *Stabilization, Safety, and Security of Distributed Systems: Proceedings of Ninth International Symposium (SSS 2007), Paris, France, November 2007*, volume 4838 of *Lecture Notes in Computer Science*, pages 394–408. Springer, 2007. DOI: 10.1007/978-3-540-76627-8 5

[97] Tina Nolte and Nancy Lynch. A virtual node-based tracking algorithm for mobile networks. In *International Conference on Distributed Computing Systems (ICDCS 2007)*, Toronto, Canada, June 2007. DOI: 10.1109/ICDCS.2007.82 5

[98] S. Owre, J. Rushby, N. Shankar, and F. von Henke. Formal verification for fault-tolerant architectures: Prolegomena to the design of PVS. *IEEE Transactions on Software Engineering*, 21(2):107–125, February 1995. DOI: 10.1109/32.345827 4

[99] George J. Pappas. Hybrid systems tools wiki, 2010. URL `http://wiki.grasp.upenn.edu/hst/index.php?n=Main.HomePage`. 6

[100] P. Petterson. *Modelling and Verification of Real-Time Systems Using Timed Automata: Theory and Practice*. PhD thesis, Department of Computer Systems, Uppsala University, 1999. Technical Report DoCs 99/101. 4, 5

[101] A. Pnueli. In transition from global to modular temporal reasoning about programs. In K. R. Apt, Ed., *Logics and Models of Concurrent Systems*, NATO ASI, pages 123–144. Springer-Verlag, 1984. 93

[102] A. Pnueli. Development of hybrid systems. In H. Langmaack, W.-P. de Roever, and J. Vytopil, Eds., *Proceedings of the Third International School and Symposium on Formal Techniques in Real-Time and Fault-Tolerant Systems (FTRTFT'94)*, Lübeck, Germany, September 1994, volume 863 of *Lecture Notes in Computer Science*, pages 77–85. Springer-Verlag, 1994. 18

[103] J. W. Polderman and J. C. Willems. *Introduction to Mathematical Systems Theory: A Behavioural Approach*, volume 26 of *Texts in Applied Mathematics*. Springer-Verlag, 1998. 25

[104] C. Robson. TIOA and UPPAAL. Master's thesis, MIT Department of Electrical Engineering and Computer Science, 2004. 6

[105] J.M.T Romijn. A timed verification of the IEEE 1394 leader election protocol. *Formal Methods in System Design*, 19(2):165–194, 2001. Special issue on *FMICS'99*. DOI: 10.1023/A:1011284000753 45

[106] R. Segala. *Modeling and Verification of Randomized Distributed Real-Time Systems*. PhD thesis, Department of Electrical Engineering and Computer Science, MIT, May 1995. Also, MIT/LCS/TR-676. 103

[107] R. Segala, R. Gawlick, J. F. Søgaard-Andersen, and N. A. Lynch. Liveness in timed and untimed systems. *Information and Computation*, 141(2):119–171, March 1998. DOI: 10.1006/inco.1997.2671 4, 24, 34, 88, 89, 104

[108] J. Sifakis. Modeling real-time systems – challenges and work directions. In *Proceedings of Embedded Software, First International Workshop (EMSOFT '01)*, Tahoe City, CA, volume 2211 of *Lecture Notes in Computer Science*, pages 373–389, October 2001. DOI: 10.1007/3-540-45449-7_26 1

[109] J. Sifakis. Modeling real-time systems. In *Proceedings of the 25th IEEE Real-Time Systems Symposium (RTSS '04)*, pages 5–6. IEEE Computer Society, 2004. Invited Talk. DOI: 10.1109/REAL.2004.34 1

[110] D.P.L. Simons and M.I.A. Stoelinga. Mechanical verification of the IEEE 1394a root contention protocol using Uppaal2k. *International Journal on Software Tools for Technology Transfer (STTT)*, 3(4):469–485, September 2001. DOI: 10.1007/s100090100059 45

[111] Mark Smith. Formal verification of communication protocols. In Reinhard Gotzhein and Jan Bredereke, Eds., *Formal Description Techniques IX: Theory, Applications, and Tools (FORTE/PSTV'96: Joint International Conference on Formal Description Techniques for Distributed Systems and Communication Protocols, and Protocol Specification, Testing, and Verification, Kaiserslautern, Germany, October 1996)*, pages 129–144. Chapman & Hall, London, 1996. 5

[112] Mark Smith. Reliable message delivery and conditionally-fast transactions are not possible without accurate clocks. In *Proceedings of the 17th Annual ACM Symposium on the Principles of Distributed Computing (PODC 1998)*, pages 163–171, Puerta Vallarta, Mexico, June 1998. DOI: 10.1145/277697.277728 5

[113] E. D. Sontag. *Mathematical Control Theory — Deterministic Finite Dimensional Systems*, volume 6 of *Texts in Applied Mathematics*. Springer-Verlag, 1990. 14

[114] E. W. Stark. A proof technique for rely/guarantee properties. In S. N. Maheshwari, Ed., *Foundations of Software Technology and Theoretical Computer Science*, volume 206 of *Lecture Notes in Computer Science*, pages 369–391. Springer-Verlag, 1985. 93

[115] S. Tasiran, R. Alur, R. P. Kurshan, and R. K. Brayton. Verifying abstractions of timed systems. In *Proceedings of the Seventh Conference on Concurrency Theory (CONCUR)*, volume 1119 of *Lecture Notes in Computer Science*, 1996. DOI: 10.1007/3-540-61604-7_75 93

[116] Shinya Umeno. Machine-assisted parameter synthesis of the biphase mark protocol using event order abstraction. In J. Ouaknine and F. W. Vaandrager, Eds., *7th International Conference on Formal Modelling and Analysis of Timed Systems (FORMATS 2009)*, volume 5813 of *Lecture Notes in Computer Science*, pages 258–274, Springer, Budapest, Hungary, 2009. 5

[117] Shinya Umeno and Nancy Lynch. Safety verification of an aircraft landing protocol: A refinement approach. In Alberto Bemporad, Antonio Bicchi, and Giorgio C. Buttazzo, Eds., *Hybrid Systems: Computation and Control (HSCC 2007), Pisa, Italy, April 3-5, 2007*, volume 4416 of *Lecture Notes in Computer Science*, pages 557–572. Springer, 2007. 4

[118] Vladimeros Vladimerou, Pavithra Prabhakar, Mahesh Viswanathan, and Geir E. Dullerud. STORMED hybrid systems. In Luca Aceto, Ivan Damgård, Leslie Ann Goldberg, Magnús M. Halldórsson, Anna Ingólfsdóttir, and Igor Walukiewicz, Eds., *Automata, Languages and Programming, 35th International Colloquium, ICALP 2008, Reykjavik, Iceland, July 7-11, 2008, Proceedings, Part II - Track B: Logic, Semantics, and Theory of Programming & Track C: Security and Cryptography Foundations*, volume 5126 of *Lecture Notes in Computer Science*, pages 136–147. Springer, 2008. 5

[119] H. B. Weinberg and N. A. Lynch. Correctness of vehicle control systems - a case study. In *Proceedings of the 17th IEEE Real-Time Systems*, pages 62–72, 1996. DOI: 10.1109/REAL.1996.563701 4

[120] H. B. Weinberg, Nancy Lynch, and Norman Delisle. Verification of automated vehicle protection systems. In R. Alur, T. Henzinger, and E. Sontag, Eds., *Hybrid Systems III: Verification and Control (DIMACS/SYCON Workshop on Verification and Control of Hybrid Systems, New Brunswick, New Jersey, October 1995)*, volume 1066 of *Lecture Notes in Computer Science*, pages 101–113. Springer-Verlag, 1996. 4

[121] S. Yovine. Kronos: A verification tool for real-time systems. *International Journal of Software Tools for Technology Transfer*, 1(1/2):123–133, October 1997. DOI: 10.1007/s100090050009 6

[122] S. Yovine. Model checking timed automata. In G. Rozenberg and F.W. Vaandrager, Eds., *Lectures on Embedded Systems*, volume 1494 of *Lecture Notes in Computer Science*, pages 114–152. Springer-Verlag, October 1998. 42

Authors' Biographies

DILSUN KAYNAR

Dilsun Kaynar is a postdoctoral researcher at CyLab, Carnegie Mellon University. Previously, she was a postdoctoral research associate in the Theory of Distributed Systems Group at MIT's Computer Science and Artificial Intelligence Laboratory. She received her PhD degree from the University of Edinburgh at the Laboratory for Foundations of Computer Science and her BSc in Computer Engineering from METU in Turkey. The broad area of her research is the specification, programming, and verification of distributed computing systems. Her PhD work focused on the design of functional programming languages that support mobile computation. She investigated the application of type-based analysis in this context, in particular to improve safety and security of systems. In her postdoctoral research at MIT, she worked on the development of I/O automata-based formal modeling frameworks for distributed systems, with collaborators including Nancy Lynch, Roberto Segala, and Frits Vaandrager. She is currently pursuing research at CMU CyLab, developing methods for analyzing security guarantees offered by contemporary secure systems and establishing foundations for data privacy, based on specializations of general formal frameworks for distributed computing such as I/O automata.

NANCY LYNCH

Nancy Lynch is a Professor in the Department of Electrical Engineering and Computer Science at MIT and heads the Theory of Distributed Systems research group in MIT's Computer Science and Artificial Intelligence Laboratory. Prior to joining MIT in 1981, she served on the faculty at Tufts University, the University of Southern California, Florida International University, and Georgia Tech. She received her B.S. degree in mathematics from Brooklyn College, and her PhD in mathematics from MIT. She has written numerous research articles about distributed algorithms and impossibility results, and about formal modeling and verification of distributed systems. Her notable research contributions include the well-known "FLP" impossibility result for distributed consensus in the presence of process failures (with Fischer and Paterson), the "DLS" algorithms for stabilizing fault-tolerant consensus (with Dwork and Stockmeyer), and the I/O automata mathematical modeling frameworks (with Tuttle, Vaandrager, Segala, and Kaynar). Prior to this monograph, she wrote two books: on "Atomic Transactions" (with Merritt, Weihl, and Fekete) and on "Distributed Algorithms". She is a member of the National Academy of Engineering and the American Academy of Arts and Sciences, and is an ACM Fellow. She is a winner of several prizes for her work in distributed computing theory, including the Dijkstra Prize (2001 and 2007), the van Wijngaarden Prize (2006), the Knuth Prize (2007), and the IEEE Piore Prize (2010).

ROBERTO SEGALA

Roberto Segala is a Professor at the University of Verona, Italy, and heads the Formal Models and Verification group at the Department of Computer Science. Prior to joining the University of Verona in 2001, he was research associate at the University of Bologna. He received his Laurea in Computer Science from the University of Pisa as a student of the Scuola Normale Superiore, and his Masters and PhD in Computer Science from MIT. As part of his PhD work, he made contributions to the theory of liveness and receptiveness for real-time systems and he designed the model of Probabilistic Automata for the formal analysis of randomized distributed algorithms. After that, he worked with Lynch, Kaynar, Vaandrager and others on the hybrid extension of the I/O automata framework. He also worked on model checking of probabilistic real-time systems, contributing to the design of some of the algorithms used in the PRISM model checker. One of his long-term goals is to design a general mathematical model that can be used for the description and analysis of systems that exhibit stochastic hybrid behavior.

FRITS VAANDRAGER

Frits Vaandrager is a Professor at the Radboud University Nijmegen, the Netherlands, within the Institute of Computing and Information Sciences. Prior to joining the Radboud University in 1995, he was group leader at the CWI in Amsterdam and held postdoctoral positions at MIT in the group of Nancy Lynch, and in the group of Gérard Berry at the École Nationale Supérieure des Mines in Sophia-Antipolis. He received his M.S. degree in Mathematics from the University of Leiden, and his PhD in Computer Science from the University of Amsterdam. As part of his PhD work, he made major contributions to the general theory of structural operational semantics. After that he worked with Lynch, Segala, Kaynar, and others on the theory and applications of the I/O automata framework. He has been and is involved in a large number of projects in which formal verification and model checking technology is applied to tackle practical problems from industrial partners. His group has been and is closely involved in the use and development of the timed automata model checker Uppaal. In part due to these efforts, Uppaal is now routinely used for industrial case studies and has thousands of users, both in academia and industry.

Index

Printed in the United States
by Baker & Taylor Publisher Services